Turkey:

Bridge

to Freedom

Escape from the 1979 Islamic Revolution of Iran

Parviz Hakimi

Turkey: Bridge to Freedom (Escape from the 1979 Islamic Revolution of Iran) © 2019 Parviz Hakimi

This book is offered by the author to the readers which is his story and his experiences.

Printed in the United States of America

Cover art and interior design by: Cyrusfiction Productions.

Library of Congress Control Number TXu 2-080-271.

Writers Guild of America, West, under the name of Parviz Hakimi Registration#: 1909517."

First Edition Paperback
ISBN: 978-0-578474-47-2

Printed in the United States of America

DEDICATION

This book is dedicated to those who love freedom, and those who have the will to escape from dictatorship, whether it's religious or political, into the free world. Many made it, but many did not. Some were captured by fanatics and dictators and executed on the spot, while others were able to find their freedom. Freedom is a basic human right given to man by the Almighty, and no one has the right to deny it or take it away from another.

This book is also dedicated to my wife and my two sons, who had to endure the hardships brought on by the revolution in Iran, as well as the anguish they experienced, including excruciating days and nights riding horses or walking through the thick winter snows over mountains from one village to another during our escape. I can't express the distress they felt when there was no sign of civilization for miles, and no one to rely on except a trusting group of human traffickers trying to get us out of Iran and into Turkey.

I want to especially thank my wife, who never made the smallest complaint and wholeheartedly trusted and supported me in making this dangerous decision and journey for our family. Also, I would like to extend my fullest gratitude and appreciation to my son, Arash, who assisted me tremendously in putting this story together.

In this book, I reveal impartial and unbiased truth, and nothing but the truth, regarding different nationalities or religions.

CONTENTS

INTRODUCTION

Turkey and its famous Bo-ghazi Bridge, which connects Asia to Europe, was also the "Bridge to Freedom" for my family and thousands of other Iranians who escaped from their homeland to get away from the oppression of religious extremists. At the time, it was so sad to escape from my birthplace where I speak Farsi with my family, relatives, and countrymen. Whenever Iranian friends get together, either in their homes or any other public places they usually gather, Farsi is the spoken language. Any non-Iranian who approaches us when hearing our language typically asks, "What language are you speaking?" not, "What is your religion?" Being an Iranian Jew, it's such a pity that I had to leave my country where my ancestors have lived for more than 2,700 years. They were part of the Great Persian Empire and assisted in the development of the history, civilization, and education of the land.

The Jewish people of Iran have always been law-abiding citizens. Turkey was a beautiful country rich with history. Then and now it continues to bare panoramic views of cities, islands, and mosques, decorated with tall *minarets* from which one can hear the sounds of the *Azan* (Muslim Prayers) five times a day. Also, it is a major vacation destination for tourists from all over the world.

Turkey has famous bridges and bazaars with unique arched architectures. Its political role expects equality for men and women and was brought into the modern age by Turkish president Mustafa Kemal Ataturk at the beginning of the twentieth century (1923 to 1938). Ataturk is known as the father of Turkey, because his progressive vision transitioned the country into a more westernized state.

Unfortunately, a few recent years ago Turkey had an influx of religious extremist radicals. I recently traveled to Turkey as a tourist (unlike my first time as a fleeing refugee), and I noticed many religious extremists among the Turkish people. The fanatic women covered head-to-toe with Islamic dress had grown in number tremendously since the last time I was there. Men with beards and the sign of dead skin on their foreheads resulting from the *Mohr-e Namaz* (a prayer during which a stone literally imprints the stamp-of-prayer on the forehead, known as a *Turbah*) had become common amongst the masses. According to Sharia (Islamic) Law, Muslims must pray five times a day. Wouldn't it be better to pray three times a day? And then spend the rest of that time reading about the economy, politics, science, and educating oneself about the world in which we live?

It is so sad to see another ancient country like Turkey revert to the Stone Age, as my country Iran did thirty-nine years ago.

When I escaped to Turkey with my wife and two small sons, I immediately recalled the country during the era of World War II, back when I was little. At that time, Turkish citizens who were Jewish were rounded up from all over Europe, especially in France. The Turkish government tried frantically to save its Jewish citizens from the German Gestapo. The biggest advantage the Turkish diplomats had in Europe was a sort of "Turkish neutrality" during the war, which helped enable them to save thousands of Jews from Nazi genocide. Turkey was the bridge between Eastern Europe and Israel (at the time called Palestine) and was under British mandate.

About 10,000 of the 300,000 Jews living in France at the beginning of World War II were Turkish Jews. The Turkish diplomats serving in France at the time dedicated many of their working hours to the wellbeing of the Turkish and French Jews. They provided official documents such as citizenship cards and passports to thousands of Jews, and in this way they saved the lives of many of them.

Throughout its history, Turkey has never set the scene for anti-Semitism, which was seen at different levels in other countries. At the time of the Nazi occupation of northern France, Jews living there fled to the southern parts of the country, which had not yet been occupied. But when it too was invaded, everything became even worse for the Jews. The first thing the Nazis did was fill trains with as many as Jews as they could find and then sent them to

German concentration and labor camps.

Let us hope one day our planet is rid of those who are wicked, so that all human beings can live in a free and healthy environment.

From the first day we arrived in The United States of America, I wanted to write this book. But I hesitated because I never wanted to expose the route, or the work of human traffickers, or the kind of disguises we had to wear to get out of a revolution-stricken country ruined by a bunch of traitors who wanted nothing more than to destroy our twentieth century foundation. Unfortunately, the fanaticism of religion brought our country back to where it had been fourteen hundred years ago.

While I was in Europe after weeks in the wilderness of the mountains, I was offered a good sum of money to share my escape story with organizations that wanted to make an escape movie, but I didn't accept that. It would have been very self-serving on my part to reveal the ways that thousands of people could get out of an imploding Iran and escape to their freedom. Now that the borders of the country are open and Iranian people can get out at will, I decided to write my story and dedicate it to all the freedom-loving people of the world.

—Parviz Hakimi

CHAPTER 1

The Start of an Uprising in Iran

February 13, 1978

It was Friday afternoon around six o'clock. I held my older son in my arms, watching the demonstration of people passing by on Aria Mehr Street. They were carrying placards written with slogans against the Shah and his government, and chanting *"Marg bar Shah, marg bar America"* ("Death to the Shah, death to America"), as well as, "Shah is the puppet of America." The traffic completely shut down. Cars had to move to the side as quickly as possible, otherwise the demonstrators would assume the drivers were pro-Shah, and thus attack their car with clubs and stones, breaking windows and lights. The demonstration by now was all over the country and getting stronger every day. Major Streets in big and small cities were filled to capacity with demonstrators.

My God, what is happening to my country? And in which direction are we going? What about our lives, families, our children and their futures? I thought to myself.

While I pressed my son to my chest, I remembered the first time I came to this house—my father's house—back in 1968, when I was on my college summer vacation. I went to school in America at California State Polytechnic University. I arrived at the airport in the evening and by the time I got home, it was already night. My father brought me to this very same spot and showed me the street full of lights, with many cars passing by. He proudly showed me his beautiful garden with a fishpond centerpiece filled with goldfish, as though the fish were happy I was home. A dancing fountain in the center of the garden, one could see drops from the fountain glowing in the light. To the right and left of the fountain were two sour-cherry trees, full of ripe and shiny red cherries. They were my father's favorite fruit trees. There were colorful flowers in full bloom, as though my father had asked them to specifically bloom at that time. The garden looked like a picture painted by a professional artist.

My father prohibited anyone from touching the cherries, until "Parviz returns from America for summer vacation." He told me, "Now that you are here, go pick some cherries and say the blessing of *Haess* (for the fruit of a tree) and give some to everyone to enjoy."

I can still taste those cherries and even feel the temperature of that day. All my family was around me filled with love and happiness. My father asked, "Go ahead, tell us, how do you like this new house? When you left for America, we were in the old house. Don't you think this house is better than the other one?"

I replied, "Of course, this one is much nicer and more modern than the other one." He pointed out the grape wine canopy in the driveway over the parked car. He told me with excitement, "Look at this one. It has already given us a lot of sweet grapes. I am so proud and happy with my garden and fruit trees."

Suddenly, my thoughts and happy moments were invaded by my wife's angry voice warning me, "Come in and bring the child. Don't you know it is dangerous outside with all the demonstrations going on?"

Many years had passed. My father was gone. The garden was now not as beautiful as it was in his time, the flowers were not in bloom, the fish pond did not have goldfish anymore, the cherry trees were asleep, and even the vine tree seemed it had taken an easy way out by getting drunk and falling into a very deep sleep.

While looking at that vine tree, I thought, "How much I envy you. I wish I could get drunk like you and forget everything." I wished that all that was happening were only a dream.

Once again my wife rushed to me with an angry voice persisting, "Didn't I tell you to come in and bring the child? It is dangerous outside with all the demonstrations and sometimes bullets fly. We came to get your mom and grandma, as well as blankets, pillows, and other items, and take everyone and everything to our apartment, which is on the fourth floor, far away from this terror, until the demonstrations are over."

We knew this was the beginning.

I rushed inside and picked up everything they had gathered and brought them to the car, which was parked in the alley right outside the back door of the house. Everyone got into the car in a hurry, even the eighty-eight-year-old grandma whom had no problem walking fast. I locked all the doors and closed all the windows, and then started the car. I noticed my neighbors were leaving their homes as well. Some of the neighbors were civilians, some were army colonels and even one was a general. It was a very sad moment. All of us used to live like one big family, but now everybody was leaving their homes. We did not know when and where we would see each other again. The army men were away from their families, and had to tend to their responsibilities either in the office or perhaps on the street trying to stop the demonstrations. On the way to the apartment, I noticed some of the vandalized buildings burnt by the demonstrators. The walls of homes were covered with graffiti and the pictures of different *mullahs* (clergymen).

While I drove through the guttered streets and buildings to my apartment, trying to pass the disaster area, I asked everyone in the car to keep their heads down so they wouldn't be noticed by the mob of demonstrators.

As soon as we got to the apartment, I rushed to the fourth floor with the children carrying everything inside with us. One of my neighbors rang the bell of my apartment. I opened the door, and noticed that both husband and wife were terrified as they told me about the demonstrations. The city of Tehran was on fire.

I told them to come inside and stay put. I locked the main entrance door of the apartment and turned on the television. The BBC radio broadcasting from England was in Farsi. There was a beautiful one-hundred-eighty-degree view of the city lights from our apartment, but now all we could see were flames burning in different areas of Tehran.

While listening to the BBC, I remembered there is an old saying in Iran that says, "Anytime there is any demonstration against the government led by a *mullah*, it is the work of England." We could feel the broadcast of exaggerated news by the BBC supporting the revolution. By now the sky was dark and the flames had grown stronger with the shouts of *Allahu Akbar* (God is great) coming from the rooftops of the homes around us.

Everyone was praying in their hearts for the future of our country, and their families.

My wife asked me if I would be going to work tomorrow. Saturday is the first day of the workweek in Iran; Thursday is a half day, with Friday as the only weekend day off.

I replied, "Of course, due to the announcement on television, all the government and oil company employees must go to their jobs as usual. I should go to work, too"

Worried, she told me about all the streets filled with debris, and demonstrations all over the city, and the many dangerous situations. She asked me, "How can you go to your job?"

I tried to calm her down and replied, "I thought you made tea for us to relax. Maybe by tomorrow, they will announce that we can stay home." Jokingly I asked, "Aren't you happy you quit your job? You don't have to go to work tomorrow." I could see she was very nervous. My mom and grandma came to my rescue and tried to calm her down.

In the morning, I decided to go to work by bus or taxi so I wouldn't have to worry about a parking space, or in case of any hazardous situation arising I could walk home. I said goodbye to the family and went out the door.

Immediately my wife started shouting advice after me, "Please do not pay any attention to the people demonstrating. Do not get involved in any political discussions. Stay away from any dangerous situations, and remember that we are all waiting anxiously for you to come home."

I said, "I promise, I promise."

In an hour I was in my office, walking part of the way and having ridden the taxi the rest of the way.

As I walked in, I saw the picture of the Shah hanging on the wall in front of me. Every office had a picture of the Shah on the wall. I looked at the picture and thought, *How much longer is that going stay there?* I sat behind my desk tending to my assignment of the day. There was a knock on my office door, and Hajji Morteza, who is responsible for the coffee room, walked in with a fresh hot cup of coffee.

I stood up, shook his hand, and thanked him for the coffee. He kept looking at me with a thousand questions in his mind. He is a very hard-working and religious man with a wife and four children. His older son was about to graduate from high school with very high grades, and all the teachers had great hopes and expectations for him, saying "for sure you will pass the entrance exam of Tehran University Medical School and in seven years' time you will be graduating as a doctor, to help your countrymen." Hajji always talked to me about the progress of his children in school. They were all good students. Hajji's wife also worked as a cleaning lady in some homes. They manage their finances together and were very hopeful for the future of their children.

Hajji started with the comment, "Look what they have done to our beautiful city. I am very worried for the future of our country, and our children." He was about to say something else when two men, whom I had never seen before, opened the door of my office. They jumped in with loud voices saying, "You still have the picture of that S.O.B. hanging on the wall? He is not the Shah anymore. Bring it down at once!"

I replied, "I have nothing to do with that picture. I did not put it up in the first place, and it is not my responsibility to bring it down. The office has a responsible employee who will take care of that."

One of the men angrily shot back, "Again, I am telling you to bring it down, or I will do it myself."

I quietly said, "You are welcome to do whatever you want to do with it."

One of them jumped on my desk and reached for the picture, tore it down, smashed it on the ground, and walked over it, adding, "So you are one of his followers? Very soon everything is going to change for you, too." They then walked out of my office.

Hajji Morteza was very angry and disgusted and quietly said, "I am a religious man. Every day I do my prayers as a Muslim. I don't know what kind of Muslim these people are."

I said, "This is not the first time we've had to go through an uprising and destruction in our country. Every twenty-five years they play the same game with us. Do you know who I am talking about?"

Hajji was very upset and started citing some verses from the Holy *Koran-e Majid* (the Muslim Holy Book). Then he added, "This is not the Sharia Law I learned, or have practiced my entire life." As he shook his head, he left my office and closed the door behind him.

My office was close to his coffee room and he could see anyone that came to my office. There were a lot of loud voices in the hallway with angry political comments and sometimes with dirty slogans about the Shah and his government.

Again, Hajji knocked on my office door, and before I got a chance to invite him in, with a fresh cup of coffee in his hand, he entered and said, "I noticed you did not get a chance to drink your coffee. It must be cold. I brought you a hot fresh one." He placed the cup on my desk, and quietly added, "There are new faces in the building that are making all that noise and commotion you hear. You better stay in your office. God help us." And then he left.

I opened one of the files on my desk and pretended to read

it. I took a couple sips of coffee, when my office door suddenly flung open. One of my colleagues burst in with excitement and exclaimed, "You are working? Come on! Forget about work! Come see what is going on in front of our office building. Come on!"

"I will be there in a minute," I replied. "This file is almost finished."

He walked out leaving the door open. Ten minutes passed, and he came in again with the same request, but this time ordering me to close the file and come with him to the conference room, where everybody had gathered. I left with him.

Most of the employees were jammed against the windows throwing down large plain sheets of paper, cardboard, and highlighters, to the demonstrators for them to write anti-Shah slogans. Demonstrators on the street chanted, *"Marg bar Shah"* (Death to the Shah), their most favorite slogan.

I stood by quietly. There were others who were also in the room against their wishes, watching the situation as well. Suddenly everyone became a political analyst as though they were commentators for a newspaper. My colleague, the one who brought me to the room, approached me and said, "You see, this is the end of the Shah, and his government, and his followers. No more Pahlavi Dynasty. I can see the day that this no good S.O.B. gets lost and leaves our country. Then Iranians can find peace, freedom, and tranquility!"

I went back to my office, thinking about my so-called friend and colleague telling me about freedom, peace and tranquility. He was dreaming. He worked for the most important organization in the country; the Iranian Oil Company. He received the best salary, benefits, and retirement program. His wife worked as a teacher in high school, and they had two children attending high school. They owned two cars and a beautiful house together. The whole family could afford to spend a whole month every year vacationing in Europe. But now he talks about freedom and tranquility?

Hajji Morteza seemed to be my guard in the building. He walked to my office again with his beautiful Turkish accent and said, "Peace, freedom, and tranquility?" Shaking his head, he asked, "What do you think about that?"

I asked Haji to sit down and relax. "The big industrial countries noticed the Shah is getting strong. Every year, fifty thousand educated young men and women come to the job market from the universities in Iran and other countries. They all have jobs waiting for them with good salaries and benefits, because our country is one of the best-located logistically in the world market with all the raw materials, including oil, gas, copper, coal, and many others that need technical, educated manpower. The Shah is hiring technical experts from the other countries, too. This is not good news for the big industrial countries. Their market in Iran is jeopardized. The Shah is not giving them the satisfaction of cheap oil, gas, and other raw materials anymore. So, they have decided to topple the Shah and his government. It is as simple as that. We must see when and how this change will come about, but it is not going to be without bloodshed, destruction of our economy, and destruction of the country. All you can do is try to stay away from the demonstrations and store as much goods as you can. Get food, oil, rice, bread, and other necessities. Store them because there will be shortages of everything very soon. Haven't you heard the speech of the Ayatollah Khomeini, who now lives in exile in Iraq? It is distributed on cassettes, which were smuggled into Iran and then duplicated by the thousands to be spread throughout the mosques among the people in our country. This encouraged and agitated the Iranians to demonstrate against the Shah, telling people they shouldn't work so hard for so little money, shouldn't pay for their gas, water, and power anymore. The proceeds from selling gas and oil to foreign countries will be divided among the people of the country, not just the "Thousand Families," which is the Shah and his relatives. You will get your share from our representative delivered to your home. Khomeini pictured a very rosy and beautiful easy life for the people of Iran."

After I finished speaking, Hajji Morteza left my office even more nervous and confused.

Then my *friend and colleague* (the man who ordered me to come watch the demonstration) came to my office *again* and sat on the chair facing me with a smile on his face. He said, "Everybody knows you acquired your higher education in America. Every week you receive *Time Magazine* delivered to your office. You love America, but you don't participate in demonstrations, don't share the excitement of the toppling of the Shah and his government. Someone even said you could be a member of *Savak* (Secret Service of the government). I am telling you as a friend, you should change your behavior and cooperate with the revolutionaries."

I couldn't keep my cool anymore and demanded, "Which S.O.B. called me a member of *Savak*? The hell with them, and the hell with *Savak* all together. Our country is going down the drain and you talk to me about revolutionaries? They are a bunch of thugs! They have been hired by those who want to see our country and economy destroyed. Look at yourself. You have a good job. Your wife is an educator. Your son and daughter are in good high schools with bright futures. Every year you have one month of *paid* vacation. Last year all of you traveled to Europe for a month to enjoy Italy. The clothing you have on is all from your trip to Italy. You think all this is going to stay the same, or get better? I am so sorry that as an educated engineer of this country doing well, you have fallen for such nonsensical, revolutionary stories."

"But what should I expect from an illiterate man who has come from a small village to work, save money for his family back in the village, and who doesn't know from A to Z about politics? Doesn't even know where Europe, America, or even north or south of Iran is? Yes, my educated friend, they gather him and thousands just like him in the street. With just very little money, a lunch and dinner, they ask the uneducated man to just listen to whatever the guy says on the loudspeaker and then repeat it to others. They even give him a picture of Khomeini and tell him he is the *Imam*, and that he is the representative of *Allah* (God). But even if they put a written placard in his hand, most likely he can't even read it, because he is likely an uneducated person who can't read and write." I couldn't believe his ignorance. I knew I should've stopped talking, but I just couldn't help myself. "That is what you find there. Do you know those guys who invaded our offices today with their *Allahu Akbar* slogan? They took the pictures of the Shah down, crushed them, and even looked at you like you are the traitors of the revolution. Do you know at least one of them? No, you do not. Neither do the others.

"Wake up my friend, look around you. God helps us for the plans the developed countries of the world have arranged for our future."

My friend and colleague left the office with a puzzled look on his face. I could not figure if he agreed with me or he thought I was an anti-revolutionary.

It didn't matter, because nobody cared what was going on in the office or whether the employees were working or not. I decided to leave the office very quietly. Due to not having a telephone in our apartment, before leaving I called my neighbor and asked her to let my wife know that I was fine and would be home in an hour.

I had to change taxis three times to get home. When I arrived, I saw my wife standing by the window with my younger son in her arms looking for me when my taxi pulled up in front of my building. I waved to her. From afar, I could see a huge sign of relief on her face. I was home with my family.

When I walked in, the television was on. The B.B.C. radio, which played a very big part in the uprising of the people against the Shah, exaggerated the news regarding demonstrations in Tehran, Esfehan, Shiraz, Abadan, and the clash between the government army, police, and the demonstrators. For the first time they reported the killing of a young man in front of Tehran University by the army of the Shah. The university is located on Shah Reza Street. There was vandalizing, as well as the burning of government buildings, restaurants, liquor stores, and movie houses. By now everything was out of control. There was no control over employees or businesses, so many did not bother to show up to their jobs. Everyone chose to stay home with their families.

Most of the shops were closed, and for those that were open there were long lines, with limited supplies that one could buy at much higher prices. I waited an hour or more in the line to buy bread one day. The baker knew me well, and respected me very much, because I had helped his son get to America for higher education. The baker told me quietly, "I will come to your house later and bring some more bread to you. I remember two years ago you helped my son go to America to study. I haven't forgotten it. I am so happy he is not here now." After he closed his bakery he came to my apartment with one of his employees, brought me more bread, and said, "Don't bother coming to the bakery anymore. Before I go home I will bring you some." He was so grateful, he tried to show his appreciation.

Soon it was dark again. The sound of *Allahu Akbar* shouted from the rooftops of the homes pierced the night like howling coyotes. The people in our complex were mostly educated university graduates, such as teachers, engineers, businessmen, and bank employees. However, one of our neighboring families was a very religious couple that did not mingle with the rest of the complex. No one from our building went on to the roof to join the others shouting *Allahu Akbar*. At least that was a good sign. Our next-door neighbor and the neighbor below us were both Jewish. The rest of neighbors were Muslim or non-religious. We all moved into our apartment complex almost at the same time. The complex was a brand-new building at that time. All the people in the complex were friendly with each other like a big family, without ever thinking about religion. Everybody considered each other an Iranian. Religion was out of the picture. Sometimes we enjoyed getting together with good food and alcoholic beverages—until the uprising started, which put an end to such festivities.

The next morning, I woke up earlier than usual. Right away I turned on the radio, and of course it was tuned to the famous B.B.C., the best friend of the revolutionary people and worst enemy of the Shah and his government. I dressed to go to work with a little change in my clothing—no tie. My family questioned me not wearing a tie, and I just told them this is the way everyone dresses up these days.

I left for work again with a taxi. I was late but no one questioned me or cared. Some of the employees did not come to work at all. As soon as I got to my office, there was a knock on the door and Hajji Morteza, with a fresh cup of hot coffee, entered greeting me. It was the first time I saw him so tired, with casual clothing and a hairy, unshaved face. He always dressed professionally, clean and well.

I asked about his family, his children's school, and his wife. He said "Thank you. You have always been a great friend to my family and me." He added, "Did you hear the people on the rooftops of their houses, shouting with all their might *Allahu Akbar?*"

"Yes," I replied. "It is not only in your area, it's all over the Iranian cities through the orders of the Ayatollah Khomeini via the tapes sent to the mosques and the other Akhonds."

"What is happening?" he asked sadly. "Why is this happening? Everybody has jobs, homes, cars, plenty of food, clothing, good parks to go to for a picnic, good restaurants, everything. And many villagers come to the city to work and send money back to their families in the villages. I don't understand. Please, you are educated, you know politics, and you have traveled to other countries. Please tell me, what is going on?"

"Sit down," I offered, "so we can talk as two Iranian friends with different religions, which never before has been an issue. We have shared the same history in this land and have enjoyed the same good and hard times of history. When our country was conquered by Alexander the Great and the Mongols people were butchered, our libraries were burned down, and they tried to diminish our civilization. But they couldn't, because we had one of the oldest and strongest civilizations in the world, which dates back twenty-five-hundred years."

I looked at my friend, and asked him thoughtfully, "Remember what it was like around here thirty or forty years ago? We had no drinking water in our homes. No electricity, no paved streets, no radio, no television, nor many other necessities that we have now. Remember we had to get up at three o'clock in the morning to put the dirty water running in the small ditches by the road in our special reservoir, built for washing dishes? And remember we washed dishes with *chuback* (shredded wood) instead of different regular washing materials on the market today? We had to buy drinking water, which was delivered by carts and pulled by a horse? And then there were the people who had wells dug in their yards so they could get water from underground reservoirs, which caused so many deaths of their children when the kids fell in and drowned inside them. Remember ice delivered by a donkey to store in a wooden box instead of today's refrigerators? There was no running hot water to take a bath and families had to go to public bathhouses once a week to clean themselves. Cooking had to be done on a very primitive brick or stone stove oven by burning wood."

Hajji nodded at the thought of our primitive, not-so long-ago history.

"Now we have showers in our private bathrooms with running hot water in our homes," I continued. "Look around you, in your house you have fresh, running, drinking water, plus connected gas with a modern oven. With the click of a switch you have lights throughout your home instead of small candles or oil burning lamps. Different radio stations, televisions, modern buildings, paved streets, and buses take you to work and back. You have cars on the streets, taxis, and modern buses to travel all over the country, railroads for easy and enjoyable trips to different parts of the country, even those connected to the European network. Beautiful parks in different parts of the cities for picnics with your family. You have more money to spend on food, goods, meat, fruit, vegetables, and good restaurants to enjoy your friends and your family."

"Although Islam is the main religion of the land, minorities such as the Jewish, Christian, Zoroastrian, and Bahai communities live together without any problems. Every religion has their own worship houses observing their rituals without any problems. And above all, we all speak Farsi, the national language of the land. We

21

are all Iranian and belong to Iran. Whatever is going on, it is not a happy time for Iran and the Iranians."

I noticed Hajji was deep in thought, as though he was in my office, even though he was miles away. I asked him, "Are you alright?"

He replied, "Yes, yes. I was drowned in your comments. The more I listen to you, the more everything becomes clear and understandable. Tell me how this uprising started."

"It goes back to many years." I replied. "It has become part of our culture to have an uprising against the different issues within our government. Ever since Reza Shah Pahlevi took over from the Qajar Dynasty, the last three Iranian leaders of the twentieth century have all been the source of crazy turmoil. What they all fail to understand is how much their posturing and desire for power affects those of us who are regular citizens just trying to live our lives as freely as possible.

"I know you are a God-fearing man, Hajji. A very honest, family man, who cares about his family and looks forward to the future. All we can do is to pray for the good of our country and our people." I looked at the clock in my office. "I think it is the time for us to go home."

Hajji left my office with his head down, as though his shoulders carried the weight of the world.

As I walked out of the building, some people stood by the front door watching everyone come in and out. None of the faces were familiar to me, nor to my friend who was walking with me. We noticed they gave everyone a suspicious look. We left the building and had to walk almost two blocks before we found a taxi. And even then, someone followed us until we drove away.

When I got home, my wife stood in the window as usual, holding one of my sons in her arms looking for me. As I got out of my cab, I raised my hand showing her a gesture of my love. Within a couple of minutes, I was inside my home. I greeted everyone hugging and kissing them as though another harsh and unpredictable day had gone by without any incident.

I looked at my wife and said, "My dear, do not worry so much. It is not you and I, it is the whole country, and we are a small part of it. As we always say, 'Put your trust in God, he will help you.'"

Another night and the same sound of *"Allaho Akbar"* filled the darkness.

As those terrorizing sounds rang through the night, my next-door neighbor rang the bell. I opened the door and noticed she was very nervous, holding her scared children. "Sorry to bother you," she said. "We are alone and my husband has not come home yet. My children are scared from all the commotion." Right away I invited them in to have a cup of tea. I left a note on their door for the husband.

Every night it was the same scenario; the wife and her kids would come over, scared. I am sure most of the people known as *Aksariate Khamoush* (silent majority) were in the same situation. We watched television and listed to the BBC routinely.

The one night, the doorbell rang as usual, but this time the husband was standing by the door with a disappointed look on his face. I invited him in to join our family and have a cup of tea. As soon as he settled in, he told us about a demonstration attack on the building at which he worked. "There was a loud voice coming over the speaker," he said, "shouting, 'Why are you here? You should be on the street, joining your brothers and sisters who are getting killed by the criminal Shah and his army, go outside and join them!' They did not even give us a chance to close our books and finish the work we had started," he continued. "They threw everything on the floor, trashing it all. Worse than that, they made us join their demonstration for more than five hours. Demonstrators watched us, walked next to us, making sure we repeat the slogan against the Shah and his government. I do not remember in my entire life such humiliation and agony as I've had to put up with as in the last a few hours. As soon as I had a chance, I went to one of the small side streets and disappeared. This was my day at work. I do not know what happened to the company and the building. As we left we could hear the sound of breaking the windows."

Every day, demonstrations grew in numbers and became stronger in power, which scared the people.

This became a routine way of life all over the country.

Days passed quickly, and demonstrations had become part of life. By now everyone was busy buying rice, cooking oil, meat, chicken, and fish. Whatever they could find at any price since the prices were practically rising by the hour. Everyone spent long times in long lines waiting for bread, they had no choice.

I had another job. One of my friends who had good contact in the government through his father-in-law (who was an army general) established an Educational Services Company and needed a partner with good communication skills in English. I had joined him before the turmoil in the country had begun. We were able to send high school graduates to college in different countries, mostly the USA, where I already had good relations with different colleges and universities due to the fact they knew my credentials. I knew the requirements of the colleges and universities, so as soon as there was an applicant, I had a good idea of where to apply. Through DHL and by phone calls to the foreign student advisors, we were able to request admission acceptance and receive it within a week.

As a result of the chaos in the country, many families decided to send their high school graduates out of the country. Suddenly, our business grew very quickly. Then the protest against the Shah's rule continued and worsened during the spring and summer of 1978. The Iranian government declared martial law on September 8, 1978, known as *Jom'e-ye Siyah* (Black Friday). A shooting occurred at *Maydan-e Jaleh* (Jaleh Square) despite the fact that the government had declared martial law the day before. Soldiers ordered crowds to disperse, but the order was ignored. When the protestors pushed towards the military, the military opened fire upon them killing and wounding several people.

Black Friday marks the point of no return for the revolution. It is thought that many Palestinians were brought to Tehran, Iran, in plain clothes as Iranian soldiers to create a massacre and blame it on the army. The number of dead and wounded varied from eighty to 1,500 by the different media and opposition groups. It was known later that those killed on Black Friday included sixty-four killed at Jaleh Square, which among them was one woman and a young girl. On the same day, and in other parts of the capital, a total of twenty-four people died in clashes with martial law forces bringing the total casualties on the same day to eighty-eight.

Days after the Black Friday incident, most of the companies and businesses working in Iran restricted their activities and some even shut down completely. Many of our college admissions did not arrive to us due to cancellations by DHL. Instead they were sent to the DHL office in London. My partner decided to go to London to get them. He left for a few days and happily returned with all the admissions. All the young men and women came by the office to retrieve their acceptances from the colleges and universities. They had appointments to acquire visas from the American embassy.

There was a change in my business partner's appearance and behavior at work; he grew a beard and changed his name to an Islamic one. I knew he was an opportunistic person who felt that the country was heading towards an Islamic regime so this was the time for him to change sides.

The day the Shah and his family left Iran, the people danced in the streets congratulating each other. Cars had tissues on their windshield wipers, which were turned on dancing them around. I was in our private office tending to the student admissions. My business partner danced in happily and shouted, "Finally the S.O.B. got lost!"

I could not believe how fast he had changed one-hundred-eighty-degrees. When everyone left, I turned to him and said, "You better take it easy. Don't forget you are the son-in-law of a general of the Shah's regime. Although you are just acting, you might want to tune it down a bit."

But he was not acting. He was serious.

That night I was happy for the many young students who left our office safely, knowing they would be leaving soon to study abroad and get out of this mess. They kissed me and thanked me for the great job we had done for them. But deep inside, I was very disappointed by the behavior of my partner. I asked myself how an educated, well-to-do man with all the opportunities he had and who enjoyed all the benefits of the title of his father-in-law, could suddenly change so much. If that's the case, what can we expect from everyday people who had much less?

I went home to my family with a very heavy heart.

CHAPTER 2

The First Two Years of the Revolution

It took us two years (1978 and 1979) to get through what happened in Iran as the result of the revolution. Everyday a new unpleasant episode occurred to someone we knew.

One day, as soon as I got home, one of my neighbors rang the bell of my apartment. As I opened the door he came in with his finger on his lips gesturing silence and said, "I just want to let you know that you should remove all the alcoholic beverages from your apartment because our next-door neighbor, who is very religious, had an argument with me and got very angry. He told me, 'I am going to tell on you and your Jewish friends to the *Komiteh* (Islamic Guard) for drinking alcoholic beverages, which is forbidden by the Muslim religion. You are all *infidel* (none-believers) and you all should be punished.'" He then hurriedly left our apartment.

Grateful for the advance notice, I filled several boxes and a few large pots and pans with all my alcoholic beverages, covered them well, and transferred them to my car without attracting the attention of anyone in the complex. I then drove the car to my mother's house, hid the boxes and pots and pans inside the cellar of her home. After that I covered them with anything I could find. When I got home, I could hear the same Muslim man arguing with his wife regarding the neighbors of the complex. Mostly they argued about those who are not happy about the Islamic Revolution, especially referring to the three Jewish families who live on the third and fourth floors.

It was amazing how fast people change. These were good friends and good neighbors not that long ago, but now we had become *infidel* to them. The irony about the whole thing was that both the husband and wife were university graduates and had taught high school.

Almost every day at work, Hajji and I talked about the Islamic Revolution. Our country had gone through a lot of changes in a very short time, and the prime minister of the Shah's regime, along with many other high-ranking army generals and officers, were executed. Every morning, when my wife and I woke up, it was on the news that a new execution had occurred with more horrific pictures in the newspapers and on the television. The war between Iran and Iraq had its own share of the horrible and dreadful pictures, as well.

One morning, I walked into my office, and one of my colleagues, who was very pro-Islamic revolution and always said aloud, "The Shah, that son-of-a-bitch, should leave the country," rushed into my office, his face pale and very nervous looking. "I need your help," he said. "My family and I are in a lot of trouble. Yesterday, the *Komiteh* Guard arrested my brother and my brother-in-law. They both were part of the *Mojahedin* (anti-Shah regime), and apparently helped the revolution and the fall of the Pahlavi Dynasty." He was so furious, and angry, but at the same time cried like a baby.

I tried to calm him down and said, "If I were you, I would sell my house, or get a good chunk of money and find some influential clergy, bribe them, and get a release for both of them as soon as possible. Do not waste any time. This has become a new routine for extorting money from the people."

He then asked, "Remember the time Khomeini declared in his speech that all the political parties were free to practice their political ideology? We revolted for the freedom of speech and the freedom of political ideas."

I replied, "Yes, I remember." I then asked, "You really did not think he meant it, did you?"

He replied, "Of course, everyone believed him. He is the highest religious authority. He is the *Imam*. The *Komiteh* told us that they would release them in a week, but we are not sure about anything yet."

I said, "A week is too long to wait. You have to go for their release now with a lot of money."

He left my office and a few minutes later, Hajji walked in. Hajji shook his head with a fresh cup of hot coffee in his hand. He said, "Do you recall that he was the one who said, 'That son-of-a-bitch should go!' about the Shah?"

By now Hajji's son had graduated high school with very remarkable grades, but unfortunately, he had been drafted by the army and sent to the south region of the country, the cities of Abadan and Khoramshaher, where the battlefield of the Iran/Iraq War was currently situated. Everyday Hajji came to my office and expected me to give him hope and positive speeches.

One week passed, and I did not see my unfortunate friend and colleague whose brother and brother-in-law had been arrested. No sign of him at work, and no news of him in general. Another week passed, before he finally showed up my office. He must have lost at least ten to fifteen pounds since I had last seen him. The first thing he said to me was, "Unless this old Satan dies [referring to Khomeini], we cannot have any freedom." He was in a very bad mood. He called different authorities bad names when he spoke and did not care who heard him.

I tried calming him down and asked him to lower his voice, because there were "Islamic Brothers" all over the place. I said, "It could be dangerous for you and your family to say such things."

He said, "Nothing is dangerous anymore. They called us to go to Evin Prison (the most dangerous prison in Iran). When we got there to see my brother and brother-in-law, we were told that they would be coming out soon. We were so happy that they were going to be released, but they brought us two shot dead bodies instead." He paused and then asked, "Do you think I care anymore?"

I was speechless. I felt as though I was dreaming. *How could this be?*

He left and I did not see him again for a month.

Everyday Hajji came to my office to talk to me and I always told him, as the old saying goes, "No news is good news." Days and weeks passed, and Hajji's son was still in the warzone. Finally, one morning Hajji came to my office very upset, with an extremely tired expression upon his face. I could see he had not had a good night's sleep. I was very anxious to hear what he had to say, and could feel my heart pounding so hard I could hear it. I asked him, "What is going on Hajji? Talk to me, please."

He replied, "Do not worry, it is not that bad. My son was injured by a bullet in his kneecap. He had a surgery and is going to be fine. The good news is that they will release him from the army. We are hoping to see him at home in about a week." He approached me, and for a minute, lost his control. He put his head on my shoulder and cried.

I asked him to sit-down, and rushed to his coffee room to bring him some water. I returned, and said, "Listen to me, my good friend. There is a saying that goes, 'God always leaves room for us to pray and be grateful.' Thank god that your son is alive and will be home soon. You know, in our office some of our colleagues lost their brothers, sons, and other relatives."

Hajji said, "You are right, we should be grateful. It could have been much worse."

I remembered that day was one of the worst days of the revolution. Hajji's son was a very gifted young man, but now instead of being in university with all the hopes and wishes life had to offer, he was forced into war. Now he'd be crippled. The choice was not his own. I told Hajji, "Please let me know when he comes home. I'd like to pay him a visit and talk to him."

In a week he came home and I did visit him. I gave him encouraging advice and said, "Hopefully next year, you will be admitted to university to become a doctor in future." I tried to motivate him a little more.

Everyday there was a different issue with different people that we knew due to the tense situations in the country. By now more and more people considered leaving the country, or at least looked for a way to send their youngsters abroad in fear that they would be drafted into the war. Many people already had Islamic Republic passports. All they needed was to find a connection in the government that could give them permission to leave the country. It soon became a business for scalpers who had government connections to accept bribes to issue permits for leaving the country. I have to mention that many instances occurred in which these scalpers did not hold up their 'illegal' agreement accordingly and asked for more money to perform their jobs and close the deals. Also, there were instances in which the scalpers said the government confiscated their clients' passports, which wasn't true. Instead the scalpers sold them to influential people of the Shah's regime who were in hiding and also trying to get out as soon as possible under fictitious names.

It was even harder for Jewish families who wanted to leave, because they had unannounced restrictions placed upon them. In reality, the scalpers had good connections with the *Komiteh*, the passport division, and all of the Islamic revolutionary guards at the borders of the country. They also had a very strong network to arrange the sending of the clients out of the country legally. Some high-profile Iranians who were sought by the new revolutionary guards handed over all the deeds of their homes, businesses, and all their livelihoods to these scalpers for the freedom of their families and themselves. The scalper network's top man with all the legal power was usually a clergyman. There were cases where governmental institutions (who were really mostly *Komiteh* individuals) tried to force the Jewish escapees that were caught leaving illegally to use Muslim names and convert to Islam. Then they allowed them to leave with a higher charge added to their escape deal. This scenario was a typical scam that occurred over and over again and was another trick the scalpers used to get more money from the Jewish people who wanted to get out.

Jews in the Islamic countries usually are not political. Mostly they are good businessmen, educated, and always per instruction of their holy book of the *Torah*, faithful, and respectful to the government of their host country. During the Shah's time, Iranian Jews had more opportunities and were therefore more successful in their businesses, and had better chances of attending universities, or to obtain responsible positions in government organizations. Due to their honesty and devotions to the land, they had a long history as very good citizens, although they were always referred to as *second-rate citizens*.

The change of the regime via the revolution, and the rise of fanatic clergies in charge with anti-Israel and pro-Palestinian agendas was one the biggest negative impacts upon the Jewish population of almost 40,000 Iranian Jews. Right before the revolution, and during its first year, many Jews left the country. Some left their fortunes behind to save their lives, because they were known for importing new technological industries to the country and creating jobs and opportunities for university graduates, as well as everyday ordinary workers who benefited with good salaries and health insurance. This was meant to move the country toward the developed twentieth century, which was the utmost wish of the Shah. Some of these Jewish citizens were able to save a part of their fortune, but many did not even consider leaving the country. These were the employees of government organizations with higher education whose fortunes and life savings were tied up in a small house with a mortgage, a car, and a small savings in the bank for the rainy days. A good example included my wife and me, both of us with university educations, both of us middleclass, and both with responsible and respectful jobs in government industries.

Among many industrial businessmen who helped Iran's economy and movement toward the industrialization of Iran was Mr. Habit Elghanian, who introduced the plastics industry to Iran. Creating plastic products established organizations that cared for the needy, the drug-addicted people, orphans, as well as supported hospitals, schools and many more similar organizations. Mr. Elghanian never thought about leaving the country, although he had been asked to do so by his advisors. His answer always was "I helped my country and my fellow Iranians by creating jobs in the twentieth century. I will do the same under any other circumstance or government. This is my country, and these are my people."

He continued his activities as usual, until the day when the revolutionary guards walked into his office and arrested him. Within twenty-four hours, and by the order of *Khal-Khali* (one of the leading clergymen of Khomeini's cabinet.), he was executed by firing squad.

There were many other cases of harassment as well as the confiscation of properties and belongings of the Iranian people by the revolutionary guards and *Komitehs*. For example, a husband and wife, with two kids, who were both engineers (one on the board of education and the other as an architect for the government) and parents (of a son and a daughter who were both honor students) lost everything after they had worked many years, and had even purchased an apartment with a mortgage.

After the revolution and by the start of the Iran/Iraq war, many concerned parents tried to send their sons between the ages of thirteen and twenty away from Iran, for fear the kids would be drafted by the revolutionary guard for the war. This same family of four was equally concerned and so obtained passports through scalpers at a very high price, and then went to Turkey. From there they sent their son to his uncle's home in the United States.

When the parents returned to Iran (without their son) they went back to work as usual. A few days passed, but the *Komiteh* eventually questioned them about the whereabouts of their son. The *Komiteh* wanted to draft their son into the army, even though he was only thirteen years old. Their neighbor's son, who was also thirteen years old, was drafted and sent to the warzone where he was wounded two months later and then died at a hospital. The *Komiteh* returned again and again looking for the couple's son.

After a while, they finally arrested the father and took him to jail. He spent about a month incarcerated without being charged with a crime, and finally received seventy-two lashes across his back as his punishment. They also had him fired from his architect position.

The wife, who had twenty-five years' experience as a high school teacher, had been asked by the Jewish community leader to take over one of the high schools that had recently been built by the Jewish community. This high school was one of the most modern and had the facilities of a synagogue on its second floor where Jewish people would carry out their religious rituals.

The *Komiteh* eventually ended up looting the school and taking anything and everything valuable that they could find in the classrooms, including all the small and large equipment used in biology, chemistry, physics, and sports classes. The high school also had one of the more complete libraries in the community, which was also looted and destroyed. The *Komiteh* burned most of the books in the schoolyard, many of them belonging to the era of the Shah and the twenty-five-hundred-year history of Iran.

Now that the husband could not work and the wife eventually lost her job as the principal when the school was taken over, the couple and their daughter decided to leave Iran and join their son in the United States.

Another episode involved a government employee during the Shah's regime. He was tipped off by a friend (who was also member of the *Komiteh*) that his house was going to be raided in the near future. They would look for any alcoholic beverages or commendations of the Shah's regime that he might have in his house. If found, all alcoholic beverages would be dumped into the sink and toilets, and fire would be set to any commendations found.

Three days later, they raided his house and although they found nothing that would incriminate him, they took anything and everything antique-like and expensive, such as Italian made chandeliers, furniture, paintings, statues, crystal vases, china sets, and very rare Persian rugs. Eventually they came again and arrested him a week later, taking him to jail for being a follower

34

of the Shah's regime. Through a clergyman who knew him, he was finally freed, but fined millions of dollars as his punishment. The same clergyman, through some smugglers he already knew, was ultimately able to transfer the man and his family to Turkey. Later on, his house and all of his real estate was confiscated by the *Komiteh*.

The *Komiteh*, or the Revolutionary Committees as they sometimes call themselves, were active in the Iranian Revolution of 1979. They arose in the fall of 1978. Two processes brought them under the control of the fundamentalist clergy who employed them as a coercive organization. Members who had supported a democratic outcome to the revolution voluntarily left these organizations with the increasing oppression by the authorities. By the summer of 1979, the clergy began an ideological purge of the *Komitehs*. The purified *Komiteh* members were largely drawn from the lower middle class, the urban poor, and the recent rural migrants. With the collapse of the monarchy in February of 1979, the *Komitehs* assembled offensively to arrest and punish any and all officials of the Shah's regime. Many *Komiteh* members had armed themselves with weapons confiscated during attacks on army barracks within the last two days of the revolutionary conflicts in February. During the first six months of the Islamic Republic, the *Komitehs* arrested a large number of officials and executed more than 220 police and army officers, SAVAK (secret police officials) members, and politicians linked to the monarchy. Liberal and nationalist political leaders who remained in government repeatedly complained about the arbitrary nature of the *Komiteh's* activities.

The Ayatollah Khomeini stated in late February 1979 that as soon as the government was in complete control of the cities the *Komitehs* would relinquish their power and avoid involvement in any other government affairs. In mid-April, however, Khomeini recognized the threat posed by the mounting social and ideological cleavages. He modified his stand and declared that the *Komitehs* needed to be purged, not dissolved. He said that as long as corrupt individuals existed, there was a need for the *Komitehs*.

The *Komitehs* were significant in terminating the Workers' Councils, which had sprung up in factories as protectors of labor. They also closed down colleges and universities throughout the country beginning in 1980. They continued to repress liberals aligned with president Bani Sadr in 1981, and the armed struggle against the socialist Islamic group, the *Mujahidin-I Khalq*, during the early 1980's. A new wave of threat and rampage was started by the *Komitehs* against the people, spurred on by a grudge they had previously held against them. It was the perfect time for the *Komiteh* to harass the people and rob them of everything, and of course, they were supported by the revolutionary clergymen and different Ayatollahs.

Many citizens suffered losses, including their homes, their livelihoods, businesses, and of course, their lives. Neighbors probed each other to coerce information they could use to incriminate one another through the *Komitehs*. Brothers turned against each other. One could not trust their own relatives. Many people who were government employees and had positions in the Shah's regime, were harassed by their subordinates. There was no respect between bosses and employees anymore.

Many times, I was stopped by these hoodlums while driving with my wife and children, asking me for proof of being a family. I could not stand the way they looked at me, nor their attitudes, but could not do anything about it. Life was becoming hell for the citizens of the country. Most of the *Komiteh* and *Khaharaneh Zainab* members had come from low-class parts of the cities, especially from the villages. They harassed the citizens and the educated peoples of the country. They received good salaries and benefits for their awful work. They went to the mosques to pray five times a day, and lived in the confiscated homes of those who had left the country to save their own lives.

A few weeks went by and my boss walked into my office holding a letter in his hand telling me that he had just received a note with my name on it. Right away, I thought I was going to be fired by the revolutionary guard who had studied my ten-year service at the Abadan refinery and its Tehran office. It had become regular practice by the revolutionary guard to fire the educated and experienced employees by gaining access to their employee files, and making a decision about firing them.

He handed me the letter and I was happy to find out that it was an invitation to join the Ajnace Company, which was going to be established as a subsidiary to the National Iranian Oil Company. The contents of the letter included the appointment date and time, which had already been set for me.

Although I was happy about the invitation, I was somewhat disappointed that I was not fired, knowing the tense and hard-working conditions that I would have to continue to endure. Even though my boss was very satisfied with my work and wanted me to remain in his department, he knew he could not stand in the way of such invitations. The appointment time for the interview had been set for 7:30 the next morning, on the eleventh floor of the new National Iranian Oil Company building in Tehran.

I arrived half an hour early the next day, and introduced myself to the secretary of the Ajnace department, which was now headed by an economics analyst with an American Ph.D. The department head invited me into his office and we sat down and he told me about the purpose of establishing the Ajnace Company. He was about 6'4" and 250 pounds, with a big stomach, which obviously was the result of the many American steaks and beers he had enjoyed in the U.S. He also had a beard he had been growing for three to four months. He told me that there were currently three hundred English employees in London who purchased the required equipment for the National Iranian Oil Company refineries, and they worked for very high salaries with a high cost upon our country.

Therefore, the National Iranian Oil Company had decided to close the England-based company and establish the Ajnace Company in Tehran. They had studied the employees of the oil companies, which were university graduates from America and England, and those who already had good experience working in the oil industries. The Ajnace Company was offering 200 different positions with specific qualifications. Among more than 1,000 candidate files that had been reviewed, and I had been chosen as one to be interviewed for an available position.

From the line of questioning, I could tell that he had already studied my ten-year experience at the oil company which included four years in Abadan refinery with the rest in different offices of Tehran and that he had reviewed all of my commendations. He already had a good idea about my experience in the oil company. He then handed me a twelve-page, legal-sized stack of questionnaires and the application and requested they be filled out and returned within twenty-four hours.

Looking at the application and questionnaire, I found myself overwhelmed by the questions. The majority of the questions were politically oriented regarding the Islamic Republic, the occupied Palestine (Israel), and the mistreatment of the Palestinians by the Zionist, rather than about my experience or education.

I returned to my office with the questionnaire and application, and while I was busy trying to fill out my answers, my boss entered the office to inquire about the interview. I asked my boss to take a look at the questionnaire and he too was surprised by the line of questioning and left my office shaking his head in dismay. The questionnaire started simply enough, asking me to fill out my name, date, and *shenasnameh* (identification booklet), the county, and the city it was issued from in Iran. My *Shenasnameh* was issued from the city of Sanandaj, in the county of Kurdistan.

There was a war between the Kurdistan of Iran, and the Islamic republic, so it created sort of a red flag in my case. I used very sophisticated vocabulary and sentences that someone of lesser education would have to spend a lot of time trying to make sense of. Again, I have to mention that the situation with Israel and the Palestinians had nothing to do with the job and the Ajnace Company whatsoever. First it crossed my mind to return the application blank, but then I suddenly realized being Jewish would immediately brand me as a Zionist if I didn't complete it.

In that case, they would not only fire me, but my chances of going to prison would be very high due to the Islamic Republic and their *Komitehs* looking for the smallest excuse to persecute me.

It took two hours to fill out the application. I decided to walk to the secretary of Ajnace Company, and handed her the completed application. She opened the folder and was impressed by how extensively the application had been completed. She made the comment that among all the applications she had received, none had been as complete as mine. She also told me that she would let me know the appointment time for a formal interview. I thanked her and left the office.

I decided to walk home to analyze whether they would accept or reject me, and if they would call and want me to elaborate on my answers. It was even possible that my answers might create some sort of a danger for me. I was about a hundred feet from my apartment when, as usual, I saw my wife holding one of my children looking anxiously down the street waiting for me. As I got closer she noticed by my face the hard day I had before coming home. As soon as she opened the apartment door for me, my children ran up and hugged and kissed me. I tried to forget about work, the revolution, and everything else that was going on around me.

She asked me about the interview. I went through everything with her extensively, including my answers and those I had concerns about. But I reminded her. "We know what the current situation in the country is like; we might have jobs today, but tomorrow, we might not." For the first time the thought of leaving the country came to mind and I asked my wife to think about it.

She was so surprised by my comment and both of us right away knew that it would not be possible. We brought my mother and grandmother to my apartment for their safety. My mother had worked a lifetime and now she was retired and had the responsibility of taking care of her own mother who was ninety years old. I just couldn't leave them alone. For ten years she was a teacher and principal of a high school in Sanandaj, and then both my father and mother worked in Abadan for another ten years. After that they transferred to Tehran and worked for the oil company until they retired. My father passed away four years after his retirement. A few years after my mother's retirement, the revolution started and her leisure time, which was supposed to be spent enjoying her life in her house after so many years of hard work, and having taken care of her family, were behind her. Now she had to be consumed with taking care of her old mother and coping with the revolution.

This house was the savings of my parents' lifetime in which they would someday enjoy the rest of their lives. My mother loved her house because of the good memories, and she did not want to move out even though the upkeep was too much for her. She loved her neighbors, who did not care about the differences in religion. They all cared for each other as Iranians who had a country, and who spoke one language (Farsi) with a very strong feeling for the history of Iran. Sometimes I tried to convince my mother to sell her house and move to a new modern apartment for her grandchildren's sake, but she refused. I was happy for her due to the fact she was within walking distance to a small, mom-and-pop grocery store, and a bakery that was known its devoted customers.

Because of the revolution, the shortage of food and high prices made it difficult for everyone. For older people, some of the goods such as milk and dairies had already been rationed through the clergy of the mosques of the neighborhoods. Retired people had to go to the mosques with their identification booklets to be personally approved by the clergy, who before revolution had no jobs, and no respect. Before, a person like these types of clergy tried very hard to read some parts of the holy book of the Islam Koran to people on the street just to make some money. But now these same illiterates became big men with power. And in their new positions they tried to make up for the past by taking out their revenge upon everyday ordinary people.

One day I took my mother and grandmother with their photo identification booklets for approval for a twelve-ounce carton of milk for my grandmother. Finally, it was approved. With a special paper my mother had to stand in line to pick up milk at 6:00 a.m.

for my grandmother. Many times, she spent two hours standing in that line, and by the time she got to the cashier, either they did not have milk left or when she got it home it was already spoiled.

By now whatever anyone wanted to buy had to be purchased on the black market with inflated prices. I urged my mother not to go to the shop and that I would buy it from the black-market myself. Every day, I paid a visit to my mother trying to help her with her responsibilities. As long as I can remember, my parents worked very hard all their lives to have an enjoyable retirement. My father's passing with a massive heart attack came just a week after I arrived back to Iran to join the National Iranian Oil Company as a second-generation member of the oil company family. Now my mother's life was in turmoil over the revolution. Fortunately, I did not have to be financially responsible for my mother or grandmother, due to the fact my mother was retired from the National Iranian Oil Company.

But as a son, I was responsible for my mother's and grandmother's well-being and that was why I just could not fathom leaving the country without them. Plus, I didn't want to abandon the country where my ancestors have lived for more than 2,700 years. This was my birthplace and this was the land in which I had grown up. I even came back after acquiring a higher education abroad for the betterment of my country.

Right away, I said to my wife "Forget about what I said. After all, your family and relatives are all here." Those who had already left the country were able to do so with most of their wealth. I told her, "Don't forget we live here as four generations, my grandmother, mother, us, and the kids. It's impossible for us to even think about leaving the country."

My wife tried very hard to be positive about my application at Ajnace and told me, "With your resume with the oil industry and command of English and German, I'm sure they will hire you for one of the sensitive positions that they have available."

We all had dinner and while my mind was occupied with the day's events, I listened to the BBC and watched television regarding the war between Iran and Iraq, the Kurdistan war, and the scenes of the warzone with dead and wounded soldiers. It all had a negative impact on everyone.

The next day, and as soon as I arrived at my office, there was a telephone call from the head of the Ajnace Company for me to be in his office in half an hour for an official, formal interview. I was both excited and nervous, because I didn't expect them to call so soon. Right away I thought maybe they had questions regarding my elaborations on Israel and the situation with the Palestinians, which I had written about on the application questionnaire. I notified my boss and left the office. He was also anxious about them having called me so soon for the interview.

I waited half an hour in the Ajnace office for the head of the company to finish reviewing my application, which seemed like hours. He read it silently to himself without saying a word as he sat there in his chair behind his desk. He told me he was very impressed by the quantity and quality of my answers, especially my elaborations on the Middle East. But he didn't mention the Israel and Palestine situation specifically. He made a comment about my knowledge of politics, even going further to ask if I had ever taken any sort of political science courses while at university.

To this question I replied, "Of course, we had to take several elective classes, and I always chose political science when I could, because I was always interested in politics." I didn't know whether it was the right decision to answer him so straight-forward, due to the fact comments of that sort were not appreciated by the revolutionary people.

We spent a few more minutes talking and finally he said, "I have the most important question for you. You haven't written your religion on the questionnaire. Why is that?"

Before he finished the sentence, I quickly replied, "Your questionnaire didn't have a part for religion, but I am sure a man with your experience and knowledge has already reviewed my ten-year file of service with the oil company. In the first questionnaire ten years ago, which I filled out for the first time during the Shah's regime, there was a question about religion and I answered 'Jewish.'

I was born Jewish, I live Jewish, and I will die Jewish." Even though I was stating the sentence sternly, in the back of my mind, I felt that I probably shouldn't have said it that way, because it might ruin my chances of getting the job with them, and maybe it would even get me fired.

He replied, "You're absolutely right, it doesn't have religion." He then added, "According to the Ayatollah Khomeini the Jewish minorities are our Jewish brothers." But then, I noticed that on the margin of my application he wrote the word *Kalimi* (Farsi for *Jewish*).

The interview lasted about an hour and then he said, "We are going to make a decision very soon, and will let you know." As I left his office, he came by and shook my hand and in English said, "Glad to have you aboard."

I got the feeling he was not one of those religious Muslim types who think of Jews as *najes* (dirty). That moment took some pressure and anxiety off my mind. Even though he had told me he was going to decide very soon, he was subtly hinting to the fact that I had already been hired.

I arrived back at my office and as usual, right away Hajji came by with a fresh cup of hot coffee and asked, "So they are going to take you away from us?"

I replied, "No matter where I go, we will always be friends. I am going from this building to the next building in the same vicinity. It is not very far."

Within a minute, my boss walked in and asked, "Tell me, what happened?" Hajji left, and I started to explain to my boss the events of the whole interview with the Ajnace Company.

He then told me they had already contacted him on my way back to the office asking for my transfer to their office within a week or two, so that I had enough time to wrap up my projects and appropriately hand them over to my colleagues. Even though it was only half a day into the workday, my boss insisted that I take the rest of the day off due to the fact that I had gone through such extensive processes and pressures of the job interview. He said, "Go home, relax with your family, and we'll see you tomorrow."

CHAPTER 3

The Start of a New Job at the Ajnace Company

The week was finished and the next Saturday morning my boss handed me a letter stating that I should go to the Ajnace Company as soon as possible for the formalities necessary to familiarize myself with the new position. Within a few minutes, I was there and of course the secretary very graciously asked me to take a seat and wait for the boss to come by and take me to my new office. After about fifteen minutes, he came out of his office and out of respect I stood up ready to shake his hand, but to my surprise he asked me "How are you?" in German.

I replied, "Thank you, I'm fine," in German.

He shook my hand and said in English, "Welcome aboard." He then showed me two large offices that each held eighteen positions, just empty desks and chairs at the time, with no employees. He pointed at a separate private section between the two offices and said, "This is going to be your room. You can see all the employees behind their desks and the separate section for the secretary from here." He then took me to a storage room and opened it, giving me the key to the door and asked, "Do you see all these files? They are all the orders made to different countries and many of were paid for in part from the *Bayt-al-Mal* (money of the treasury), which we have not yet received. They add up to millions and millions of dollars. Your job is to fill all thirty-six positions with new employees. We will send you the applicants. You will interview them and make a decision to hire them or not." He shook my hand and told me that his secretary would arrange anything I might need. He also told me that he had notified the rest of the employees at the Ajnace Company that I would be taking over this department and that by now, everybody had heard of and knew a little about me.

Being Jewish, I wasn't happy starting a new job on a Saturday, but this was the rule of the country. And during the Shah's regime we also had to work on Saturdays, so I was accustomed to it. I sat behind my desk holding my head in my hands. I thought about the gravity and responsibilities that had come with the new position. Being Jewish and holding a sensitive position such as mine meant that I would be watched very carefully by the Islamic Republic revolutionary guards. I started planning and scheduling for getting all the files in order until I would have more assistance from the other employees that I would later hire. I made a list of stationeries I needed for the new office and handed it to the boss's secretary. She notified me that a secretary had been already assigned to me whom would arrive the next day.

I didn't know how the time flew by so quickly, but as soon as I looked up, it was already time to leave and I knew my wife would be excited to find out how my first day at my new job went. As usual, it took nearly an hour to get home, both walking and riding in a taxi.

It had become like a schedule for my wife to stand by the window looking at the end of the street to see a sign of me. I shook my hand from afar gesturing sending her a kiss and ran fast toward the apartment. I stepped inside, hugged her and the children, greeted the rest of the family, and finally discussed my first day at the new position. Everybody listened very anxiously, even my ninety-year-old grandma and my children. I took a shower to relax and clean the sweat of the day from my body, had dinner and tea, and of course topped the night off with the BBC to update myself with the news.

I made a comment regarding our passports to my wife. One of them was my passport with my wife and children as companions, which was customary in Iran. The other one was for my wife with the children as companions. Both still had six months' time and were valid, but they had to be exchanged with the new ones issued by the Islamic Republic of Iran. I said, "We have all the required documents including pictures. Please make time in the morning to go to the passport office for their exchange. Just pay the fees so we have new ones in case of an emergency."

She did not like to hear the word *emergency*.

I said, "Listen honey, we must always have valid passports. Who knows what is going to happen in the future? They might close the passport office. Most of the time after a revolution, the passport office is usually one of the offices immediately closed by the government. I think it's only smart to have updated passports." I got all the papers, pictures, and old passports ready, put them in an envelope and handed them to her.

I noticed my grandma did not like the idea of us leaving the country by her comments such as, "You want to leave us behind and go?"

I replied, "No, of course not. If the time comes for us to leave our homeland, first you two and my family will go, then I have to attend to the house, the apartment, and many other things that need to be taken care of. And that is not easy."

My wife said, "I will go for the exchange of the passports, but I tell you now in front of your mom and grandma, I will not leave with the children without you. I understand being concerned about your mom and grandma, but that is a decision up to them completely."

I tried very hard to make sense of my proposal by assuring them it was just as a precaution, and that I would bring their old, expired passports to the department to apply for new ones. I said, "I don't think they will have any issues with two old retired women."

I didn't think this would have created such a situation in the house. I will never forget that when we went to bed that night my wife kept asking me, "What happened at work today? Is there anything you do not want us to know?"

I had to assure, replying, "I am not hiding anything." But I told her that she understood what was happening much better than my mom, and especially my grandma. No matter what, we had to look forward, especially having small children.

My wife's boss had a PhD from France and was married to another PhD in political sociology, also from France. They had been married for fourteen years. Both were very healthy with no children. When I once asked them why they didn't have any kids, they replied, "We are very much capable of having children, but the world we live in is very dangerous. Therefore, we decided not to have children." I did not understand that then, but now I get what they were talking about.

To my wife I said, "Again, honey it doesn't hurt to have passports. You know me, I always am cautious. We are going to have a very hard time ahead of us in the future."

I tried to change the subject, and said, "You understand my position at work. Now, it is three positions higher than my previous position. Don't forget that this new boss offered a position like this to a non-Muslim minority, not only a minority, but a Jewish minority at that. That's a big deal. Either he really doesn't know the true Islamic Republic or he lives in a fantasy world. He acts like we're in the U.S.A. We just have to wait and see. I hope everything goes well. I have already made my schedule of jobs to be done as soon as I have some help. I will run the operation very well and try to bring in all the lost money over the course of this revolution."

My second day at work started by making two big empty desks and chairs presentable. I also got stationary for my office and some for the empty desks. In fact, all sorts of new stationeries kept coming in. The boss's secretary knocked on the office door and stepped inside. I could see she was amazed by the look of the office. She made a comment regarding the big boss, saying how happy he was regarding my joining his department.

The first week passed mostly with just getting the office ready for new employees, as well as the scheduling of the work process. But the first day of the second week at about 9:00 a.m., a bearded, young man with a khaki jacket and a note in his hand came in looking for me by calling me *brother*. He looked just like one of the revolutionary guards.

I asked, "What can I do for you?"

He presented me with his note from the human resources department regarding working in my section. He looked to be around twenty-three or twenty-four years old.

I said, "Well, tell me about yourself, your education, experiences, and your knowledge of English."

He said, "Brother, I am a high school diploma graduate, and when I graduated I got a job at the police department. My main duty was to stand on the corner of a busy street and jot down the registration numbers of wrong-doing passing vehicles and then give those numbers to an officer to write citations." That was a common trick to stop the cars, show that their registration number was already written down to be given to officers for a citation as a means to coerce the driver into giving him a few bucks to erase the number. I could tell where this was going. I was certain this guy was now a proud member of the revolutionary guard,

He continued, "Then the revolution started and I joined the revolutionary guards. Last Friday, I was in Tehran University for a mass prayer service and listened to the *Imam Jomeh* [the clergy who performed the mass prayer and made revolutionary speeches], when someone distributed forms to apply to the oil industry, which has always been one of my lifelong dreams. I brought it to the human resources department and they sent me to you."

I said, "Well, I am happy for you. But I have a question. How is your English?"

He replied, "My knowledge of English is what I learned in high school from seventh to twelfth grade." Then he changed the subject. "But human resources told me there are English classes. I have to be at work at 7:30 a.m. but at 11:00 a.m. I have to go to the main hall for praying and to listen to the Imam of the day and eat my free lunch, which is part of my benefits. By 1:00 p.m. I have to come back here to work and then at 2:30 p.m. I have to attend the English class."

From what I heard, I wanted to pull my hair out. I kept my cool, and said, "Well, it's almost the time of prayer. I will see you at 1:00 p.m."

He returned at 1:00 p.m., well-fed, and relaxed with an English book in his hand. He approached me and said, "Brother Mehdi gave this English book to me. He also told me that you can help by reviewing my homework assignments before I return to the classes. He reminded me that every Friday my friends and I have to be at Tehran University for the *Namaz-e Vahdat* (prayer of togetherness), praying along with delicious sandwiches provided for attendees after the services." It's important to note that these "delicious sandwiches" always had some sort of paper money hidden inside their wrappers to attract both young and old. This creates a big crowd for propaganda purposes.

I worked with him for an hour then he went to the English class. When he left the office, I remembered the time Khomeini made speeches and agitated the Iranian public by asking them not to pay their water, power, and gas bills, because they as the people had shares in the country's oil and wealth. He had also claimed that while he remained in power and the *Taghut* (which is what he called the Shah) was gone, everything was going to be free. He also claimed that the government employees would deliver the check of each person's share in oil to their homes regularly.

My boss's secretary came by my office asking about the new member of my department. I told her the background of the new employee and she was also surprised. I said, "Millions and millions of dollars of the country is buried among those files, and he has to go to English class?"

She asked, "So what are you going to do with him?"

I replied, "Are you kidding me? He is a *Komiteh* member. He has to have a job. Don't worry. I have already set up two weeks work time scheduled for him. Of course, I have to find the time to help him with his English homework, too. I showed him the storage room and asked him to set the files in alphabetical order."

She wished me good luck and left.

The next morning, I was in the office earlier than usual. The inside of the office had been completely changed. All the walls of the office were covered with colorful posters of the Iran/Iraq War as well as with pictures of Khomeini and many other clergies, some of them whom were already dead. Under my desktop glass someone had inserted all sorts of pictures of different Imams. The new employee was already there and noticed I was shocked by these findings. He said, "Brother, these are our Imams, our holy leaders. Some of them are *Shahids* (martyrs). They are in heaven now among the holy ones." Colorful posters of the soldier's dead bodies, some without heads, some without legs or hands, some burned beyond recognition with the color of blood all over the place, including young soldiers standing on top of the bodies with headbands on their foreheads and some verses from the Koran in their hands while holding their machine guns upward to give encouragement to the young inexperienced drafted soldiers; all these horrible images covered the walls.

The slogans on the posters read, "These Shahids received the key to heaven from our Imam Khomeini and now they are in heaven being received by seventy-two young, beautiful virgins." A plastic key made in Hong Kong was given to each soldier to wear around their necks as the key to open the gates to heaven if they died on the battlefield. These keys were imported by the government specially for the purpose of sending the *Shahids* that wore them under their uniforms to heaven. For some of the lucky ones who were injured in war and released due to not being able to be productive anymore, they were told by their superior officers to not forget their key of heaven, and to keep it around their necks—that it was more important than their rifles, because it had been given especially to them by the Imam Khomeini.

My young employee then said, "A group of us brought all

these posters and placed them in every office. Aren't you proud of the Imam soldiers? Now brother, I am ready to work."

I opened the storage room, and gave him instructions written in both Farsi and English and returned to my office. I looked at the walls of the office one more time imagining the previously tranquil and happy environment I had created for my employees and now how it had been changed to a war zone. By looking at these posters you would get all possible negative energy the moment you stepped into the office.

I heard the telephone ring. It was a call from the big boss's secretary asking me to come to his office right away. This was the last thing I wanted, but I was there in a few minutes. He opened the door, asked me to enter, and then said, "Don't say anything, I know all about it. The new employee, the posters, and also the English classes. By the way, congratulations with the new scope of jobs added to your job description as an English teacher." He was being sarcastic.

I said, "Well, we have to do what we have to do."

He said, "If you don't want the guy, I can get rid of him for you. I have already notified human resources what qualifications we are looking for. Make him work for the time being with the schedule you have given him. I just wanted to thank you. Good luck."

The next day was a usual workday with the new employee's schedule, not mine, ruling the day. Praying in the main hall, listing to the Imam, having a free lunch, relaxing and finally coming to work for another hour for me to help him with his English homework, and then off to his class. With this schedule, another week concluded.

Our weekend holidays changed from two days to one and a half days off. The Thursdays and Fridays off were reduced to Thursdays a half-day work. As a result, the employees' monthly salaries were reduced by twenty-five to thirty percent. In many families, both the husband and wife worked together. But now in these cases, the wife was sent home to take care of the family and prepare food for the husband and children, government decree saying that the woman's place was at home in the kitchen and not at work, which had a very harsh impact on many families. Friday was the time for shopping for goods at inflated prices.

I assigned our hard-working new employee "brother" a desk with the necessary stationary items and a direct telephone line by the window on the eleventh floor to enjoy the view, and thank the revolution for giving him his wish to be part of the oil industry. Most of the time he was on his feet simply setting files in order.

The following day, I had four new employees join our team. Only one was a university graduate, with a fairly good command of English, whereas the other three had experience in different refineries and were familiar with the equipment. We needed that expertise on our team. Everyone picked their own desks. I assigned files to each of the employees, which I had already reviewed according to their expertise in the field. I was impressed by their knowledge.

The next member of the team was the secretary who had a separate desk away from everyone. She came by the office toward my private area with a note in her hand calling me *Aghaei-Reis* (Mr. Boss). No "brother" or any slogan as such. I invited her in and she handed me the note and said, "I am Sara, the secretary of your office." Sara was an Armenian, but with the Vail and long dress she looked like she was a *Khaharan-e-Zaynab*. No shaking of the hands. I just led her to her desk and told her the scope of her duties.

She listened very carefully and finally said, "I have been in the oil company almost ten years, and my typing in Farsi and English is very fast. I am very much familiar with formal letters, and very good at answering the telephone in both languages. I am sure you are not going to be sorry about me being part of your team in this office."

I said, "I am sure you are correct. I am glad you are here. Good luck."

Everyday new personnel joined us in the office. Large empty offices with only desks were suddenly occupied by employees, filled with files piled on their desks, and calls regarding the contents of those files came pouring in. There was excitement in the rooms, and questions and answers occasionally led to loud voices out of frustration. In the last step, the completed files were brought to my desk for a final decision. It was rewarding and became challenging for the old timers of the industry. That very first, unskilled employee now had five others like him in a corner, mostly talking about the revolution, the Iran/Iraq War, and attending 11:00 a.m. prayer services to get their free lunches and listen to the Imam of the day before going off to their English class. It was pretty obvious to everyone they were not in the office to work. They were from the revolutionary guard assigned to every office to keep an eye on all the employees and report any talk or action against the Khomeini.

One of the most interesting figures at the office was a university graduate who as soon as he came in picked up the phone and called the top man of the company quoting him some verses from the Koran. Everyone looked at him as if he was a showoff and a two-faced person. One day, he came by my desk and said, "You know, I am a brother of a *Shahid.* I lost my brother in the war last month and the top man likes me very much."

I said, "I am sorry to hear about your brother, but I am happy for you." The very first time he came by my desk he said, *Sohbah-Komolahol Balkhair* (Arabic for "good morning"). I thought to myself, suddenly we are not Iranian anymore? Farsi is not our language anymore? It seems not. Everyone quotes verses in Arabic now and I could see from the sign of dead skin on his forehead, because of the *Mohr-e Namaz,* that he was a fanatic Muslim. There was definitely a negative outside impact from the revolution threatening the Iranian culture and its country.

The follow up on the files continued and ended with me reviewing every single one of them thoroughly, analyzing their contents, including the descriptions of the items, costs, deposit monies, times of deliveries, terms of payments, delays, systems of payment by either American dollars, English Pounds, German Marks, or the Japanese Yen, and so on. Every file had to be approved by me, and at some point required the signature of my immediate boss or more rarely the signature of the top man, depending upon the amount of the contract. Occasionally, I had to go to a special Islamic committee to support my approval of a file with facts, figures, and other facets such as the rates of exchange in monies. None of the files were to be finalized by any of the employees themselves. The final decision papers had to have my signature or my boss's signature on them. We had access to the telex department for our communications and according to their guidelines, each telex had to have separate authorization from the man in charge of the office so that no one could send a telex on their own.

A new week started and business was as usual. I had a bunch of files on my desk waiting their final approvals and was already reviewing them, when suddenly my concentration was interrupted by a voice that asked, "*Aghay-e Reis* [Mr. Boss] or shall I call you *brother*? Or whatever you'd prefer I call you?" I could sense a sarcastic tone in his manner of his speech. I looked up and saw a very well-dressed man with a beard, suit, tie, a smile on his face, and a note in his hand extending it towards me. He continued, "Human Resources asked me to come to work at one of the positions you have available in this office." I took the note and the name on it surprised me right away, because it was one of the most talked-about on the news. It was the name of a high cleric in the government.

I asked about his education and experience.

While smiling, he said, "I graduated from Oxford, one of the top universities in London. I have three years' experience in business. Recently, my father who is a clergy asked me to come back to help out the country and the revolution."

I said, "I am happy to see you joining our group. Please go ahead and choose a desk. Settle down and later we will discuss the requirements and the scope of this job."

He looked at the nearest desk to my right and said, "Can I have this desk?"

I replied, "Of course, but there are some others available by the window and the view of the city."

He said, "No, thank you. This will do."

It was almost 11:00 a.m., and time for the Group of Six to go for their usual prayer services, free lunch, and positive speeches by the Imams of the revolution. As they left the office, they called upon the newcomer sitting to my right to join them to the services. To my surprise, the newcomer refused due to the fact he had already done his prayers before coming to work. He approached my desk with a smile on his face and made the comment, "These people, as well as the revolution, are hurting Islam, because they have no education," referring to the Group of Six, as I had privately come to know them.

I said, "Now this is the law of the land. I cannot approve or disapprove of it. Besides, I have told them from the beginning that I am Jewish and if they have anything against working with a minority, they should look for something else in other departments."

Again, with his smile remaining on his face, he said, "I was already told by the boss all about you. It doesn't make any difference to me. The boss told me he is very happy about having you on his team. He even told me to cooperate with you as much as possible due to the lack of educated manpower in this office."

I said, "I am sure you will be a great help to this office." I then assigned him two files, which required a good command of English.

The Group of Six returned discussing and elaborating upon the day's speech by the Imam and they were very excited. The rest of their working day was already over. They continued with the studying of their English homework, and then they left for the day. This was a big shock and surprise to the newcomer who didn't expect such opportunists, like the Group of Six. They claimed to be fighting for Islam and the revolution, but instead they made a mockery of it, and took advantage.

I was again approached by the newcomer, now with a file in his hand, asking me questions. We studied the file together and came to a sound result. He asked me about the next step in the file's processing. I told him that in the procedure this specific file needed both my signature and my boss's signature and that only then could he take it to the telex department with a cover letter that also required my approval on it so that they can take care of it. I must say I was impressed by the fast and complete job he had performed. In the coming days I noticed bad blood was beginning to brew amongst the Group of Six and the newcomer, which was not pleasant for the overall office environment.

It was again the start of a new week. It was early morning, and as I got closer to my department, walking through the hallway of our building, I heard the sound of the Koran being read coming from the general office. As I got closer to the office, the sound became louder and louder. I opened the office door and to my surprise the newcomer had some of the office mates sitting facing him as he was seated on a chair located on top of one of the desks looking down at the others. Everyone had a copy of the Koran in front of them and he was asking them to read portions of it out loud. I could not believe what was going on in the office. Very quietly, I walked to my desk and sat down. While one of the pupils read an assigned part, he made a mistake and the newcomer with his eyes closed read the whole page from memory with a beautiful voice and no mistake. Then he called on me to join them and participate in the reading of the Koran, although they all knew that I was Jewish and could not read or write Arabic.

I answered him respectfully and said, "You read it and I will enjoy it and I will pray along with you." I noticed he winked at me with a smile on his face. I had a feeling he had something on his mind, which was not agreeable with the others, but because they knew who he was and who his clergy family was, so no one dared to go against his wishes.

By 7:30 a.m., the working hour started and the Koran reading class was over. Everyone got to their desks to tend to their assignments. One of the Group of Six came to me with a file in his hand asking questions. As he approached my desk he raised his voice and said, "Oh no, brother! You have covered the face of the Imam Khomeini with a file. We have put these pictures under the glass of your desk so that for every minute you work, your eyes may see heaven by looking at the Imam Khomeini." He pushed and mixed up the files I had arranged in order to assign or finalize.

I could not stand so much aggressiveness and said, "This is a working desk. These pictures are of holy ones and should not be here. They should be on the wall so that everyone can see them and become energized by them."

He said nothing.

I waited a moment and asked, "Do you have a question for me?" He handed me the file and I looked it over giving him instructions for its completion along with a written cover letter. At this time, my telephone rang and the boss's secretary was on the other line asking me to be in the boss's office in ten minutes. That was a call I really needed to receive under the circumstances so I could get out of the office for a few minutes.

I arrived at the boss's office and as usual he greeted me with a handshake, a smile and said, "I understand you have the Koran class, too?" He added with a sarcastic grin, "Apparently you don't have to go to class. They have already brought the class to you."

I said, "Yes, of course. They read and I listen. It is fine. No complaints, as long as they take care of the business and we can recover some of the lost monies of the *Bayt-al Mal* back to the country, I will be happy."

While pointing towards the ceiling he said, "I was in the top office reviewing some of the completed files from your department. You have completed them in such a short time and with so much recovery that the top man is very impressed with you and he just might come by your office without any notice to see you and your group, and to shake hands with you and talk to the rest. I want you to know we are aware of everything that goes on in every office." He called the secretary and ordered two cups of American coffee and some sweets and said, "It's good to have some American coffee instead of Turkish coffee all the time." I spent about half an hour with him and came back to my office relaxed. I noticed it was almost time to go home. Everyone had already left and I finally left the office, too.

On the way home, thoughts of the newcomer and the addition of our scheduled Koran reading classes kept my mind occupied. As I got home, my wife again asked, "What is new in your work and office? Your face tells me something new has come up."

I explained the whole day's work, even the cup of coffee with the boss and concluded by telling her that we just had to wait and see what was going to happen.

I asked my wife about the new Islamic Republic Passports and if she had already taken care of them. She hadn't. I said, "Please put it into your schedule to go get the passports exchanged tomorrow morning. It is very important to have the passports exchanged, because as I mentioned before, they might close the passport office without notice."

By two weeks' time, my department was almost completely filled up with new employees. I could see that amongst them were both members of the leftist group (the *Mojahedin-e Khalgh*), who helped the revolution bring Khomeini into power, but were later betrayed by him (many of them being captured and executed), and the *Fadayi*, who were the followers of Communist China. Another group I could distinguish within the employees made up the followers of the Shah's regime who kept silent and to themselves.

The latest employee addition to the office was a six-foot tall gentleman who approached my desk wearing a military uniform and presented a human-resources note that had assigned him to my office. He had a full beard grown and with the uniform looked exactly like one of the *Komiteh's* revolutionary guards. He handed me the note and greeted me with "Brother Boss" when he introduced himself. As usual as with newcomer employees, I asked about his education and work experience. I also asked him the reason why he came to the office wearing a military uniform.

He told me that he had just arrived back from the Kurdistan warzone that same day and that the human resources department had instructed him to report to my office as soon as possible, without having a chance to change his uniform. About his education, he told me he had graduated from Tehran University with a major in

English and had later continued for two years working in England eventually working in the field of business in different countries around the world. I welcomed him to the office and asked him to choose one of the few desks that were still left available. He pointed to the one closest to my desk to my left-hand side. I asked the secretary to provide all the necessary stationary for him and assigned him two files, which needed a good command of English. The day went by fast and everyone left the office.

The next day as usual when I arrived at the office I could hear the sound of the Koran reading in the hallway. As I walked into the office, the newcomer with the military uniform arrived a few minutes earlier than his starting time wearing a suit, very professional and businessman-like. The Koran reading class finished and everyone got back to their desks to start on their assignments. I received new files from storage and started reviewing them and assigning them to different employees when the door of my office opened and a man wearing a goatee beard, suit and tie, and carrying a business briefcase, walked in. He stared at me, to my right, and then to my left and began to laugh. Sarcastically he said, "Look at you. One bearded guy on your right, and another on your left."

I didn't know who he was, but I was rather surprised by his comment. I asked him "How can I help you? Are you in the right office?"

Before he had a chance to answer, the guy sitting to the left of me stood up hugged and kissed him telling him to stop joking around with the people in the office. A few members of the Group of Six had already heard the comment and were quite upset about the remarks. The employee apologized on behalf of his friend and introduced him to me as his brother-in-law, who hadn't had the chance to come see him the night before to welcome him back from the Kurdistan warzone. So, he had dropped by the office now to see him.

The employee then ordered coffee for me and a few of the other colleagues.

CHAPTER 4

Obtaining Our Islamic Republic Passport
to Leave the Country

Finally, my family and I received our new Islamic Republic passports and the only thing left for us to do was to get permission to leave the country through the passport office. To obtain permission, a special form from the passport office had to be filled out. Many people rushed to the passport office to get this form including my wife, who went back and forth several days before finally acquiring one. There was a limited number of permit forms available and the office always ran out by the time she arrived and made her way through the line. It was obvious to me that the situation resulting from the revolution was getting worse every day, especially for minorities.

The thought of leaving the country became more and more of a reality, and I constantly spoke to my wife about it, trying to convince her to agree with me to leave. I also had to talk to my mother regarding the fact that the situation was getting worse for everyone, especially minorities, and this was not the retirement life for her after a lifetime of hard work. I tried very hard to speak to my mother and although she was very reasonable and could appreciate the circumstances, she was continuously opposed by my grandmother's decision, who said, "Don't let your son make your decision for you. Eventually, everything is going to be normal again." I knew dealing with my grandmother would be very difficult. Although my mother agreed with me, she asked me to give her mother time to eventually realize that it was not going to be normal any time soon, and that it would get worse before it got better. I tried to convince my mother to sell her house and move into our apartment complex in one of the other available units. Again, my grandmother was against everything I suggested and ended the argument with the same statement, "Don't let your son make your decisions for you." She repeated that over and over again.

The rest of us, however, filled out the forms for the passport office to get permission to leave the country. It was then we realized that they would not issue any permission for Jewish people to leave the country.

I had a very serious talk with my wife and my mother. As a result, my wife and I decided to sell our apartment and move to the second floor of my mother's house, although both of us were not really happy about this decision. Selling any real estate by a minority was a dangerous red flag, because the government kept a closer eye on minorities for the chance they might flee the country. Therefore, we had to keep a low profile when selling, letting only close friends who might be interested in purchasing know anything about it.

My wife finally agreed with me, under one, and only one, condition; the four of us would leave the country together. In many other scenarios, the father of the house would send the mother and the children out of the country first, while he stayed behind to sell their real estate and other belongings before joining his family later. But that was not what my wife wanted. Sometimes the husbands were arrested by the Islamic *Komiteh* (before they had a chance to sell their belongings) without any prosecution, the only crime being Jewish and a part of the well-to-do in the business world. They were normally thrown in jail and threatened to be executed by a firing squad, and if they were to be executed, were first given seventy-two lashings from a whip, the number seventy-two originating from the time of *Hasan* and *Husayn* (two grandsons of the Prophet Muhammad) who along with seventy of their followers were killed in Karbala. Many of these people lost their lives. Some were lucky and were able to pay off large sums of money to save themselves, while others gave away everything they had for the chance to get out of the prison.

The Islamic *Komitehs* were stationed inside the police stations and every one of them acted like an independent government, so that the real police had no power at all. The only people who remained safe were those that had high clergy connections.

It took us about three months to sell our apartment through a friend who was acquainted with the buyer. The buyer proposed to pay off our mortgage and the balance in American dollars through his relatives who resided in America. At the beginning it seemed like a very sweet deal, but eventually with the Iranian *toman* (Persian currency unit) losing its value to the American dollar, the buyer took advantage of the situation. He not only sold us more expensive dollars, he also threatened us by saying he was going to report us to the Islamic *Komiteh* for planning to leave the country and take our money with us. We had no choice but to go along with his demands. This was not something new for the educated part of the country or especially for minorities. Every day we heard about different true stories about hardships of other people.

The neighbors in the complex noticed the sale of our unit, and they approached us asking the reason. I explained to them that due to the fact my wife was not working our family income was slashed by thirty percent, and because of two children to feed, the high cost of living, a high mortgage, and many other plausible reasons, we decided to sell our apartment and move into my mother's house, who along with my grandmother were old and needed our attention anyway. Some believed my story, but many did not. One of them, who was religious and not friendly with most of the neighbors, asked, "If you are moving to your mom's, why are you selling all your furniture and other household belongings?"

I told him, "We don't need any of them because my parents already have everything. We sold everything that wasn't necessary, including the furniture." One of the saddest days was when buyers came and my children tried to stop them from taking things away, crying, "Where are you taking our stuff? These are ours, you must not take them." I had to tell them, "We are moving to *Mamani's* house [a nickname the kids called my mother], and they are delivering them for us to *Mamani's*."

It was about two weeks before we had the confirmation of the money from the U.S.A. and then we delivered the apartment to the buyer. I had no idea that it was going to be the start of a three-year period moving from one place to another till we finally got a chance to leave the country, which was a very difficult and dangerous journey.

The boys enjoyed having a big backyard in which to play. We tried to keep their minds occupied with different hobbies. One day, while the family had gone shopping, we saw someone selling small chickens and ducks in the street bazaar. The boys asked if we could buy some to keep in the backyard. We agreed, and provided a secure cage for the chickens and ducks, and the boys took care of them. They let them play in a fishpond, which had no fish anymore, and watched the chick and ducklings grow, and of course, make a mess of the backyard. One can do strange things to keep one's mind occupied under stressful conditions. Just like a prisoner who keeps his mind busy with odd work so he does not feel the passing time.

Stress at work was building up. There was more pressure on everyone by the Group of Six and the Brothers of the Islamic Republic. Their regular work schedule was only two hours, most of which they passed with discussions elaborating on the Imam Khomeini's latest Islamic Law or speech. And of course, they never missed the prayer of the day. However, they now listened to the Imam with a minor disappointing change in their programs. There were no more free lunches, and they had to come into the office a little sooner than before.

The *Shahid's* brother collected money from everyone who

wanted to eat a hamburger and purchased them from an Armenian man who everyone called Mosiuo. For a very reasonable price he made burgers with his own tasty recipe. Everyone loved and enjoyed them. The *Shahid's* brother was very good at his self-appointed assignment of buying hamburgers. During their thirty-minute lunch breaks, one of them would recite verses (previously heard from one of the Imams) to the rest of the group..

It quickly became obvious that there was bad blood between the Group of Six and the one whose father was a clergy and whose uncle was an important Ayatollah. Every morning, the Koran class from 6:30 to 7:30 went on in full force. Sometimes there were heated discussions amongst them, which disturbed the rest of the office members. I often had to interrupt and remind them that 7:30 a.m. to 4:30 p.m. are working hours and that if they wanted to have a Halal salary, which is paid to them from the *Bayt-al-Mal*, their time should not be spent on political or religious discussions. The Group of Six did not appreciate this from a Jewish boss, but they had no choice but to cooperate.

Days, weeks, and months passed and yet my wife and I still did not do anything regarding our plans to leave the country. The circle around minorities was getting tighter and smaller. Every day, we heard about different families who had tried to leave the country, and even though they had valid permissions for their trips, their passports had been confiscated and the husbands arrested and taken to jail. Of course, it was obvious that the first punishment was going to be seventy-two lashes of a whip for him. And to get out of jail he would have to pay a big sum of money to the Islamic *Komiteh*. As a result, people turned to human traffickers, which had become a new trade for many who had good connections in the Islamic *Komiteh*. Every *Komiteh* had its own Ayatollah who had his own connections in different government agencies.

There were different options for different people to get out of the country. One way, and the most expensive, was to simply fly out of the country through Mehrabad Airport. Another was to go from the border of Iran to Turkey by bus. All of it was high risk due to the fact that the connections in the airport and those at the borders of Iran and Turkey were not cooperating with one another. In fact, they caused problems for each other. It was a very frustrating procedure. The main concern of the people leaving was not the money anymore, but rather their own safe passage without getting caught.

Finally, my mother agreed to sell the house. She realized the country had changed. It was not easy for minorities in the Islamic Republic. The city, the streets, and the behavior of the people had also changed, especially those who had lived with us for so many years as Iranians, and not as Muslims, Jews, or any other minorities.

It took three months to sell my mother's house. The buyers allowed us to stay in it for another two months after escrow closed, because we needed time to find a new place. One of the most heartbreaking moments for me was when my mother delivered her house to its new owner. She had many years of happy memories. She walked around the empty rooms telling me about the time she and my father first saw the house with a broker. It was under construction then, but as soon as they walked in and saw the layout and its general location, both were excited about the house. She said, "We both said to the broker, 'This is the house we are looking for, although the street is not paved and a lot has to be done.' Your father and I went to the escrow office and made an offer. Within a month the house was ready. We sold the old house, everything happened so fast. Moving in this house was one of our best days of our lives. But now everything has changed." She walked from room to room touching the walls, remembering fond memories, especially when they prepared a room for my arrival after I finished my studies in America.

At this time, my uncle, who was a bachelor and happened to have a two-bedroom apartment, insisted we move in with him for as long as we needed. We stayed at my uncle's place for about five months. He enjoyed having a family and children around. Although all of us were very happy living together, it was still difficult for seven people from four different generations to live in a two-bedroom apartment.

After a while, we accepted an invitation from my mother-in-law to come live with her in her house. My mother and grandmother ended up moving into my mother's brother's house. The kids were very excited to move back to a house with a backyard. They once again could have their pet chickens and ducks, which they had previously given to Amaman (a nickname the kids called my mother-in-law). Until then, they had seen the chickens, ducks, and their grandmother only every once in a while.

The move from my uncle's apartment to my mother-in-law's house happened during a very cold snowy winter day. We lived in her house for around two years. We were very happy, because the house became the center for family gatherings. My mother-in-law took every chance to convince us not to leave the country, because she loved her children and grandchildren very much, and she was very happy having all of us around.

When the school year started, we took our older son to first grade and the younger one to pre-school. In the morning before the start of classes there was a prayer ceremony for all the students in the yard and it became customary after the revolution for the students strike themselves upon the heart (*Sineh-Zani*) with their right hand as a sign of mourning for the so-called *Shahids* (martyrs) of the Iran/Iraq war. The slogans most commonly used by the students in this service were *Marg Bar America* (Death to America) and *Marg Bar Israel* (Death to Israel). This was repeated a number of times. This ceremony usually took about an hour.

Four months passed and my eldest son became one of the best students in his class learning Farsi so fast that every time they had an exam, he passed with an 'A' and came home excited to tell his grandmother his score. He would shout, "Amaman, Amaman, I got another 'A'."

Meanwhile, we started looking for someone who had connections in the government agencies to get permission for all of us to leave the country. At the same time, we found someone who had good connections in the passport office. He got passports for my mother and my grandmother after we paid him a large sum of money. His name was Nader and after he received payment and our old passports, he promised to return in two weeks with new passports that contained everything we needed to leave the country legally by way of the Mehrabad airport.

He didn't come back until three months later.

We had to track him down through friends who had also made deals with him for members of their family. Once we found him, Nader said somebody turned him in and he was jailed for two and a half months. He was able to only get a passport for my grandmother, and not my mother, because for my mother the authorities said her passport would have to be issued in Hamedan, the city in which she was born. Therefore, my mother and some friends had to travel to Hamedan to get their passports. At least, that was some good news. My mother and her friends had their passports waiting for them in Hamedan to be picked up in person.

As soon as we had the passports for my mother and grandmother in hand, I purchased airline tickets for both of them from Tehran to Istanbul, Turkey. Within two weeks we were in Mehrabad airport to see my mother and grandmother off. On the way to the airport, my mother constantly gave my wife and I advise, reminding us that I had agreed to sell the house and leave the country. My mother said, "With all your hard work and worries, thank God we are on our plan now, and in a couple of hours we will leave the country. You two have promised me that at your earliest possible convenience you will join us." She looked at me and said, "Please take care of your family and yourself. Ignore any comments or situations regarding the revolution."

"I promise," I said.

"I also want to thank you and your wife for all you have done for me," my grandmother chimed in. Then she looked at me and said, "I have eighteen grandchildren. None of them bothered to help me except you. Therefore, I promise I will be around until you and your family join us." Even though my grandmother had been in a wheelchair and both my mother and grandmother were covered from head to toe in Islamic scarves and robes, they were still required to get naked and be completely searched by the women *pasdars,* called the *Khaharaneh Zaynab.* That was very embarrassing and traumatizing for both of them. Their checked luggage was emptied onto the floor. The *Khaharaneh Zaynab* went through every piece of clothing and personal items that the two women had brought with them. Everything was checked piece by piece, just because they were Jewish. It took the *Khaharaneh Zaynab* forty-five minutes to complete their search and most of the time the two old ladies were naked standing in the room. This terrible treatment was almost as bad as that of the Gestapo of Nazi Germany during World War II. Most of these *Khaharaneh Zaynab* were prostitutes during the time of the Shah's regime and now they had become "holy."

When my mother and grandmother came out of the room to board the plane, both were crying from their treatment by those cruel animals. Finally, they were able to get inside the plane and take off. My eyes were focused on that plane from the moment of takeoff until it disappeared in the sky, cruising toward freedom.

In the next hour and until I had heard from the airport officials that the plane had finally left Iran's border I worried that it would return, remove all its passengers, and arrest some of them, because this kind of scenario had happened many times before. I stayed at the airport the entire time, until I was certain they had arrived in Istanbul.

But all went well and they were picked up at Istanbul Ataturk airport and brought to a hotel by some friends with whom I had previously made arrangements. Two days later, they went back to the Istanbul Ataturk airport and flew to Israel. My brother was waiting for them there.

As my wife and I drove home from dropping off my mom and grandmother at the airport, I started crying very hard. As I looked around at the changed landscape, I remembered the summer of 1968 when I came home from my studies for a vacation. The Board of Education of Iran had arranged a visit to Maydane Shahyad for the students who had come to visit their relatives. A group of around two-hundred-fifty students were brought to the Maydane

Shahyad on some very modern buses. It was interesting for all of us to see the improvements and developments of our country. It was the Shah's desire to encourage Iranian students to come home when they completed their educational programs to serve their country. My wife also cried and said, "My God, look at what they've done to a beautiful piece of architectural art," as she pointed at the Maydane Shahyad. It was now covered in Islamic Regime graffiti, along with the pictures of different clergy members, including the Ayatollah Khomeini. The beautiful landscaping that once covered its grounds was now reduced to only a dirt lot.

Underneath the grounds was once a beautiful historical art center. We could only guess at what its condition was now, especially concerning the expensive art pieces that it held. I said, "This beautiful building is a symbol of freedom and represents development toward twentieth century when the Shah tried very hard to modernize the country. The history of our country has many glorious chapters and unfortunately some dark ones, too. Unfortunately, this revolution was the second attack by Islam upon the Iranian people, this time brought upon us by the Ayatollah Khomeini who tried, through religion, to bring the country back to the Stone Age.

CHAPTER 5

Nakhostvaziri

Now that my mother and my grandmother were out of the country safely I started working on getting my family and myself out, as well. The next day, when I went to work I must have seemed preoccupied, because the educated son of a clergyman, the one who sat to the right of me, was very friendly. He came by and asked me what was going on in my mind.

"Nothing," I answered.

He told me he thought the Group of Six was causing problems for me.

I replied, "No, I don't have any problems with them. I know why they are here and what their mission is. They are here to watch every employee so that there is no talk against the Islamic regime."

Then he asked me, "Why are you so disturbed? I can see in your face that you are not acting as your usual self?"

I knew I could trust this guy, therefore I said, "When you want to have a lunch break, let's have a talk."

At lunch, we walked on the street and talked and he asked, "Tell me, what is going on with you. I know times are difficult for minorities, and you being Jewish, you are not exempt."

"Do you promise me to keep a secret about whatever I am going to tell you?" I asked.

He sincerely promised and said, "Anything I can do for a good friend is my pleasure."

"Unfortunately, my wife is sick," I replied, "and here they cannot do anything for her. My uncle, who is a big surgeon in Germany, has asked me to send her to him and his family along with my children. But it is very difficult for us to gain permission to leave the country even though we have Islamic Republic passports. I am just looking for somebody to help me with this situation."

He said, "Let's go back to the office." When we got there, he made a phone call. Then he asked me to meet him after work at a specific location so I could drive him to someone he knew to discuss the situation.

When we left later, he brought his nine-year old son and we headed to the city of Shemran in northern Tehran, and ended up in one of those secluded homes in the mountains. To get there we drove through very narrow streets with old walls of ranch-type houses and freshwater mountain rivers. All the houses had very large private backyards. We came to a gate in front of a house, got out of the car and walked through a beautiful landscaped yard full of blooming, colorful flowers. The flowers led to the entrance of the house, which had an old, antique, wooden door. He knocked on it. A woman covered in scarves and a *chador* (Iranian women's Islamic clothing) opened the door. Two feet behind the door was a curtain, which prevented anyone from seeing the inside of the house. We waited a few moments until she said, "When you enter, the first door on your right is the room prepared for you." She then left.

My friend pushed the curtain to the side and directed me into the room. But before entering, we had to take our shoes off. He entered the room first with his son and I followed. There was another curtain hanging at the entrance of the room behind the door. As we walked in, the large room's floors were covered in Persian rugs and *mokhatehs* (Persian-style futons). He offered me a specific place to sit, and then there was a knock on the door. The curtain went back and a man servant walked in with a tray of Persian tea. But before drinking, a clergyman wearing a white turban walked in and we had to stand up in front of him. I had to watch my friend to see what he did and then follow suit.

My friend called him by the name of "Uncle Ayatollah." They greeted each other and my friend introduced me saying, "This is one of my best friends who is also a Jewish brother." I didn't know whether I should shake hands with him and waited for Uncle Ayatollah's first move.

He took a couple steps towards me and stretched out his hand to shake, which I very respectfully accepted. He said, "Our Jewish brothers are amongst the best minorities and friends we have in this country since centuries ago."

I was very surprised by his comment especially coming from a man in his position. He offered for us to sit and started talking to his nephew about his disagreement on some issues, pointing to Ayatollah Khomeini's large picture on the wall. He explained, "I left my position in Esfahan as the top Ayatollah and came to Tehran to bring my dissatisfaction with the *Komiteh's* behaviors towards the people. Through many letters I have brought the matter to Khomeini and he has ignored all of them and that is why I am here now." He turned towards me and told me about Jewish businessmen in Esfahan who were unfairly arrested, their homes and businesses confiscated, and that in some occasions were given seventy-two lashes by a whip and threatened with execution. He was the main Ayatollah to make any final decisions on any incarcerated people. He said, "When they brought the case to me for final judgment, I was so upset with the behavior of the *Komiteh,* that I decreed all of these mistreated people to be released at once and all their homes and businesses restored to them with no further harassments. But of course, I heard by the time the poor people got their houses back that most of their possessions were gone, and their homes had been stripped of all their curtains, light fixtures, and even the attached items, such as doors, windows, toilets, showers, and kitchen appliances. They told them they had to give everything to *Sazeman-h Mostasafin* (a department created after the revolution that supposedly took care of the needy). The only good news for the Jewish people was that after they got released from jail and had their businesses returned, they had the opportunity to make up for the big losses they had suffered."

He continued, "Due to the unjust behavior and lack of trust with this new government, many of Jews have tried to leave illegally to Turkey using smugglers. Some escaped successfully, but some were caught at the border by the *Komiteh* and thrown in jail or shot to death. This really made me angry so I started writing letters to the top man." He meant Khomeini. "No response," he said. "So, I decided to come here to talk to him directly. It's been three weeks since I've been here, and I have no appointment yet."

By now he was curious about my presence and turned to his nephew and asked, "Why have you brought your friend along?"

My friend said, "He has a problem which I think you can help him with. As I told you, he is one of our Jewish brothers with very strong feelings about Iran. But now unfortunately his wife has a problem the doctors cannot help in this country. He has sent a copy of the medical file to his uncle in Germany who is the head of a big hospital. The uncle in Germany asked him to send his wife where she can get the right medical attention. He has two boys aged five and six years old. They did not allow them to leave the country and he has even asked to let his wife and the boys go, but they denied the request and that's why we are here, asking you for your help in the situation."

Uncle Ayatollah stood up with anger in his face. I could not tell if his anger was regarding the *Komiteh* or me. While rubbing his beard he asked, "Why should a man not be able to take his wife to get the right treatment with his children? What do they expect him to do? Send his wife alone without the husband and children? He is the husband. He should be with her. Who is going to take care of the children?"

My friend replied, "They said the *Komiteh* might review the medical file and might let the wife go by herself. The husband told them let my wife and children leave, because he cannot take care of the boys by himself."

The Ayatollah kept rubbing his beard, again after a few moments of silence he finally said, "I have a friend in the passport office who would like to do something for me, because I helped him very much in the past," He looked at me and said, "I can give you a letter and his telephone number. You call him at home and tell him you are my friend and that you have a message from me. He charges about half a million *tomans* (Iranian currency). Do you have that sum of money or do you need time to get the money?"

I said, "I need a week to get the money."

We shook hands and he said, "You speak to my nephew and when you're ready to go along with the plan, then we'll continue." Then he left the room.

While driving back, we talked about other subjects, mostly the Group of Six and his differences with them. I took him to his house and drove home. While driving home, I was very confused about the result of our meeting. It seemed so easy given the situation in the country and at the same time it was a high risk.

When I got home my wife and I reviewed my meeting thoroughly, but could not make a decision. My wife and I kept this meeting and its outcome between the two of us, due to the fact we did not have that kind of money at the time. I had some money coming in from a friend who had borrowed it for some hospital expenses. He needed the money urgently just for a short time because his house was on the market and there was a serious buyer for it. In the morning I contacted him for the money. But unfortunately, his buyer had backed out and therefore he could not repay my money for at least for another month.

Under these circumstances, we had no alternative but to wait. Besides, even though it seemed like an easy solution, it still could involve a very high risk. If anything went wrong it could be very dangerous for us. Not only would we lose the money, but at the same time it could create a legal situation for my family and me.

By now, some of my very close relatives knew about our search for connections to get permission to leave the country legally. One of my close relatives came to us with good news about a sergeant in the police department who was a very good friend of a business partner of his, who had very good connections within the passport office. He said, "If you have a valid Islamic Republic passport, he can get you permission within a week for fifty thousand *tomans*."

I showed him the valid passport.

He said, "I will talk to my business partner in the morning to ask the sergeant to meet me then. I will bring him to the house so you can talk to him, then you can make up your mind."

Another week passed. I talked to the nephew of the "Uncle Ayatollah" at work and told him that the earliest time I could get the money would be in three to four weeks. I just wanted to keep that option open.

Office work was as usual. The Group of Six watched everyone's move carefully. Every week we had new horrible pictures of the warzone with bloodied dead soldiers on the walls of the office, placed there by the group, along with new slogans or speeches of the Ayatollah Khomeini. Everyone got used to seeing the new pictures of dead soldiers, which did not really bother us anymore. Everyone in the office knew me as being a cooperative Jewish guy that helped everybody by trying to meet the work schedule on time. My immediate boss and the Big Guy were really big supporters of the office employees and, of course, not of the Group of Six. I made sure everyone got credit for their hard work by mentioning their names to the Big Guy so he would recognize them.

Most everyone trusted me a lot, therefore they shared their problems with me. I always listened to everything they shared privately and tried to give them advice or help them if I could. I gathered from the comments that most of the office members were not happy with the revolution, especially the promises made by the Ayatollah Khomeini regarding freedom, peace, and cheap water and power. In fact, during the Shah's regime no one had to pay very much for these services, because they were part of the country's resources, and every Iranian had a share in them. But now the prices were tenfold.

One of the members of the office, who had years of experience in the Oil Industry and a good command of English, approached my desk with an assignment he had finished for my approval. By going through the file, I made a comment about his good analysis. Also, I was happy he was a part of our team.

He looked in my eyes and said, "My mentor was an educated man from England with many years of experience in the oil industry. He was hired to work in the Oil Company. He trained a lot of good men in this company, but unfortunately he was executed by the Hanging Judge."

I said, "Keep your voice down, because we are being watched." I approved the file and thanked him for his good work.

The Hanging Judge, or Mohammed Sadeq Givi Khalkhali, was a hardliner Shia cleric of the Islamic Republic of Iran and a Chief Justice. His happiness in executions earned him a reputation as Iran's Hanging Judge. Khalkhali was known to have been one of Khomeini's circles of disciples as far back as 1955 and constructed the former secret society of Islamic Assassins known as the *Fadayan-e Islam*. Khalkhali was chosen by Khomeini to be *Hakeme Shar-e* (Sharia Ruler), which was the head of newly established Revolutionary Courts that made Islamic rulings.

From the start he sentenced to death hundreds of former government officials on charges such as spreading corruption on earth and warring against God. Most of those executed did not have access to a lawyer or a jury. Reza Shah's mausoleum was destroyed under the direction of Khalkhali with Khomeini's approval. Khalkhali also made a trip to UAE and stated that the Persian Gulf should be renamed as The Muslim Gulf. He was one of those who openly hated Iran, Iranian culture, and Iranian history.

Khalkhali ordered the execution of Amir Abbas Hoveida, the Shah's longtime prime minister and Nematollah Nassiri, the head of SAVAK (secret police). Because pleas for clemency poured in from all over the world, Khalkhali was told by telephone to stop the execution. He said, "Hang on, let me find out what is happening." He then put the phone down, went to the imprisoned Amir Abbas Hoveida, and shot the man dead himself, then returned to the phone and said, "I am sorry, the sentence has already been carried out."

Khalkhali was known for his antipathy towards pre-Islamic Iran. In 1979, he wrote a book that branded King Cyrus the Great as a tyrant, a liar, and a homosexual, and called for the destruction of both the Tomb of Cyrus and the remains of the 2,500-year-old Persian palace in Shiraz, in Fars Province, Persepolis. Khalkhali came to Persepolis with a band of thugs and gave an angry speech demanding that the faithful torch the silk-lined tent city, and that the grandstand built by the Shah be destroyed.

Khalkhali later investigated and ordered the execution of many activists for federalism in Kurdistan and Turkmen Sahra, and sentenced up to sixty Kurds to death every day. Later he was forced to resign from the revolutionary courts because of his failure to account for $14 million seized through drug raids, confiscations, and fines. Many sources believe that by the time of his death, he had sent 8,000 innocent men and women to their deaths. In some cases, he was the actual executioner in which he killed the victims using a machine gun.

When my co-worker mentioned the Hanging Judge, his eyes filled with tears and I could see the anger in his face as he returned to his desk, while at the same time glancing over at the Group of Six as though he wanted to challenge them.

I called him back to my desk and opened the file again trying to calm him down so we wouldn't have some sort of crisis on our hands. Softly, I asked him to go for a walk-in order to stay away from trouble. As he stood by my desk I said, "When you mentioned the Hanging Judge, your story played in my head like a movie. In fact, we should be going home very soon. Please close your desk and go home early today with a smile on your face. This is the reward for your good job today on your file."

I was happy to see him leave early. Otherwise, there was a

chance of trouble between him and the Group of Six who had heard his comment regarding the Hanging Judge. As the Group of Six left the office, I kept myself busy on the phone with one of the files in process. They stood by my desk waiting for me to finish the phone call. I excused myself by hanging the telephone up and asked, "Can I help you, gentlemen?"

The very first member who joined the office angrily mentioned he heard somebody say the negative slogan about the Hanging Judge, adding, "This is not an expression we appreciate, used for our brother Khalkhali who worked so hard to rid our society of the anti-revolutionary people."

I said, "I understand your concern, but he heard someone in the lobby saying that slogan and he also was upset about hearing that no-good comment." I had to make up something or right away there would have been an uprising just to disturb the office environment. We had experienced this kind of situation in our building before.

I left the office heading home with thoughts of leaving the country becoming stronger each passing day. Every small incident made me think more and more about Uncle Ayatollah's suggestion. I tried to convince myself to go along with his plan.

There was also the new alternative of the police sergeant to consider. He would be coming to meet with us very soon and he was much cheaper and recommended by the partner of our relative.

When I got home, my wife said, "Our relative and the police sergeant are coming tonight and hopefully we can make the deal with him." After an hour, they arrived. The police sergeant wore a civilian suit so that no one would recognize him. The meeting lasted only thirty minutes and involved the inspection of the validity of the Islamic Republic passport and its final approval. We gave him the money and the passport and he promised to bring it back with the necessary permission no later than seven days from that day. He even told us to start packing because we would be on our ways very soon. He was so positive and assured us by adding, "Consider it done."

My mother-in-law had mixed feelings about the meeting. She

was happy for us, but at the same time she was saddened by the fact her grandchildren were going to be taken away from her. "I am missing you already," she said to the kids.

My wife and I promised that there would be a day when all of us would be together in America.

The next seven days went by very slowly and every day we expected the sergeant to come back with good news. Our relatives were sure the sergeant would give us what we needed, but nothing happened. Finally, it was the end of the seventh day. No sign of him. No news. Nothing. We contacted our relative who had set it all up for us. His partner assured us that the job was going to be taken care of. The partner said, "This is not the first time he has taken these sorts of jobs. He has done it many times before and knows what he is doing. Just give him more time"

Unfortunately, another week passed and still no news from the sergeant. Finally, the third week passed and then we knew something was wrong.

By this time the partner was, like us, concerned about the delay. And then the bad news. My relative showed up at our house with a small part of the money and no passport. He told us, "The guy in the passport office was arrested just two days after receiving your case. A big chunk of your money and your passport was confiscated by the authorities." In other words, we had lost most of our money as well as our valid family passport. But worse than anything else, the authorities now had our passport and all of our information about us.

A new week started and I went to work very upset and was really not in the mood to work. As usual, I got to the office and the Koran class was in session. New posters of bloodied bodies of recently killed soldiers replaced the old ones. I walked to my desk and without realizing it I had not said "good morning" to anyone. The Koran class was over and everybody got to their desks to work.

I noticed a Turkish coffee landed on my desk, which was brought to me by the guy on my left, the one wearing his army uniform from the Kurdistan war zone on his first day of work. I thanked him for the coffee.

He said, "Drink it and relax. If you need someone to listen, I am here."

"If you're available for lunch, let's go downstairs and talk for a few minutes," I suggested.

He nodded, and headed to his desk.

At lunch we went down to the lobby and I noticed a *Komiteh* member with four bodyguards enter. Everybody got out of their way. The *Komiteh* member's eyes focused on me and for a minute his face seemed familiar.

With a surprised loud voice, he shouted "Brother Parviz!"

Suddenly I did remember him. We used to work together in Abadan.

The man walked up to me with a large smile and his arms opened wide. He hugged me and for the first time in the Islamic Republic he kissed my face three times per Islamic custom. I was confused by his action due to the fact he knew I was a Jew. He said, "My friend. It's been such a long time. Where have you been hiding? I haven't seen you since the time you left the Abadan Refinery. Are you in this building now? We should get together. What is the number of your office?"

I just listened and nodded as he rambled on.

Then he looked at his watch and said, "I am sorry, I have to rush. Otherwise, I will be late to my appointment with the top man. Call me if you need anything, my friend." He kissed me again three times and left.

My co-worker friend and everybody else in the lobby looked at me strangely.

"Please let's go before we have another surprise," I said.

We walked toward the street and he asked, "Do you know who this guy is?"

I nervously ran my fingers through my hair. "We used to work together in Abadan."

"He's the son of one of the biggest Ayatollah's in the

government," my friend exclaimed. "You must have been very good friends that he hugged and kissed you twice Islamic-style."

I was getting more confused and concerned by the minute. "I know I can trust you," I confided to my friend. "Even though you came to the office in an army uniform straight from the Kurdistan warzone your first day at the office."

He nodded in agreement. "I was drafted and sent to the Kurdistan warzone. I had no choice but to go. You can't imagine what I went through, what I saw. Sometimes, our young Kurd brothers were executed by machine gun." He paused to relive the memory and then shook it off. "But we are here to talk about your problems, not mine."

"I was born in Sanandaj of Kurdistan," I admitted. "I am a Jewish Kurd." I let the enormity of my statement sink in. "Remember, you promised our conversation is going to remain our secret."

He nodded in agreement.

I then explained my current passport situation and described what happened with the police sergeant.

"Remember that I told you many of my relatives are in different law-observing positions?" he asked. "It was through their influence after many months in Kurdistan that I was finally able to get a release from the warzone." He then added, "My uncle is a colonel in the police department and he is quite fond of me. I will call him and tell him about your situation. If there is anything he can do, he will do it as a favor for me.

As soon as we got back to the office, he called his uncle, the colonel, and quickly and quietly explained my situation to him. The colonel asked my friend to send me to his office at 6:30 a.m. tomorrow. He would be waiting for me.

The next morning, I left very early to be on time for my appointment. I had to change three taxis just to get to my destination and arrived at the colonel's office minutes ahead of time. I introduced myself to the guard and he asked me to follow him. He knocked on the door and went inside, and said, "Sir your appointment is here. Shall I bring him in?"

The colonel got up and approached me with a smile. "I asked my nephew to send you this early so that we could have breakfast together." He dismissed the guard and said, "Hold my phone calls."

While we ate he explained, "My nephew told me everything in detail and asked me to help you as much as I can. He thinks very highly of you and the way you handle the office under the eyes of the revolutionary guards. He already let me know that you're Jewish. If they discriminate against you, look at those who have lost their lives and life savings. I see all sorts of unbelievable unjust criminal acts by these revolutionary *Komiteh*, who are backed by different Ayatollahs."

I explained everything to him thoroughly, and he asked, "What is the name of the officer?"

"He introduced himself as Azadi. When he came to visit us, he was wearing civilian suits with an Islamic-style one button shirt and no collar, looking very Islamic."

"Is he a skinny fellow with a mustache?"

I nodded my head.

He was furious. "That son-of-a-bitch is an opium addict." He then called his guard in and said, "Go to the department of personnel and ask for Azadi. Find out what time he is coming in and tell his boss to send him to my office as soon as he arrives."

The guard left and it took him about fifteen minutes to come back with the answer. "His boss said Azadi came to the office early and requested a two-week vacation to tend to his sick child and left in a big hurry."

The colonel shook his head and said to me, "When he is back, I will take care of him. Unfortunately, I have no connections in the office where your passport is now, but I will ask friends for any connections they might have and find out how we can get your passport back. The guy who is handling that department is one of those sons-of-bitches criminals who shoots the final shot into the head of the executed prisoners. It seems the more vicious and criminal they are, the more important their positions in the revolutionary government."

I asked the colonel, "Can you tell me about the office that confiscated my passport?"

He said, "It's one of the offices of Nakhosvaziri (which is the office that directly reports to the Prime Minister) and the guy's name is Sadri." He continued with disappointment by saying, "Very soon they will get in touch with you, by now they have all your information. It usually takes them about two to three weeks for someone in your position, and I am sure they will review your experience in the oil company, your vacations and if you have been out of the country, which countries you have traveled to, the purpose of your trip to any specific country and so on. What you have to do now is sit with your wife and prepare yourselves. Have you traveled to Israel in the last ten years? Prepare a good logical answer for it"

I said, "I am not in my own apartment now, they don't know where I am living."

With a smile, he said, "But they know where you work. Who knows, by now through the personnel office of the oil company they have your office address and your room number and very soon you will hear from them."

I thanked the colonel and left his office in a very miserable mood thinking about the tense situation I created for my family and myself. I had heard about the office of Nakhostvaziri and the guy who is in charge of the office. He hated Israel and didn't like the Jews at all. The smallest thing about Jews bothered him as a criminal act against Khomeini's revolution, especially if they had traveled to Israel, which they referred to as Occupied Palestine. I was so angry at myself and blamed myself for not turning to my friend's Uncle Ayatollah instead. I even considered smugglers who traveled by the border of Pakistan or through Afghanistan in a pickup truck, by S.U.V., or even camouflaged in sheepskin among hundreds of grazing sheep with shepherds.

But it was too late now. I lost our passport and some money. But above all, I created myself a criminal case and became what they called a *Mofsede-fel-Arz* (Criminal on the Earth), which jeopardized everything.

It took me an hour through the morning traffic to get to the office with an hour delay. Everyone was concerned about my delay except the colonel's nephew. One of the Group of Six walked to my desk and said, "You are late, brother," as though he was the boss and I was his employee.

I said, "My boss knew where I was." Then I asked, "Can I do anything for you?"

He got the message that I resented his question. Without a word he went back to his desk and continued talking to the Group of Six.

My friend approached my desk with a question about the file he was holding and said, "I need your opinion on this specific case." He laid the file on my desk and pointed to a note that said, "I will see you at lunch break downstairs." We acted as if we were studying the file and made different comments about it. Then he walked back to his desk. Everybody in the office worked on their assignments quietly, the only interruption was the voice of the Group of Six quoting verses of the Koran and translating them for the members of the office.

At lunch I met my friend on the street. He was very anxious about the outcome of the meeting between the colonel and me. He asked, "How was the meeting?"

I answered him, "Your uncle was very gracious, he offered me breakfast, and I could not refuse. I explained my case thoroughly and he listened carefully. Then he told me I have to prepare myself and my wife for when the authorities call on us to explain why we wanted to leave the country. Overall, it's not good news. I created a mess for my family and myself and I have to live with it and face the consequences."

My friend was very sorry about the situation. He said, "Don't worry. You haven't done anything wrong. You are not a criminal. You haven't killed anybody and you always have been a very law-abiding citizen. There is not even the smallest action against the revolution in your record, either. And in this position you have proven yourself to be an honest, hard-working man with the support of the big man and even the top man. So, your wife is sick and you wanted to send her to be taken care of, that's all."

I looked at him and said, "It's easy for you to say. The people who handle that specific department are a bunch of animals. They try to make everything out of nothing, especially if you are Jewish and have traveled to Israel, or as they call it, *Occupied Palestine.*"

We headed back to the office. When I was in the lobby I remembered the *Komiteh* brother whom I had met there not long ago, and thought he might be able to help me, but I had no information about him except his name.

The day was over and I headed home with a very heavy heart. I felt like I wanted to go into the mountains, where nobody could hear me, and shout as loud as I could and curse everybody and everything. I was so disappointed because everything went wrong for me and I had to go through a lot of problems to overcome them. I imagined getting home and breaking the disappointing news that came out of my meeting with the colonel to my wife. I dreaded her reaction.

When I told her she listened to everything and asked, "What is going to happen to us now? I am not worried about the children or myself. I am worried about you. If they make a criminal case, or as they say *Mofsede-fel Arz*, they'll take you to Evin Prison and after a short time they'll release your executed body to us. Is this what we are heading for?" She was angry, furious, disappointed, and disgusted with the situation we were in.

I tried to reason with her by saying, "Believe me, nothing like that is going to happen. We have to plan and prepare ourselves for the questions they most likely will ask.

CHAPTER 6

A Summon to the Office of Nakhostvaziri

The next day I had a visitor in civilian Islamic suit in my office with a letter in his hand summoning me and my wife to the office of Nakhostvaziri. I was not surprised, but I hadn't expected it to happen so soon. He asked me to go to the hallway with him to speak with me. For a minute I thought he would arrest me, but to my surprise, he asked me to appear with my wife the next day at 8:00 a.m. in for some questions. At least I was happy he did not create a commotion in the office in front of my colleagues. I thanked him, he left, and I went back to work. A very excruciating day passed before I left.

I got home with the bad news. My wife read the letter and asked me, "What are we going to do? Are we going to Nakhostvaziri tomorrow or are we going into hiding?"

Although I was nervous myself I said, "We are going and we will tell them the truth. We haven't done anything wrong, the worst they can say is 'You are not allowed to leave the country.'" That wasn't anything new. We knew that already. I added, "We have to be very calm and show no sign of weakness. It's going to be all right.

In the morning my wife and I left the house for our appointment to meet Mr. Sadri, the head of the department. We arrived at his office on time, and the same man who met me the day before in my office was waiting for us. He asked us to remain in the waiting room. We waited for about fifteen minutes then they called us in.

Sadri was a bearded, medium-built gentleman with a very vicious look. I saw a real criminal in front of me, with the blood of so many innocent people on his hands. His look created a very avenging feeling in my heart, and in a split second I cursed him a thousand times in my mind.

With a sarcastic humiliating voice, he asked me, "Is this your passport?"

I answered, "Yes."

"How did you get this passport?" he asked. "I see this is good and genuine issued by the Islamic Republic."

"Of course, this is a genuine issued by the Islamic Republic, what did you expect?"

"Then why did you go through those scalpers to get permission to leave the country?"

I looked straight into his eyes and said, "Because the passport office denies minorities permission to leave the country."

He acted as though he was surprised. "That's not true, why do you accuse them with this nonsense?"

"Mr. Sadri, my wife and I filled-out the passport form and my wife went to the passport office three days in a row until she was finally allowed to submit the form. Although they accepted the application and the fees, they denied us due to being Jewish. I ask you sir, isn't it the order of the leader of the revolution Imam Khomeini that our Jewish brothers are our minority brothers? If so, then why are they denying us permission to legally travel? Saying Jewish people cannot leave the country? Someone introduced me to a sergeant in the police force and said, 'He knows people in the passport department and will take care of it,' and we ended up losing fifty-thousand *tomans* and our valid passport because we trusted him." I looked at my wife; she was biting her lip giving me the sign that said, *don't go too fast, this guy is not a responsible and understanding person.*

Suddenly his face became red and I could see he was upset about my comments. He said, "I have to ask you people some questions separately." Referring to me he added, "You can wait outside. I will interrogate your wife first and then it's going to be your turn." He called his assistant and said, "Take him to the waiting room." The secretary led me out.

I tried to listen to the questions and answers through the broken window of the door. As I had anticipated, the questions were about Occupied Palestine (Israel). Asking my wife, he started with, "Have you ever traveled to Occupied Palestine?"

My wife answered, "Yes."

"When and how many times?"

"Three times, once when I was single, with my mom for medical attention because she was sick, and the second time with my husband when we had just married, to ask the Almighty for a healthy and happy life by visiting the holy land of Jerusalem…"

As soon as she said 'Jerusalem', he angrily corrected her, "*Al-Ghods*, not Jerusalem, there is no Jerusalem. What about the third time?"

"The third time, I was pregnant and we believe in the power of the Almighty to visit his holy land and ask for a healthy baby."

There was a silence and the next question he asked was "Do you have any relatives there?"

"I have some relatives who have lived there for many years, but we are not in contact with them."

"This question is very important and I want you to think about it before answering. Are you a Zionist?"

She answered, "I don't have to think about it to answer that. No, I am an Iranian and my ancestors have lived in this country for 2,700 years. I speak Farsi. I studied in university and worked in this country. I call myself Iranian Jewish and I practice Judaism by observing the orders of our holy Torah." She spoke very confidently without any hesitation.

He called his assistant in and told him, "Take the *sister* to the waiting room and bring the husband in." He led my wife out of the room and asked me to enter his office.

When I stepped inside, he said, "You have a very smart and brave wife. She answered my questions without any hesitation and very straight forward. You are a lucky man."

I thanked him for his compliment.

"Are you going to be truthful like her?" he asked.

"I don't have to lie about anything, why would I have to lie?"

"I know you have a very responsible job and your boss is very happy with your performance, because we already talked to him and his boss. They think you are an asset to the oil company, you work hard, you are very precise, you run your office very smoothly without any friction with different people and different ideas. But the question is why do you want to leave the country?"

I said, "No one wants to leave his country, his job, his years of accomplishment and just walk away. I have a good record of my accomplishments here and more than anything else among a thousand interviewed employees I was the only minority who got the job in the Ajnas department. My bosses, as you know, are very happy with me because I care for my country and the future of my country".

He kept looking at the passport and a file, which he had requested from the personnel office of the oil company. "Tell me brother, how many times have you traveled outside of the country?"

"I don't really know the exact numbers, but many times. The very first time I traveled to the U.S.A. I went there to acquire my higher education and during a summer vacation I came back to visit my family"

"Were you ever part of any political groups in the U.S.A.?"

"What do you mean by political group?"

"I mean with American government, like the C.I.A.?"

I laughed. "You must be kidding me! The C.I.A.? Of course not, what do I want with the C.I.A.? I was just a foreign student who had to work and study hard."

He asked, "Why didn't you continue your higher education in Iran?"

"Because there weren't enough universities to accommodate the number of graduating high school students back then. Therefore, many went abroad to work and study. Is studying abroad a crime? If I hadn't gone and didn't obtain that knowledge, I wouldn't be useful now to my country like I am now. May I ask what gave you the idea of this ridiculous C.I.A. notion?"

"The Islamic Republic of your office has a note in your file that the president of the United States of America, Ronald Reagan, signed your graduation diploma."

I was beyond frustrated by his ridiculous remark and replied, "No offense, but whoever wrote that note must be the most stupid, idiotic person on the face of the earth."

He was angered by my comments. "If I were you, I would watch my language. This note was written by a very dear *brother*, whom I've known for many years, and together we were among the revolutionary people who brought down the filthy Pahlavi. Therefore, no more such comments will be accepted."

"I'm sorry," I said, "but when someone accuses someone else of something they don't understand, and then incorrectly relates it to how it's going to hurt the image of the revolution, the result can be very dangerous. The reason the signature of President Ronald Reagan is on my diploma is because at the time of my graduation in Los Angeles in the state of California, he was the Governor of California and the President of the Trustee. His signature is not only on my diploma, but also thousands of others who graduated during his term as governor. You see, *brother* Sadri, anybody in your position without your knowledge and understanding could have made a very drastic mistake, but I am happy a man of wisdom like you are handling this situation. That's why I lost control and got upset and made that comment."

He looked puzzled and I was sure he didn't know anything about being an American Governor or the President of the Trustee, but he acted as though he understood and knew whatever I was telling him.

"I have to look into this matter very cautiously," he said. "I have other questions to ask you. As I recall you said earlier, you traveled to other countries many times before, is that right?"

"Yes."

"Can you name me the countries you traveled to?"

"Of course," I replied. "I was twenty-one years old when I traveled to Israel on my way to the U.S.A. and visited the holy land to pray for success in my studies and a successful future."

He interrupted me and said with an angry voice, "There is no Israel! We call it Occupied Palestine, and from here on, you should call it Palestine, do you understand? No more Israel, Palestine!"

I said, "Fine, it is *Palestine*, not Israel, but do you think the problem of the area is going away by calling it Occupied Palestine or Palestine?"

I could feel in his voice he was getting annoyed by my answers. "Did that piece of land help you in your life?"

I replied, "Muslims go to Kaaba in Mecca, Saudi Arabia, for Hajj, to become Hajji, and as far as I know many of my Muslim friends have made the trip. It's something that has been in our culture for generations in Islam or Judaism. You as a Muslim and I as a Jew believe in that"

Angrily he asked the next question "How many times have you traveled to Palestine and why? The first time you went to pray for your future. What about the other times? Do you have relatives in Palestine?"

"Yes"

"Did you visit and spend time with them?"

"Yes."

"Are they Zionists?"

"I don't know what they are. I hadn't seen them since I was a school boy and just for a very short time"

"Are you a Zionist?"

I replied by asking, "How do *you* explain Zionism brother Sadri?"

He replied, "There is only one way to explain it and that is Zionists are occupiers and murderers who have brought misery on our Palestinian brothers and sisters, taking over their lands and making them leave their homes. That is the meaning of Zionism and one day that name is going to disappear from all the maps and dictionaries of the world.

"Yes, that is Zionism to me in my book, as well," I said. "No, I am not a Zionist in the sense that you are talking about." I was getting restless and he was frustrated with my answers.

He looked at the clock on the wall in front of him and said, "I have another appointment that I am already late for. We have to have another appointment. My brother secretary will make an appointment for you for next week. But I tell you now, don't you get any ideas about leaving the country, because if you do and they catch you, you will be shot by the firing squad, and I will put the last bullet in your head myself."

I kept my cool, but I wished that I had a gun so I could shoot him right there in his head myself. Without waiting for him to excuse me to leave, I opened the door and walked out.

My wife saw my face and she knew right then that the meeting had not gone well. The brother secretary gave me an appointment note for the next Wednesday at 9:00 a.m. in the same office and told me, "Don't be late, he hates people coming in late for their appointments." But then he added, "I know you are a very hard-working man. I saw your office and the mixture of the staff you have and the way you get along with every single one of them. To save the *Bayt al-mal* is appreciated by your boss."

We left Nakhostvaziri, but before getting a taxi to go to my office, I explained everything to my wife, except the part of him warning me to 'not try to leave the country, if we catch you, you will be shot.'"

She listened and said, "My god! It doesn't look good. What are we going to do? We have to find someone who knows him and pay him to let us off the hook." We got a taxi and headed to my office. I paid the driver and paid him extra to take my wife home.

It was almost lunch break and most of the staff had gone for lunch. I got to my desk and noticed a pile of finished files sitting on my desk for my review and approval. My friend came to me and asked, "How did it go?"

"Not good," I replied. "Let's meet on the street before we go home and I'll fill you in."

For the rest of the workday, I kept my mind occupied with the pile of files. I called my wife and told her, "I will be home in an hour and please don't worry, everything is going to be all right."

After work I explained everything to my friend on the street while we walked. He was concerned for my family and I said to him, "You know that's my luck. I have experienced bad luck so many stupid times before. I always get what I want, but with a lot of agony, hard work, distress, and whatever you want to call it. At the bottom of my heart, I know these days someday soon will be over and they will be only bitter, harsh and nerve-wrecking memories. It's all right. My only concern is to find someone who is a friend with Sadri. I am sure he has a price, but who and how, I have no idea."

We said goodbye and I got into a taxi. I made it back home in about an hour. We had some of our close relatives visiting us. They already knew about our meeting with Sadri. I told everyone not to worry, but especially my wife, to whom I said, "Honey, in my heart I believe everything is going to be all right."

My relative told us about a mutual relative of ours who had just left with his wife and four children through a businessman he knew. They have taken so many families, men, women, children, old, and young to Turkey by the route of Khoy and Salmas. Thank God not even one of the cases got caught. He spoke very highly of the man and the connections the guy had.

I had a smile on my face. "Well, we just had a similar case, in fact, and it was a masterpiece," I said sarcastically. "The result of it was the loss of our money, passport, and the agony of meeting with Sadri today and next week, and how many future meetings I don't know."

He said, "I know you can't trust anybody anymore, but if I were you, I would at least meet with the head of this crew and hear them out."

"Fine. Given the circumstances we are in it's not a bad idea to look at every possible avenue to save ourselves."

"I will bring them here tomorrow at 6:00 p.m. Actually, they are in town now for a few days and they have a group of six people already scheduled to take on their next trip to Turkey."

He left and another nerve-wrecking idea shadowed over our thoughts and plans.

The next day at work my thoughts were preoccupied with the meeting of the new crew that had now popped up in our escape story. After work I went home, had a fast dinner, and at 6:00 p.m. the doorbell rang. I opened the door and saw our relative with a bearded man in a khaki jacket of about fifty years old and a younger man of about thirty in casual clothing. I told them, "Do not talk at all until we get upstairs on the second floor, because the neighbor on the first floor is very nosy and wants to know everything about us." We made it upstairs and closed all the doors so that nobody could hear us in the stairwell and downstairs. We all sat and my mother-in-law served everybody tea and sweets.

My relative introduced the two men as Saleh (the *Komiteh*-looking one with the khaki jacket) and Abdollah (the younger one).

Saleh noticed our two sons watching TV and said, "The children are a problem. I know because we have taken families with much smaller and younger children than these two. When are you planning to go? Because we are in the middle of winter, and all the mountains are covered with snow. The nights are very cold. It's uncomfortable for the children, but if you wait until the end of spring it will be much easier for the children and your wife." Saleh went through the escape plan completely, step-by-step, and at the end he said, "We know your feelings. You can't trust anybody after what has happened to you. And I also know that you are worried about your family, their safety, and the hardship of the trip. I am not telling you it is easy, but it's doable, and we have done it before. Thank Allah."

We did not talk about the price, because our relative had told us it would be one-hundred-thousand *tomans* per person. Now with

Sadri on our case, we had no choice. I asked my last question before they left our house, "If there is a situation, and we decide to leave sooner, is it possible to do so with Sadri?"

"We hope they don't bother you that much, but if they want to make a criminal case of it, let our friend know and we'll try to accommodate you with every possibility at our disposal." We set our next meeting for the up-coming week on the same day and same time of the week.

As soon as they left, my wife and I got in our car and went to the house of Mr. Simani, the top man who introduced this group to our relative. He was a very successful businessman and a relative of my father-in-law and he had a lot of respect for my father-in-law. My father-in-law had helped him when he had just entered the world of business, and had given him every support. Therefore, as soon as he saw my wife and me, he assured us that the escape plan through Saleh and Abdolah was safe and legitimate. He told us, "Anytime you are ready to leave, let me know a day earlier. I will contact them and ask them to come to you. In fact," he said to my wife, "now that I know you are the daughter of my mentor, whom I respect like my own father and whose help I have never forgotten, it's now my turn to return the favors by helping you get out of this hell. Go home and stay out of trouble and when you are ready, just call me and say, 'The flowers in the greenhouse are blooming,' and I will send them to you within a day."

We got in the car and I felt very relaxed. We went to a store to buy some ice cream and sweets to celebrate our small lucky break. We came home and my wife explained everything to her mother regarding how graciously the relative had treated us. Also, how kindly he had agreed to do his best for us when he heard about us and our situation.

My mother-in-law said, "Mr. Simani respected your father very much. If he assured you about the trip, then it's going to be okay."

The week passed, and again we had to go to Sadri's office. We were there fifteen minutes earlier than our appointment time. The secretary was pleased to see us on time and asked us to wait in the waiting room. A few minutes passed, and I was called in. My wife asked if she had to go in with me, but Sadri said, "I don't have any questions for you. In fact, you shouldn't have come today, but as long as you are here, sit and wait."

I walked into the office and said good morning in Farsi to him. He looked at me, and said in an unfriendly voice, "Time has changed and now we say *Sobah-Komolahol-Balkhair*, go ahead and sit down. I have a situation here which bothers me, my secretary asked many people whom you worked for and work with, we even contacted the personnel office in Abadan, and everybody talks very highly about you. Why did you get yourself involved with that stupid sergeant? You treat the staff in your office so well, the Islamic Brothers talk that you even helped them with their English studies."

I answered, "If I can help anybody, I will, it makes me feel good to be helpful."

"But we have a problem here," he replied, "which makes me very angry. You have a brother in Palestine, he was in the army and you didn't tell me about him."

"You didn't ask me about my brother, but yes, I have a brother in Palestine and he has lived there for many years."

"So that makes you a Zionist."

"No, with all due respect he lives there and I live here and when I finished my studies I came back to Iran to help my country. Iran is *my* country. My ancestors have lived in this country for 2,700 years. Our holy Torah commands us to respect the land you live in, respect the government and the leader of the land and that's the reason I work hard and help my countrymen as much as I can."

"Why didn't you go to the passport office to get permission to leave the country legally?"

"I told you before, we filed the application, but they denied us permission to leave the country legally because we are Jewish. My wife is sick, she has to go for medical attention, my uncle is the head of a hospital. He has seen her file and asked me to send my wife to him, my uncle will take care of her and the children can stay at his home with his wife. I even told them at night I would come and sleep at the *Komiteh* if necessary. We were denied again and again, and finally this sergeant came along and made it very easy for us. I am not happy about what I have done and I wish I hadn't fallen in his stupid trap. I lost the money and the family passport."

"Your passport is here with me, but I can't give it back to you because you broke the law. Remember we know where you work, where you live and how much you make as salary. In short, we know everything about you, you are being watched and your passport is here with me. I have to ask you to leave now, because I have another appointment. I will see you in a month. Make an appointment with my brother secretary. Come alone next time, it is not necessary for you to bring your wife."

We took a taxi to the office and I paid extra for the driver to take my wife home. Sadri's comment, "your passport is here with me," rang in my head over and over again until I finally decided to talk it over with my friend, the colonel, to ask him if I should pay of Sadri so he'd leave us alone.

The colonel said, "If I were you, I wouldn't think of mentioning a word about a pay-off to Sadri, because he is known to be the most brutal and trickiest people in Nakhstvaziri. If he really is looking for money to release your passport, he will send someone to contact you. You shouldn't initiate the smallest move toward him."

I decided to forget Sadri's comment about the passport and wait until our next appointment.

I reviewed in my mind the events that had occurred over the last four years of the revolution, and the charade of everyday unpleasant situations the Iranian people had been forced to encounter. Also, how these brutal events had made me stronger little by little, even in Sadri's case with the confiscation of our family passport and losing my money. Everything had become a challenge—the type of challenges that could result in jail time or even my execution if I stepped out of line. It had become a game because the revolutionary guards and *Komiteh* brothers were groups of rotten thieves who robbed the Iranian people in any way that they could. As a result of their wicked actions, every member of the *Komiteh* brothers became very rich and wealthy in a very short period of time. There were always homes to be raided based on any excuse, even if people just mentioned anti-revolution jargon, to get whatever they needed.

It had become routine for three to four of the *Komiteh* brothers and a *Khahran-e-Zainab* to ride in Toyota SUV's throughout the city looking to harass the ordinary, everyday people, especially women, making sure they wore their Islamic robes and scarves, or *Maghnaeh* (Islamic scarves), which covered the head and hair completely so they wouldn't accidentally sexually arouse men.

They wanted to make sure that if they saw a man and a woman, or a young man and a young woman, driving in a car together without any children that they were either husband and wife, or brother and sister. By stopping their cars, getting the man out of the vehicle, and asking for his identification card they also asked about his relationship with the woman sitting in the car, as well as having a *Khahran-e-Zainab* check her face for any sign of makeup or lipstick per Islamic rules. The smallest mistake would have high consequences for those pulled over, which meant being arrested, taken to the *Komiteh,* and being punished with heavy monetary fines. Most of the time all this was accompanied with many lashes of a whip across the back. The fines had become another way to rob people legally.

People were slowly becoming used to the behavior of the *Komiteh* and tried to ignore them as much as possible. I was stopped so many times with my wife in the car by the same *Komiteh* car and same *Komiteh* brothers, who asked for my identification and proof of our being husband and wife, even though they already knew us well. They always checked to make sure my wife had no makeup on and that she had her hair covered completely according to Islamic law. They were the most unreliable, unpredictable, and most irresponsible people on the road with no experience or training in handling a gun or machine gun and caused many unpleasant accidents on the road, which ended up killing or injuring innocent people. Therefore, anytime anyone was stopped by them, he or she had to be very cooperative and answer their stupid questions, while trying to stay cool and not get angry. Some of the *Komiteh* brothers were as young as twelve or thirteen years old, with no education. They had come to the big cities from the small villages. They were given a tiny, confiscated apartments or houses for their families from the Big Man (the Ayatollah) of the *Komiteh*. The Ayatollah usually had three or four *Komitehs* under his control. The *Komitehs* were paid by the local mosque of the area, which had control over them.

As usual, each *Komiteh* member had to attend prayer services five times a day at a mosque to be enlightened by the speech of the Imam of the mosque. They left the mosques mesmerized and with full stomachs of free food, prayer services, and the speeches of the Imam of the mosque. They were ready to do anything for the revolution, their bosses, and especially for their leader, the Ayatollah Khomeini.

It wasn't pleasant for the ordinary people who had been caught in the middle of the revolution, and the chaos it brought created by a bunch of hoodlums. People did not respect each other as they used to, and everyone blamed somebody else for having participated in the demonstrations against the Shah and supporting the Ayatollah Khomeini. Nobody dared say anything against the people in charge of the country. In the morning, many people left their homes to go to work, but never came back. It was not safe anymore. Children were influenced by their teachers, who were mostly from the *Komiteh*. All the minority schools, which had been built by donations from the minority people, were eventually taken over by the Islamic revolutionary guards. Minority children were often watched closely and questioned about their families, and about their conversations at home. Many parents were arrested and jailed because they complained about the revolution inside their homes in front of their children not realizing that their children had been brainwashed. We were lucky to find out about this very soon one day when we had company and were watching the news on a television broadcast of one of Khomeini's speeches. One of the guests made a remark about Khomeini and made a sign with his fist to the television.

Suddenly my older son, who was in first grade, got upset and with an angry voice said, "You said that to Imam Khomeini. He is the father of all of us and every morning before the start of our classes we pray to him."

I speedily said, "No, no. He meant the other guy who was against Imam Khomeini. We pray for him too, and we love him like our father."

We decided to let the other parents know what was going on in the schools, and with our children. We had no choice for the time being, although we were already planning to leave the country by then. We couldn't keep our children home, because our neighbors would notice if we didn't send our kids to school and they would report us to the authorities.

One month passed and I had to go to Sadri's appointment. Even though Sadri had told us, "Your wife should not come," she insisted on coming along with me anyway, and promised to stay outside of the Nakhostvaziri building. She was concerned that I might be arrested if I went alone and that her presence would not affect anything if that was the decision they had already made, which had happened to many before.

As usual, I was on time. The brother secretary asked me to sit down and wait in the waiting room. For a moment I felt really scared, and had a very bad feeling about the meeting. A few minutes passed, and I was called in fifteen minutes delayed after my appointment time, which made me more nervous.

The brother secretary opened the door and asked me to go in. I walked in and stayed quiet without any greeting, because I didn't want to say greetings in Arabic. Mr. Sadri commanded me with an angry voice, "Sit down," and pointed at the chair in front of him.

I said, "Thank you," and sat down. For the first time in his office I could hear my own heart beating as though it was going to jump out of my chest.

He looked at me and asked, "Did you come alone?" I said, "No, my wife is with me, but she is waiting outside of the building. I had to bring her along because she has a doctor's appointment later today. I have taken a day off to come to you and go with her to her appointment."

He said, "I am glad you answered my question correctly, because I saw you with her from this window." He then added, "I see you haven't left the country yet, and you and your family haven't escaped from the border, either. You know I have told you, if you try to leave the country, I am sure you will be caught. You will be executed on the spot."

I said, "I have no intention of leaving my country, my people, or my job. I have a very rewarding and responsible job and as the result of my and my colleague's hard work at the office we are recovering and saving millions and millions of dollars of the *Bayt al- Mal* money for my country. I have no intention of leaving."

He said, "But you tried to get permission to leave through the sergeant."

"You are right, but I was going to leave my wife and children with my uncle and return to my job and country within a week. I already told you this. Besides, I have no money to go to other countries. My wealth is summarized in my wife and my two sons. I am happy here with my job and my family."

He listened to every word I said. "I have to tell you about how happy your superiors are with you, and how well you manage all the brothers and how productive you are. Therefore, we want you in the country. We have good doctors in Iran, too. Your wife can get all her medical attention here. I tell you under any circumstances you and your family are not going to get the permission to leave the country, therefore every month you have to report to me by coming in to my office. The brother secretary will make an appointment for you, and don't forget that we check your office every once in a while through our agents and follow your progress at work."

I left his office and joined my wife. We walked for fifteen minutes, and I explained everything to her especially regarding whether I had come alone or with her, because he had seen us getting out of the taxi together. I could feel that the circle for me, or perhaps for the Jewish people in general, was getting tighter and tighter. Sadri was a symbol of the revolutionary people. He was a man with a very sensitive position, in a very important government office.

I said to my wife, "As you see, we have no chance with this guy, and I don't know if he is the kind to be bribed either, because he hasn't made a smallest move to release our passport in return for money. I talked to different people about the situation, and almost everybody thinks that cannot be bought. Let's think about our options."

From then on Saleh's option was in my head all the time. Finally, my wife asked, "Are you thinking about something, and not sharing it with me? Can I ask you what is on your mind?"

"Saleh," I replied.

"I thought so. I was thinking about him, too," she admitted. "He is the only choice we have, and my father's friend assured us about everything. My mind is somehow at ease with Saleh's group."

"We have two or three months' time, if we decide to go with Saleh," I said. "We will know more about their operation next week when we meet them. But we don't want to tell them anything about Sadri's comments. If they question us about him, we just say every month I have to go see him for a few minutes. That's all."

Another week passed and it was the appointment time with Saleh and Abdolah. They came to my mother-in-law's house and very quietly behind the closed doors Saleh explained the plan to my wife and me. It was so confidential that even my mother-in-law wasn't allowed to know the details of our escape. Saleh and Abdolah told us everything; details from the start of our escape trip, until we got to Turkey, and eventual freedom. To make us feel better, they shared the different missions during the last three previous months that they had successfully completed. "Trust us," they said, "we have seen this among other people, too. It is very normal to worry and think about the safety of your family. In three months', time, the spring weather will be much better than now. That's why we asked you to wait until spring, for the sake of the safety of the children." Looking straight in my eyes, Saleh said, "If it were you alone, or just you and your wife, I wouldn't hesitate to take you anytime you were ready to go. Even tomorrow. My only concern is the hardship of the cold winter weather for the children. Of course, if it is an emergency situation, and if it's a must, with a little more warm and heavy clothing for the children available, it is doable, not impossible. But in case of an emergency, and you decide to start your plan sooner than three months, just tell Mr. Simani to contact us, and we will come to you as soon as possible."

Saleh and Abdolah left. My wife and I had mixed feelings even though we had been assured so much by both of them. Finally, I said to my wife, "We both know, no matter what, we have to escape this hell that we are in. And of course, any decision we make has its share of risks. But I have a very good feeling in my heart about our chances and our success with this escape plan."

The fee of the trip was set by Mr. Simani at 100,000 *tomans* ($15,000) per person. The money would stay with Mr. Simani until we were delivered safe and sound in Turkey. Then Saleh and his crew would get their money.

The second month of the cold snowy winter had already started. I was sitting in a warm, cozy living room with a glass of homemade red wine in my hand looking at the front yard. All the fruit trees and tall rose bushes around the big fishpond were covered with fresh snow. I looked at the west side of the front yard, which was covered by a very large canopy. The canopy had been built many years earlier by my father-in-law for a small vine tree that had grown into a large one, and produced tons of grapes for red wine. The old vine tree was lying on the canopy for its winter sleep as though enjoying the cold blanket of snow, trying to recover her strength for the coming spring. I took a sip of my wine and said, "Thank you, old friend, your red wine has a very special bouquet, and the vodka from the residual of the grape makes our melancholy and anxious days bearable."

I called my wife and said "Honey, come and see what a beautiful snowy day it is today. Look at the front yard. Everything is covered with white snow. Sometimes you can see sparrows flying around looking for food inside the duck houses under the canopy." I sighed and hugged her. "Tell me, will there be a day that we see peace and tranquility among our people and country again? Will there be another chance for us to come back to our country to visit our friends and relatives to refresh our memories and create new ones?"

She listened to me very quietly and finally said, *"Khodah Bozorgeh"* (God Is Big).

CHAPTER 7

Deciding to Leave the Country as Soon as Possible

I said to my wife, "Look at us, we are standing behind the window and staring at a snow-covered front yard with a glass of red wine talking about our escape from my birthplace as though the town was safe and everything is *dandy-dandy*. As if the last four years had never happened, with no one knowing what would be in store for us in the future. We have so much work to do and at the same time can't do anything."

Again, she said in Farsi "*Khodah Bozorgeh* (God is Great)."

For a minute I lost my cool. "Those who lost their lives, homes, husbands, sons, daughters, relatives, businesses, and the many other things, where was their God? Either, their God wasn't great, or their God was different from the God of the rest of the world."

My wife got upset with me. "With that attitude," she shot back, "and weak belief in God, you want to make a dangerous and difficult journey with two small children riding horses through mountains? I am surprised at you."

Right away I pulled her close, hugged and kissed her and said, "You know that I am a God-fearing man, and any step I take I will always mention his name. I hope that with his help and wishes we can be successful in our journey to freedom."

At this time, I noticed my children in the front yard playing in snow with their ducks, which were all grown up by now. I said to my wife, "Let's go downstairs into the yard and join the children." She agreed and we played in the snow. And for a few minutes we forgot about the world and its problems.

In the morning, my wife took the children to school and picked them up as usual. I got home after a very busy workday where I had to attend meetings regarding the recovery files for the approval of the Islamic *Komiteh*. I was very tired and after dinner, my wife and I reviewed our exit plans. But then I noticed my older son rubbing the left side of his chest above his heart. I said to my wife, "I wonder why he is doing that?" And then we noticed the younger one is doing the same thing. I said to my older son, "Why are you rubbing your chest?"

He became nervous and said, "It's nothing."

I asked the younger one, "What about you?"

He also became anxious and answered the same.

I opened their shirts and noticed both of their chests, in the area over their hearts, was bruised, black and blue. "What happened to you two?" I asked, very concerned. "Did somebody hurt you?"

They said, "No, nobody hurt us. It's okay."

"What do you mean *okay*?" I said. "That is not okay. Bruises don't happen by themselves. What happened to you two?"

"Please papa," my older son pleaded. "Don't say anything to the school principal and the teachers." My two young sons were afraid to tell me what had happened to them.

"Don't worry," I assured them. "We are your parents and we love you very much. We are not going to create a problem for you. Just tell us what happened." My wife and I hugged and kissed them and tried to make them feel relaxed.

Finally, my older son said, "Every morning before the class, we gather in the yard of the school and pray for the Imam Ayatollah Khomeini, and then we have to repeat the slogans regarding the dead profits. We have to hit our fist upon our heart. At the beginning, we did not hit ourselves hard over the heart, but then the brothers came by and stood next to us and told us to hit harder and harder because we are Jewish. Otherwise we would be punished."

I was appalled. Sickened to my stomach. "How long has this been going on?" I asked, trying not to show my anger and upset my son further. "That you hit yourselves hard while the *brother* stands next to you?"

"It's been about two weeks," he replied sheepishly. "They came next to us and made us hit ourselves, yelling, 'Harder, harder!'" Both my sons became increasingly upset as my older son told his story.

My wife and I tried to calm them down and at that moment we decided that our children would not attend school anymore. From then on, my wife took our children to our relatives during school hours, so that the neighbors would not notice that our kids did not go to school.

I have had many long nights in my life, but that night was the longest one I can remember. I could not sleep at all, tossing and turning in my bed. I pictured how scared and under pressure my children must have been in school and still they were afraid to tell us—their parents—anything about being bullied by the brothers. My older son still had the highest grade-point average among his classmates, and yet he was treated like he'd done something wrong, like he had to repent, simply because he was Jewish. I was angry at everything and everybody. I wanted to go to my son's school first thing in the morning to complain to the principal, but the principal had the same mentality as the brothers, and was also a member of the same *Komiteh*. We decided it would be best for everyone not to bother with them at all, especially given the situation we were in.

In the morning I went to work as usual. I could hear the sound of the Koran Class from outside of my office. I felt like rushing into the class to scream my anger at everyone, but decided it would be better to stay calm and collected. I went to my desk and started going through the completed files stacked for my review and approval. I was so busy that I didn't realize that it was lunchtime and that my morning coffee sat on my desk without being touched.

The custodian of the coffee room came by my desk and said, "I brought you a cup of hot coffee three hours ago, and later I came by to pick up the empty cup and noticed that the coffee was not touched and was cold. I brought you a fresh cup, and again you haven't touched it. Is it my coffee that you don't like anymore? Or do you just not want to drink coffee today?"

"I apologize," I said sincerely, "I love the coffee. Bring me another and I will drink it right now."

He picked up the cold cup of coffee and left. Within two minutes, he returned and brought me a fresh cup of hot coffee. I thanked him for his genuine concern and drank the coffee while he stood there. He picked up the empty cup with a look that conveyed many curious questions and then left my office.

I continued to work and heard one of the members of the office calling me. He came by my desk and said, "Sorry to bother you, but I need your help on this project. I didn't want to bother you earlier, you were very busy and I didn't want to interrupt. According to the schedule, I have to finish this project today so that you can take it to the committee for approval tomorrow."

"I am sorry that you had to wait," I said. "Let's look at it."

"You seem very preoccupied today," he observed. "You haven't spoken a word to anybody. Everyone is wondering what is going on with you."

"As you see, I have so many files to review and I am on a schedule, too," I said honestly. "But I am glad everybody is concerned and doing their jobs on time. We have a good, hardworking, responsible team in this office, and the bosses are very pleased with our performance."

The truth was all I could see while at work were the faces of my children and the black and blue bruises on their chests. I thought I was going crazy. I could picture their scared faces standing in line in the front yard of the school, repeating the slogans with a big bully standing next to them forcing them to hit their small chests harder and harder. I wished that I could go back to school to face that stupid bully and tell him, "Why don't you pick on somebody your own size, you son–of-a- bitch?" I wanted to scream at the principal and teachers for letting this happened. Instead, I released some of my anger by talking to myself.

After work I took a taxi home. I was so happy to be with my family, and for a minute while I had them in my arms, kissing them, I forgot everything. I even didn't care about my upcoming weekly meeting with Sadri.

My wife was so surprised at my actions. "We are so glad to see that you are so relaxed and happy," she said.

"I have the three of you with me, who are the most important things in my world. I am sure the Almighty will have a good solution for our situation."

We spent a quiet and relaxed night with some quality time together. But my older son was concerned about his classes at school. He asked, "Are we ever going to school again?"

I replied, "Of course, you will. But the schools are closed for the holidays. In the meantime, your mom and I will work with you at home." It was so sad to see him missing school and his studies. My wife and I didn't want to risk the smallest chance of those stupid bullies harming our kids again. Also, we didn't want to risk anything in case the school authorities put too much pressure on the kids and found out from them that we had been moving around for the last year and half changing our place of residence. In lieu of school my wife took the children to her relatives every day, and worked on their schoolwork with them. And every week I tested them on their homework assignments and gave them a happy face and high scores, which they were happy about.

During this time one more meeting with Sadri was due. He always made the appointment on the first day of the week, which was Saturday. I was in time for our meeting, and as usual Brother Secretary said, "Sit in the waiting room, until the boss calls you."

I sat and waited. Fifteen minutes passed my appointment time and finally Sadri called me into his office. I walked in and stood by the chair without a greeting.

In a very harsh and sarcastic voice he asked, "Don't you have the manners to say greetings when you see someone?"

I replied, "Yes, I do. But I don't know it in Arabic, and I don't want to say something incorrect. Also, I know you don't want me to greet you in Farsi."

He became furious. "Don't get smart with me!" he bellowed, as if I were a child.

I stood there and said nothing.

"Which day of the week is today?" he asked condescendingly.

"It's Saturday," I replied.

"Did you go to your house of worship to pray?"

"No, because I'm employed by the government so I have to be at work."

"Then, what are you doing here?" he asked.

I replied, "I have an appointment with you."

"But you are not working eight hours today, because by the time you get back to work you will be three hours short for your workday.

"On the days I have an appointment with you, I stay after hours and make up for the lost three hours."

"I know that," he said. "I received word from our people that you stay late to make up for the lost hours."

Then why did you ask me? I thought. "I know the rules and regulations; therefore, I have to be an example for the rest of the office members. Anyone who completes his project will be given credit and will also be recognized by the bosses. This is the procedure of our office, and everybody is happy about it."

"Yes, I also received the word that your office is working very efficiently, and that all the bosses are very happy about the result of your teamwork," Sadri said. "You don't have to come to my office next month." He called in the Brother Secretary and said, "Make an appointment for him in two months," and dismissed me with, "Now you may go."

By the time I got back to work it was late. I started working on the pile of files on my desk. I stayed after hours in the office to make up for the lost hours, so it was dark by the time I got home. My wife was entertaining her relatives, who were invited for dinner. I freshened up and enjoyed a nice dinner with our guests along with some homemade vodka and red wine and tried to forget the revolution, Sadri, and work. I just wanted to enjoy a quiet and relaxed night with my dear family.

The end of a snowy and cold year was approaching and so we had more and more sunny, enjoyable days. There was not very much snow on the street. Sometimes I walked most of the distance to work and enjoyed the fresh air. It was very relaxing and helped me forget my problems. At those rare times, I subconsciously felt happy, and hopeful.

One morning as I walked to work I passed by the side of Tehran University. I stood by the wrought iron gate of the entrance for a few moments and glanced at the buildings. I had a sad feeling remembering the demonstrations, which started at the beginning of the revolution, and how much the students helped lead to it.

My thoughts were interrupted by the angry and harsh sound of a man who shouted, "What are you looking at and thinking about? What do you want? Go on, leave and stay away from the entrance of the university!"

I apologized and said, "I was just remembering… I used to walk across the university yard enjoying the flowers and chatting with the students. Of course, it was some time ago, before the revolution."

With a smile on his face he replied, "Yes, the students that you talked to helped that revolution. Some of them are dead, some are in Evin Prison (the most horrible prison in Iran), and most of them have suddenly become such religious fanatics that even the faculties are scared of them." Then his mood changed. "Go on, go away from here before you get us both in trouble."

I wished him well, and continued my way to work.

When I got to my office I heard the sound of the Koran reading all through the hallway and the office. As usual, I sat behind my desk and ignored it. Suddenly, I received a fresh cup of hot coffee on my desk. Coffee was not free anymore, you had to order it and pay for it. I raised my head and said, "I did not order coffee."

"I ordered it for you. It's been a long time we've had a cup of coffee together," said my friend who sat in the desk to my right. With a sarcastic smile, he added, "I decided to order coffee for both of us before you drown yourself in your work without a word to your friends. From the minute you come in until the time you go home, it's work, work, work for you. And all the time you're so serious."

"You know we have a very busy schedule, and we are all under a lot of pressure to finish as many files as we can," I replied, wishing he'd just drop it.

He looked into my eyes. "There are people in the same building and their production is not even half or one third that of yours and your office. Most of the times they talk about politics, and the revolution, and nobody says anything to them."

"Their jobs are not as important as ours," I offered. "If I was an authority, I would demolish half of those jobs because they are just extra costs for the company. You should be proud of the work you do and feel good for the salary you receive. You really earn it."

"How is your wife doing?" my friend inquired, cautiously changing the subject. "What happened to your plan to take her to Germany?"

"She sees doctors here because we can't leave the country. I am sorry I couldn't get back to you in time for the arrangement offered by your uncle. I did not have enough money to cover the cost. We've left everything in the hand of God, or as you say, *Allah.* There is an old expression in America, or 'the Great Satan' as these days America is called." I was being sarcastic. "Which is *Que sera, sera.* It means 'What will be, will be.'"

"Actually, a week after our meeting my uncle's friend in the passport office was removed from his position. Maybe it was your good luck that your hard-working money wasn't ready in time or you would've lost it." And then he added, "I thanked Allah many times that you didn't come up with money, because the chance of losing it was very high. I see you as a very good human being, a good friend, but most of all, a very good boss. I have noticed how much you pay attention to those sons-of-bitches," he said, referring to the Group of Six. "Even though they are spies and a bunch of scavengers, you still found time to help them with their English homework. Do you think they understand your kindness? Do you think they are really worth it? I promise you, there will be a day I will take care of them myself. They are a group of people who brought shame to our religion, our pride of being Iranian. My family has lived in harmony with our Iranian minorities, such as the Jewish, Christians, Zoroastrians, and the Bahaies, even though Bahai is not a legal religion. We still respect them because they are human beings and children of the same god." With some anger in his voice he added, "Why do you think I started that Koran class? I wanted to let the Islamic Revolution Committee know that they can't fool around with me, and that when the time arrives I will know what I have to do with them. They don't dare say a word in my class."

I noticed that one of the Group of Six watched us from afar. On a piece of paper, I wrote, "We are being watched" while I opened a file in front of him so that he would see it.

He quietly said, "To hell with them." We finished our coffees and he returned to his desk.

I was very anxious to get home and let my wife know about Uncle Ayatollah and what a disaster it would have been if we had rushed to his suggestion. Although he had helped other people successfully in the past it was right at the time I had a meeting with him that his connection in the passport office had been transferred to another office. I said to myself, "There is some extraordinary power that controls everything, and that power can only be God."

The day was finished and I headed home. I wanted to get home as soon as I could and share the story with my wife. "You have to listen to what I have to tell you," I said. "It's unbelievable. We don't have to regret about not moving on the deal with Uncle Ayatollah." My wife was all-ears and she was as stunned as I was when explained what happened. "Honey, someone is looking after us and I am sure we will overcome all the unpleasant events and will have success in our plan. All we have to do is to wait for the middle of spring and with the help of God we will get out of this miserable situation. I promise you, one day we will look back and remember these moments as bittersweet memories about our country."

That evening we went to my wife's sister's apartment for dinner and the smell of my sister-in-law's cooking filled the complex. "I can smell your dinner in the stairwells," I said to her, "I hope you have enough for a very hungry bunch, especially me!" My brother-in-law handed me a glass of whiskey and said, "Don't worry about dinner. First enjoy this drink. It is one of the presents you brought me. I have a feeling there will be a day I look at this bottle and pour myself a drink and toast to your health, my dear brother-in-law, whom I always love as my own brother." We said, "Cheers" and drank. Dinner was very delicious and again for a brief time, my family allowed me to forget about the horrible politics of my country.

When we drove home later that night, the children had fallen asleep in the car. As we carried them to bed in our arms, their beautiful, peaceful, innocent faces were so moving that we held them close and very quietly said, "Our dear angels, I promise you, that there will be a day, when you are grown up, that I will explain to you about the revolution and how we had to escape from our homeland and our people. And you will understand."

I turned the television on to watch the latest news about the Iran/Iraq war, which had been going on for the last three and half years taking thousands and thousands of lives and bringing with it destruction, misery, and economic hardship to the Iranian people. The bloody pictures and senseless killings made me sick to my stomach. Suddenly my wife turned off the television and said, "We just came from my sister's and had a good time. I don't think you want to spoil it for yourself by watching these horrible pictures and the disappointing news. Tomorrow will be another day. Let's hope that God opens the door of health and success for us."

The next day was Thursday, the last day of the workweek for government organizations. Usually everybody looked forward to the weekend, which was only one day per week on Fridays. Our company used to have Thursdays and Fridays off, but since the Islamic Republic's revolution, we had to work a half-day on Thursdays.

At around 11:00 a.m. I noticed the secretary, who was pregnant and delivering her baby very soon, crying very quietly. I thought her time had come to have the baby and so I asked her, "Why don't you go home? You might need to see a doctor if you are in pain?"

"No, I am not due for another month. I'm not in pain. It's about our new landlord. He is giving us a hard time."

"New landlord? I didn't know that you moved."

"We haven't moved yet. We found a very nice apartment with two bedrooms and two bathrooms, closer to my job, and just perfect for the time of arrival of our new child. Right now, we live in a one bedroom, my son sleeps in the corner of our living room and we have only one bathroom. Of course, the rent is higher in the new place, but we can manage. My husband is a mechanic and works for his friend who has promised a raise to cover the extra expense."

"So far everything seems to be good. Then what is all the fuss about?"

"We agreed to the terms the landlord required and he said he is going to draw the papers. Last night we were supposed to sign the lease agreement and pay for the first month's rent and a security deposit. We have already notified our present landlord about vacating the apartment by the end of the month, but last night when we went to the new landlord with cash to sign he said, 'I have changed my mind about renting the apartment because you are Christian Armenians. You are not clean people, and in fact, you are *najes* ['abomination' in Farsi]. You eat pork, which is a very dirty animal in our religion, and you drink alcoholic beverages in your homes. Therefore, you are *najes*. I don't want your presence in my apartment to make it dirty. If I let you in, in the future I won't be able to rent it to any other people.' This is our situation now.

We have to vacate our current apartment, because our landlord has already rented it to somebody else, but we have been refused by the new landlord and I have a baby on the way."

The Group of Six listened to our exchange. Then the Shahid Brother who always collected money to make a hamburger run for lunch from the Mosio of the Armenian shop shouted, "In fact, your new landlord is right. You are *najes*. And anything you touch will be *najes*, too." The rest of the group repeated his words "Yes, you are *najes*, you are *najes*."

All I could do was invite everybody to control themselves and be quiet.

I was surprised when our secretary loudly retaliated. "We are *najes*? Anything we touch becomes *najes*? And all this time you collected money from everybody and bought hamburgers from the Armenian Mosio who makes them with his hands? This hamburger is not *najes*?"

The situation was out of control and before I knew it, The Group of Six were all shouting, "*Marg bar America, Marg bar Israel*" (death to America, death to Israel). Three from the group walked to the hallway to ask the other Islamic Brothers in the other offices to join them and make some kind of demonstration.

I tried to make peace when the three remaining members of the Group of Six threatened me by saying, "You are *najes*, too. Imam Khomeini has said anybody who is not Muslim is Infidel, we can throw you out of the window to the street and no one can touch us, because we killed a non-Muslim, in fact a *najes* Jew."

I could not control myself and said, "Don't misquote the Imam. He said all the Jewish people are our Jewish brothers and sisters. And besides, if I wanted to go downstairs there is an elevator. If the elevator is out of service, there is a stairway. And if the stairway is closed, and I have to go down from the window, at least two if not all three of you, especially you, the trouble-maker, the so-called Shahid Brother, will go down with me."

That did it. My comment was too much for them to hear. The sound of *Marg bar America, Marg bar Israel* grew much louder and angrier. The rest of the office members were so stunned by this outburst, but they didn't want to get involved and into trouble with these Islamic hoodlums. My immediate boss, who had suddenly become very religious and acted very Islamic with some other bosses, rushed to the office and tried to calm down everybody by reading verses in Arabic. When that didn't work he shouted, "For the sake of Allah, be compassionate and understanding, this is an office and not the place for this sort of behavior!" He then rushed to me and said, "Brother, please go to them and kiss their faces. Apologize to each one of them so that they stop shouting and creating a demonstration."

"What are you talking about?" I yelled. "They called me *najes*. And they started with the secretary first, then they told me they would throw me out the window. And now you ask me to kiss them and make up?"

Then one of the Group of Six (the one who was the very first member hired) came to my boss and said, "In fact, the brother pointing his finger at me was not the cause of the disturbances. The secretary was the cause of the whole thing. She always made up her face with makeup, and fixed her eyebrows, and put on lipstick in front of us, and when we looked at her we got sexually aroused. I have to add that our boss has been very good with all of us and that she is the cause of all this disturbance."

I couldn't believe what I heard from this man who prayed every day and listened to the speech of the Imams after praying. He formulated a big lie about the secretary's behavior at the office, whereas she always kept her hair covered with *maghnaeh* (Islamic scarf), came to work with no makeup, and even didn't talk to the Islamic people at all.

My two friends (the nephew of the Uncle Ayatollah and the colonel) were trying to explain the situation to the big boss. The big boss came to me and said, "It's almost three and a half years you have been working here and you haven't taken your vacation, not even for a week. You have been working so hard and so diligently and saved millions and millions of dollars of the *Bayt al-Mal* monies for your country. I know that the top man knows that without you we could not manage this office. But you better take a one-week vacation. *Now.* You don't have to write the request for the vacation. I will take care of it for you. Just get out as soon as possible." He looked at my two friends and added, "Take him downstairs, get him a taxi, and make sure nobody harms him."

They both said, "They will have to go over our dead bodies to get to him."

I didn't have time to get any of my personal items from my drawer, as we rushed to the elevator. We waited about two minutes for the elevator, and by the time we got inside, one of the Islamic hoodlums saw us and asked, "Where do you think you are going? You are a *najes* traitor, and you can't escape from us. We will catch you and will take care of you."

Both my friends stood in front of me as the elevator door closed.

We got to the lobby and they walked with me (one in front and one behind me) as we made our way toward the main exit of the building. They rushed me into a taxi and told the driver, "Take him straight to the address he will give you without any other passengers. Remember what I told you, *without any other passengers*," and handed the driver more than twice the taxi fare. He added, "I have your taxi number, and if I call my friend and he tells me you had other passengers, you will be in trouble."

"The fare money you paid me is more than enough," said the driver. "I will take him straight home as fast as possible."

I only had a few seconds to shake hands with my friends and left. I did not give the exact address to the driver. "Go to the entrance of Tehran University and make a U-turn. I will get off there."

The driver parked across the entrance of the University and I got out. I stepped into a shop and made sure the taxi was gone. I came out and continued toward my mother-in-law's house. I went inside, and everybody was surprised that I was home so early.

I explained everything to my wife and said, "Honey, the day of making the decision is here. We have no other choice but to call Mr.

Simani to arrange for our escape."

"But it's ten days until the beginning of spring and we were planning to leave the middle of spring because there is a lot of snow on our escape route now."

"I know. We can't take a chance anymore." I made a phone call to Mr. Simani and told him the code passphrase, "The flowers in the greenhouse bloomed."

"I will come to see the flowers in two days," he said and hung up.

I knew then that his crew would come by as soon as two days to make the plans and set the time of our escape.

I made another telephone call to my friends at work to thank them for being so protective of me against those Islamic hoodlums. When I called, the nephew of the Ayatollah picked up the phone and once he heard my voice he said, "I am sorry your file is not ready yet. Please call me in a couple of hours. I have to go now," and hung up the phone.

I knew he couldn't talk and that the situation in the office was very tense. I was very nervous and excited at the same time. I paced back and forth the length of the living room floor thinking.

My wife came in with a cup of tea and said, "Please sit down, and enjoy your tea. I think God has made the plan for us. I am not worried about anything anymore. As soon as the crew comes and makes the arrangement, we are going to go."

Two hours passed and I made another call to my friends at the office.

The nephew of the Ayatollah once again answered and said, "Please wait until I get your file, and I will explain it to you." He then added, "Oh, yes. I have all the information in front of me and your case is finished. All the required signatures are done and we will take care of it soon." He wasn't talking nonsense. He was trying to make a conversation so that the Islamic hoodlums and the Group of Six wouldn't listen in.

I said to him, "I just wanted to thank you for being there for me. I will never forget your friendship. Please thank my other friend for me, as well." I hung up.

My wife and I started to pack two small suitcases, mostly filled with warm clothing for the children, and a first-aid kit in case of an unexpected emergency. We also took some cans of tuna fish, crystal sugar, and the special medication for my back. My uncle had said, "If you feel pain in your spine from riding horses, when you get to a place that has nurses, ask for an injection and you will be pain free." Within a few hours, we were ready. We put our packed suitcases away in the closet and decided to go to our relatives for a few hours.

The neighbors were curious why I didn't go to work. The surrounding people had changed to extremes. They wanted to know everything about everybody. Sometimes even relatives put their noses in the lives of other relatives hoping to incriminate them. My mother-in-law had a very vicious tenant in her house residing on the first floor. Even though my mother-in-law tried to help them due to their poor financial situation, the lady of the family was a very unappreciative person and always tried to create some sort of trouble. We were very careful about our children not attending school and me not going to work. Every morning after breakfast, my wife and I would take the children with their backpacks and pretend that we are taking them to school and that I was going to work. It was a pretty sad situation. Everyone had to be very careful about their everyday routines, because there were people watching constantly, sometimes even their own relatives were the watchers.

My wife and I had a feeling that as the old saying in Farsi goes, "The fish has come to its tail." In another words, it's getting very close to the end of the line, which in our situation, the time of our journey (or our 'Great Escape') was nearing. Psychologically both of us were ready. All we had to do was wait to hear from Saleh and Abdolah.

Finally, two days after I had contacted Mr. Simani with the code passphrase "The flowers in the green house are blooming," he replied with a phone call and said. "I will come to see them in two days."

The two-day time had almost passed when we received his next call. It was the one I had been waiting for. I picked up the phone and heard, "I will come to see the blooming flowers at 9:00 in the morning." Then he hung up.

I looked at my wife, and she was very elated, but at the same time I could see grief and sadness on her face.

I rushed to her and asked, "Honey, this is what we want? Isn't it?"

"Yes. Yes, but look at my mother's face. She was just getting used to our children being around every day, and who knows if we are ever going to see her again or if she will get a chance to see our children or us again." Tears welled up in her eyes.

I noticed my mother-in-law's face blush red, her own tears pouring. I rushed to her side to calm her, as well.

"I am glad for you," she said. "For all of you, but I don't know if I'll ever see you and your family again." She took a deep breath. "I understand you are a man who loves his wife, children, and his family," she said to me. "All you do is try to get the best in the world for them. That gives me a good feeling when I know I can count on you."

I hugged and kissed her. "As soon as we settle in America, I will do my best to bring you and your daughter and your grandchildren together again. This is a promise." I said sincerely. It was all I could do.

The next few days my wife and I tried to act very normal in front of the children, although both of us were so confused, excited, scared, and even more than anything else, we questioned ourselves, wondering if we had made the right decision about leaving the revolution-stricken country. A country whose clergy in the name of *Allah* had already brought misery, crime, theft, murder, war, economic hardship, and many other such atrocities to my country and people.

My wife walked to her mother and gave her a hug. While both of them were emotional and crying my wife said, "I know you believe in my husband. Any promise he has made, he fulfills. I also promise that the moment we settle down in America we will try our best to get you out of this situation."

The kids walked into the room and they noticed their mother and grandmother weeping. They rushed to them and asked, "Why are you crying?" The question quickly changed the mood, because we had to keep our escape program from the children as much as possible.

I jokingly said, "Your grandma and mom want to have ice cream and cookies. We don't have any, but I promised I would go buy them from the market so everyone can have some." Everybody started to laugh, and we spent a happy and sweet night with ice cream and cookies.

The next morning, I paced in the living room until the doorbell rang. I rushed to answer it and saw both Saleh and Abdolah in the doorway. I brought them to the second floor and then into the back bedroom to make sure no one could hear us. My wife and I were all ears, and my mother-in-law entertained her grandchildren in the living room.

"I know we're about seven weeks early from the time we originally decided to go ahead with our escape, but there is a new development and we have to get out as soon as possible. We know the difficulty of the snowy mountains, rugged trails, and the difficulties in riding horses…"

"Take it easy," Saleh interrupted. "We know you must be under a lot of pressure to make a difficult decision. We are here to help. Mr. Simani told me to take care of you because you are like his own family. Therefore, I arranged my schedule to be here from our main station in Tabriz, which is nearly an eight-hour drive."

I thanked them for being so concerned, and explained the revolt in the office and how it ended up with me having to leave work. I told them that even though Sadri's appointments had changed from every month, to every other month, I didn't want to take any chances because Sadri's spies would let him know about the office incident and that I was asked by my boss to take a vacation for a week until everything quiets down. I told them that he also asked me to call him in four days and that Sadri might try to create some sort of problem for me, such as ordering my arrest under any fictitious circumstances. I explained that is why we decided to leave the country as soon as possible.

Saleh took a piece of paper from his pocket and said, "This is the plan. We will meet you at Khoy post office, on Friday, the last day of winter, at 5:00 p.m. You have to leave Tehran very early Friday morning, which is exactly one week from today, and give yourself enough time to get there. As we agreed before, you and your family will drive in your own car. It's going to be the last day of the year and the following day is going to be the first day of *Nowruz* (the Iranian New Year). The traffic will be heavy since usually a lot of people travel to Rezaieh, or the smaller cities. I am sure there won't be any inspection posts on your way, but in case for the holidays they decide to have checkpoints with *pasdars* (which were the new revolutionary guards who controlled everyone, including traffic and borders), with your look," he pointed to my beard which at the time was somewhat thick and covered my face, "and your wife wearing an Islamic woman's robe and scarf," which was the attire for every Iranian woman to wear when leaving their homes decreed since the Islamic regime came into power, "you should be fine." Then he looked at my wife and said, "No makeup at all. Look as Islamic as you can."

"What about the children?" I asked.

Saleh replied, "Heavy and warm clothing is very important."

My wife rushed to the closet and brought the clothing we had prepared for the kids, which consisted of warm underwear, heavy wool sweaters and pants, along with a long raincoat with wool lining for each child, as well as warm socks and boots.

Saleh was surprised and very happy with the setups and said, "You won't have any problem with the cold and snowy weather in the mountains. But again, I stress, give yourself enough time with the heavy traffic, due to the *Nowruz* holiday, to be at our designated Khoy post office on time. Khoy city is fairly small with one main street, and as you enter the city you should continue for about fifteen minutes on the main road to arrive at a roundabout park-like area. Usually people sit in the park, and due to your arrival on a Friday afternoon, there will be a lot of people on the streets. Just park and hang around to kill time. After you pass the roundabout, make a left turn on the first street and you will see the post office. In front of the post office there are six telephone booths. Use one of them to call your relative and let them know that you have passed the checkpoint of Khoy, Rezaieh. This checkpoint is very important."

"Is this the checkpoint which is known as *Istanbul malid?*" I jokingly asked, which in Farsi translates to no escape-way to Istanbul.

"Allah is with you," he replied. "When you want to make a phone call, talk very simply and don't say anything about the trip."

"I actually made a secret code passphrase with my relative, which is 'We are at Khoy waiting for Amoo Ali and please take care of the flowers in the greenhouse while we are on vacation.' Then I thank them and say my goodbyes."

"Remember you are going for holiday vacation out of town and nobody can suspect anything," Saleh reminded us. "Because of the holiday, the timing is in your favor. At exactly 5:00 p.m. we will come to the post office, and you will see me in a pickup. I will give you an army salute gesture to follow us to the designated area where we will take over your car and you will be transferred to our pickup. You don't have to worry about the rest of the plan, because it has already been arranged for you."

My wife and I gave a quick look at each other and then I asked, "Is that all?"

"That should do it, simple as that," Saleh replied and then drank his tea. "I promise you, it won't be difficult at all, and you shouldn't be worried. Just relax. Because it's going to happen right at the time of the holidays, when many people travel, it's going to work to your advantage. This is a good sign from *Allah.*"

Abdolah was very quiet during our meeting. Saleh asked him, "Do you have any comments, or questions for them? You have been very quiet? You will be traveling with them from the time they join us in Khoy, and you will be their guide throughout the trip." Saleh looked at my wife and I and said, "Abdollah grew up in Khoy and Van, and knows all the trails and mountains by heart. He travels from Khoy to Van almost every week. He also knows which trail is the best route for you at the time of your journey."

I noticed Abdolah had waited anxiously for that moment. Even though he was a young man of about thirty years old, he seemed much more experienced than he let on. "I will be very happy to be the tour leader for this family," he said. "I have traveled with other people who didn't speak any other languages but Farsi. It always helps to have educated and experienced people traveling with me. For sure, our journey will be very smooth and without any difficulties. But there is only one request I have and that is when we get to my father's house in the first village inside Turkey, that you agree we deliver you close to the first *askar* station [a police station] by the border, and you and your family walk to that station and tell them that you have escaped from Iran over the mountains and want to go to Istanbul to go to America to your relatives there. They will take you in and send you with a police car to the closest city, which will be Van. The police station in the city of Van knows about the refugee program, and they will prepare the necessary paperwork and make the arrangements for you and your family to go to Istanbul under the supervision of the Turkish government. It is the responsibility of the Turkish government to take care of refugees from Iran. Because you have small children, they will come to your aid without any delay. Then you won't have to ride horses to the City of Van."

"If we did ride horses, how many hours would it take to get to the city of Van? I ask because we don't want to be arrested by the *askars*, and we want to go straight from Van to Istanbul per our previous agreement."

He replied, "About eight hours horse-ride at night, or maximum of two nights horse-ride, depending upon the situation with the border *askars*. But within a few hours you will be transferred to a police car, with a warm heater inside, and then go directly to Van. After the formalities of paperwork for the Turkish government, you will be given permission to go to Istanbul within seven to ten days."

My wife and I looked at each other and almost simultaneously said, "No, we don't want to be arrested by the *askars*, and we don't want to walk to the *askar* station to give ourselves up either."

I added, "We want to go with what we had decided before, and if we have to ride horses for two or even three nights, we prefer going straight to Van to board a bus to Istanbul according to our original plans."

Abodollah noticed that my wife and I did not appreciate the option of giving ourselves up to the *askars* and he apologized and said. "That's fine, I just thought it would be easier for the children."

In the last four years, my wife and I had been under a lot of pressure and even the slightest bit of doubt made us nervous and psychologically drained. I noticed my wife felt worse than I did. I turned to her and said, "Honey, don't worry. It was just a suggestion, and nothing more. I am glad Abdollah brought it up now, and not during the journey."

I looked at Abdollah and asked him, "Am I right?"

Right away he replied, "Yes, absolutely. It was just a suggestion, please forget about it completely. *Inshallah* with the help of *Allah*, we will start from the Khoy post office and in Van we will have the bus ticket for the four of you to go straight to Istanbul."

Saleh noticed that my wife looked overly concerned about the circumstances and he put his right hand on his beard as a gesture of giving his utmost salute and promise to her and said, "Please, don't worry. Remember, you have been recommended by Mr. Simani, and for your journey we will try one hundred and ten percent. I promise you won't be sorry and there will be days in the future when you remember your trip with us and laugh about the worries you now have."

Saleh and Abdollah left our place and we started planning for the coming Friday morning. The excitement of the trip, or *escape*, which it literally was, made us very happy, but at the same time the thought of the separation from the rest of our relatives made us sad. But this was what we had planned and hoped for to have a better future.

My wife and I decided to go to my wife's sister's place on Thursday, one day before the start of our trip. We had to move our small suitcases when the tenants of my mother-in-law weren't home, because they watched our every movement at all times. Within two days, all our suitcases were transferred to my wife's sister's place. The only thing we had left to do was to wait for the Big Friday, the day of our trip. We had to control our emotions and count the days. During the last four years, this was the first time we felt, as the old saying goes, that "there is a light at the end of the tunnel." Finally, we had some real hope.

The next day, I was walking in the front yard and looked at the melted snow. Some of the shrubs around the pond had new leaves and the surface of the water in the pond had a thin layer of ice floating on it. The old vine tree seemed very fresh, just as if it had just finished a very good sleep and was fully rejuvenated. I walked to the vine tree and said, "Old friend, I am going to miss you and your delicious grapes, and wine. More than anything else, your very strong vodka, which warmed me during the snowy and cold days of winter." I noticed the kerosene barrel, which I try to keep full at all times for the use in the heater on the cold days of winter, sitting on the front yard lawn. Looking at it, I remembered the days that the Iranian people had to wait in lines to purchase the rationed kerosene from the shops. The older homes did not have central gas heating systems and they had to use kerosene instead. Sometimes people waited hours in lines, but they couldn't get their rationed shares of kerosene because the shops had run out. Everything was available in the black market. Half of the kerosene was given to the *Komitehs* and their people who then sold it on the black market. I remembered the apartment we owned had natural gas pipes connected to it. During the Shah's time, we never had any shortages of natural gas, but as the result of the events of the revolution, we frequently had shortages. Again, the miserable times that my countrymen had suffered ran through my head like a movie. These thoughts were bittersweet, which reminded me of the similar hard times now and the hope we had to get out of our miserable situation.

My mother-in-law and the rest of the family came to the front yard and the children started playing with the ducks by chasing them around. Everybody decided to go visit relatives and spend the rest of the day with them. We spent a lazy and calm day with our relative and arrived back home late at night. My in-law's nosy tenant approached us upon arrival and asked, "Where have you been? I haven't seen you the whole day, where were you? Did you have a good time?"

My mother-in-law got furious. "Do I have to get permission from you to visit my daughter? Who do you think you are?" I knew my mother-in-law was upset about our trip and all she needed was some smart remark from her tenant to really send her over the top.

I gently grabbed her hand and led her to the second floor. When we arrived upstairs, she started to cry and said over and over again, "I just got used to having all of you here, and very soon I will be alone with only a bunch of good memories of the times we shared together during the last eight months."

Again, my wife spoke with her and promised her that if she wants to come to America, we would do our best to help her get there.

The next day I called my boss to check in and he said, "I decided to renew your vacation for another week, due to the Islamic Committee of our office who is trying to create a case for you. My boss and I are trying to stand up against them. They are looking at your resume and your fourteen years' experience, your education in America, and your trips to Israel." This was new to hear him say 'Israel', instead of his typical 'Occupied-Palestine.' "We have had a real hard time without you and hope we get it all worked out and that you will be coming back to work as soon as possible."

I thanked him and said, "Whatever happens, it was a pleasure working for you. I hope to see you very soon at work." I tried to sound as if I was looking forward to coming back, whereas I knew I was about to leave the country with my wife and children.

We had two more days until our escape plan on Friday. We reviewed our route many times so we were certain how to react to different scenarios that might arise.

On Thursday afternoon, around 1:00 p.m., the weather became very cloudy. Luckily, the tenants were not home, so we didn't have to worry about them seeing us leave. We collected a few last-minute items and for the last time glanced at the front yard, watching as the ducklings ran up to the children. They played with the ducklings for about five minutes not knowing it was to be the last time.

We got in the car and I put my hand on the *Mezuzah* by the upper right side of the door and prayed in my heart for a safe and easy trip. In a few minutes, we arrived at my wife's older sister's apartment. As soon as they saw us, they knew that the time had come. Everybody acted normal because we didn't want the children to find out about our trip. It was about 5:00 p.m., and my wife's older sister and younger sister and her husband came to our circle to say our last goodbyes. The older sister brought two toy cars for the children and they started to play with them. Everybody had dinner and before they left my brother-in-law handed me a red *Tasbih* (a special string of prayer beads the clergy pray with) and said, "Hold this in your hands until you get out of the country. If any of the *pasdars* or *Komiteh* see you with your beard and *Tasbih* they will think you are one of them."

The time had come for them to say goodbye. They left us with very heavy hearts and we all tried not to cry. It was about 9:00 p.m., and the dark night sky started to rain. The sky reflected what my heart felt. We never anticipated that our journey would start on a rainy day. I hoped that by the time we wanted to leave it would have stopped raining, but the weather bureau announced that we were going to have rain ahead of us. I noticed my wife was somewhat concerned about a rainy day starting our trip, and I said, "Honey, I've had our car serviced and tuned up. Everything has been checked. You don't have to worry about a little rain. We had planned to leave at 6:00 in the morning, but instead we will leave at 4:00 a.m., so we can have two more extra hours' time because of the rain."

We were in bed by 10:30 the night before, but I couldn't sleep. The excitement of the trip and traveling on the last day of the year with heavy traffic and rainy weather kept my mind occupied. It was about 3:30 a.m. when we got dressed in warm clothing and right at 4:00 a.m. we kissed everybody goodbye and started our trip in very heavy, rainy weather.

I had traveled to the town of Karaj (approximately twenty-seven miles from Tehran) before, and it was the first city on our way. Therefore, I knew the roads well, but the heavy rain made it very difficult. I had my headlights and flashers on the whole way. I couldn't drive more than twenty-five or thirty miles an hour and the entire time my eyes were focused on the road.

My wife put a blanket on the children in the back seat who were tired and already sleeping. She watched the road with me. Sometimes we had to slow down because of accidents as the result of fast drivers not paying attention to the conditions on the road. It took us about two hours to get to Karaj. The sky was a little lighter and we were happy to be within its city limits. I pulled into a little coffee shop on the main road and we decided to have breakfast. The kids enjoyed their hot milks and teas along with over-easy eggs and fresh hot breads baked by the coffee shop owner. Our host brought some cookies for the children and said, "You must have a long way ahead of you to start your trip so early in the morning."

I replied, "We are going to Tabriz to our Uncle Ali for the *Nowruz* holidays, and with this rainy day, we want to take our time and drive carefully."

He wished us a good and safe trip and we left.

It was still raining but not as hard as the night before. The hot, fresh breakfast had really given us a boost and while I drove, the children asked about the planned trip and "Uncle Ali." This was the first time they had heard about Uncle Ali and were curious to know more about him. I said, "I have a very good friend in Tabriz, and he has invited us for the *Nowruz* holidays. They have a big farm with all sorts of animals like horses, cows, chickens, and ducks just like the ducklings you raised at your grandmother's place. So, we are going to have a lot of fun with them on the farm. You are going to learn to ride horses. It is very fun to ride horses."

My older son asked, "Papa? Isn't it dangerous to ride horses?

Have you ever ridden a horse?"

"No, it's not dangerous," I replied. "I rode horses when I was a student in America and enjoyed it very much. You are going to ride a horse either with me or a teacher who will ride with you."

My wife asked me, "Which city is next on our way, and do you have any idea how far it is?"

"Ghazvin, and it's about sixty-five miles away. Thank God the traffic is not as bad as we thought it would be. I think we will be there in an hour and a half." I glanced at the skies for a moment and asked, "Did you notice that the clouds are breaking up and we are going to hopefully have a sunny day?"

She smiled a big happy face. "Yes, I am so happy it stopped raining. I was worried about you getting too tired, having driven all last night during the rain watching the road so cautiously. I take this as a good and positive sign for our trip."

We passed many farms where we saw cows and sheep grazing, and the farmers had already begun their usual day's work. The sun was trying to break through the clouds and it was the start of a beautiful day. We hadn't been out of a big metropolitan city like Tehran for a few years, so all the traffic and the sound of cars, the buses driving on crowded streets, and the motorcycles dashing through the traffic honking their horns loudly with the smell of gasoline and the thick smog in the air was almost non-existent.

The fresh smell of farms after the hard rains and the glow of a sunny day made us happy. I played some music from the box of tapes we brought along to help us enjoy the start of our happy day. Everybody sang with the music. The kids had a good time, and every once in a while, they asked us how much further we had to go to get to "Uncle Ali's" farm to ride horses. I had to repeat myself many times over with, "It will be in a few hours. We have to pass other cities on our way before we get to the farm." I looked at my wife and quietly said, "Farm. Uncle Ali. Learning to ride horses." The only part of it that was right was the "riding horses" part, and that was not going to be on a flat farm but on rugged mountains covered with snow.

She looked at me with an excited expression and said, "I am sure

God will help us for the sake of these two little angels. Everything will be alright."

"*Inshaallah*," I muttered, which in Farsi means "God willing."

Soon we arrived in the city of Ghazvin. This was the first time for all of us to visit Ghazvin, the first and the last time to be precise. Traffic was not as bad as the big city of Tehran, but what was interesting for the children were the carts pulled by different colored horses among the cars and buses.

I noticed a large confectionary shop with all sorts of sweets and cakes on the side of the street. I pulled over and parked. We walked inside the pastry shop and the smell of fresh baked cakes and cookies in the warm environment made everybody crave something sweet. They had four or five tables from which to choose, so we sat next to the window.

The owner's wife came by and asked, "What would you like to have? Hot tea? Turkish coffee? Perhaps hot milk for the children and cake or some other sweet?"

My wife and I ordered Turkish coffee and the kids wanted hot milk with different kinds of cookies. I also asked for one kilo of cookies to take with us. I had another cup of coffee and spent about forty minutes in the shop, which was good for me to be able to relax my feet from changing gears on the car and pushing the gas pedal and break.

We hit the road again and I said "There will not be another stop for the next three hours. We have to pass the cities of Zanjan, Mianeh, and finally Tabriz, where we will stop to have lunch." My wife had already prepared lunch back when we were still in Tehran, which included chicken with French fries, pickles, and fresh water. I said, "We are going to have a picnic on one of the farms by the side of the road."

The children fell asleep in the backseat, covered with a blanket. Drinking the hot milk and eating the sweets with the warm temperature inside of the car helped them quickly fall into a deep sleep. I noticed my wife was tired, too. "Why don't you sleep? Relax, don't worry about me," I reassured her. "The two cups of Turkish coffee really took care of my not sleeping last night. Go ahead and try to get some sleep. I promise I will be a good and careful driver, without you having to watch over me."

"I know you are a good driver," she replied. "Any driver who survives driving in Tehran traffic compared to driving on these roads should have no problems. But I like to see the scenery. It's so beautiful, especially after a rainy day. Just look at the snow. It is so white and clean, and besides there is not a bit of smog in the air. The air is so fresh, shiny, and clear, one can see for miles."

"Okay, suit yourself. But believe me, we will see a lot of this kind of weather along the way."

While she watched and enjoyed the beauty of the snow, mountains, and the fresh air, she fell asleep and I was happy to see her mind off the problems of the trip for a while.

I played the music very softly and drove cautiously to get to Zanjan, the next big city. I passed some villages and small cities before getting to Zanjan. The sound of the city traffic woke up my wife and she asked, "Why didn't you wake me? I don't want you to drive by yourself while all of us sleep."

"It wasn't very long. You slept only about an hour. I am all right. The two cups of Turkish coffee I told you about really worked. I don't feel sleepy at all. I am very fresh and ready to deliver this crew and myself to our destination with the help of almighty God, without any problems or hardships."

We didn't stop in city of Zanjan, but went through the city with the flow of the traffic and within thirty minutes we were on our way to the city of Mianeh. I said to my wife, "In Mianeh, we are going to take a break so that everyone can freshen up. The children can use the bathrooms and I can relax my feet."

As I had expected, about thirty-five to forty minutes later driving through the winding roads, we arrived in the city of Mianeh. The crisp cold weather of the city was very refreshing. We went into a fairly large coffee shop that had a wood burning heater standing at its center and three big *Samovars* (a special vessel to make Persian-style tea), standing on the counter along with hundreds of special tea cups and saucers ready for customers to use when they entered from the cold weather to enjoy freshly made tea.

I took the children, one at the time, to the bathroom and then washed my face with cold water, which made me feel very fresh and relaxed. Within half an hour, we were on our way to the biggest city on our route. I turned to my wife and kids and said, "In two hours, we will have our picnic with chicken and French fries on one of the farms, before we reach the city of Tabriz."

The children noticed a train approaching from afar and became very excited. The older one asked, "Are we going to ride the train? Does this train go to where we're going?"

"Yes," I replied. "We will be riding the train, but after our holiday." The train passed us and we heard the conductor blow the horn and saw him wave towards the kids, who were still wound up by the commotion.

I started looking for dry land without snow, not too far away from the main road, so that we could have our picnic. Finally, I found a spot, pulled over, parked the car, and grabbed the blanket and the food from the trunk. We had a nice lunch and with an instamatic Kodak camera I had with me, I shot a picture of my wife and the children while they were enjoying their lunch. It was a good break for me, too. I stretched my legs and for ten minutes I just reclined on the blanket and shut my eyes to relax. Everybody helped and got the blanket, dishes, and other items back into the trunk when we finished.

In a short while, we arrived in Tabriz. It was a very big city. I turned to my wife and asked, "I've always heard of Tabriz, but unfortunately never had a chance to visit this beautiful city. Have you ever travelled to Tabriz before?"

"I haven't been to Tabriz, either," she replied. "This is my first time. But look how beautiful it is."

Tabriz is one of the biggest and most important cities of Iran. We noticed we had two and a half hours until our appointment and decided to spend some time driving on the main streets. Most of the shops were closed because it was Friday, which is the weekend of

Iran. But still, many people were out walking. Some of the people brought their lunches to the park with some small Persian rugs to sit on. Tabriz was famous for creating beautiful Persian rugs that were exported all around the world.

The children played football while the parents played Backgammon, Chess, or just relaxed by smoking cigarettes or a *kalian* (a water pipe/hookah). Our children wanted to join the other children playing football, but I said, "We are going to be late for our appointment with Uncle Ali. It's very important that we get to the post office in Khoy and meet him on time. I promise you, you will have plenty of time to play in the future."

We headed to Khoy, which was about fifty miles from our location, but there was a junction thirty miles ahead on our route. This junction was very famous for those who wanted to get out of the country, like us, or those who wanted to escape from Iran to Istanbul. There was even a slogan for the junction that went, "*Istanbul Malid,*" which means "Those who think they can escape via Khoy to Istanbul should forget it."

This junction had two routes; one went directly to Khoy, which we eventually were hoping to take to meet Abdollah and Saleh, while the other one went to the city of Rezaieh (a.k.a. Urmia). Many families who wanted to escape from Khoy were arrested at this junction and eventually ended up in jail with punishments such as whip-lashings and big fines. I turned to my wife and said, "When we get to the junction, keep the children busy with something and cover your head and part of your face with the scarf. Try to look very Islamic, and I will deal with the *pasdar* at the junction."

We knew the success or failure of our escape depended on going through this junction. I had my sheepskin hat on with a face full of a thick beard, and the red *Tasbih* around my left-hand fingers, which I purposely allowed to be exposed to the *pasdar*.

I drove very carefully and watched the road for the sign of the *pasdar* station. I looked at my wife and said, "Honey, I can see the junction and the station. You take care of the children and with the help of God and his profit Moses, who brought the holy Torah, we are going to go through this post very easily."

She said, *"Beomide-Khoda,"* which is Farsi for *with the hopes of God.*

As we arrived at the junction, I noticed there were civilian cars, pickups, and two buses filled with passengers. It took us about ten minutes until we were able to get into the station for the inspection. There were three lanes for the arriving cars already setup. We were in the middle lane, and as soon as the *pasdar* came by and looked at me, he said, *"Alsalam-on-Alake,"* which is Arabic for "Greetings."

I replied, *"Alsalam-on-Alke, Bradar_pasdar,"* Arabic for "Greetings, brother guard." I noticed that he looked at my beard and the *Tasbih* around my left-hand fingers, then he looked over at my wife who was busying herself with the children giving them fresh fruits her head and forehead completely under the scarf with her Islamic outfit.

In Turkish he then turned to me and asked, "Where are you going?" The language commonly spoken in Tabriz is Turkish.

I answered him with the only sentence in Turkish I knew, and that was that I didn't speak Turkish.

He then pointed to the trunk and asked me in Turkish with a hand gesture to open the trunk.

I walked very slowly with confidence and opened the trunk. There were two small suitcases full of clothing for the kids and some of the boxes of cookies we had bought on the way. I opened one of the boxes of cookies and offered him some.

For a minute he hesitated and looked around, but with a sign of *"take some and put it into your pocket"* by me, he looked around one more time, then took some of the cookies and put them into his uniform's jacket pocket.

I noticed there was a car next to us with four young men who were going to Rezaieh. The *pasdars* asked them to step out of their car and they were taken into the building. At the same time, they separated the young passengers from the buses and a major chaos ensued, which worked in my favor. One of the officers looked at my face with my beard and shouted to our inspector *pasdar,* "Let that brother go and come here as fast as you can."

The *pasdar* thanked me for the cookies and said with another gesture of his hand for me to "go, go." I walked to the car very relaxed, started it up, and left the station.

For the first five minutes, my wife and I didn't speak. We were just trying to play it cool. When I noticed I couldn't see the *pasdar* station from my back mirror anymore, I held my wife's hand in my right hand and said, "This was one of the most difficult and dangerous parts of our trip." Both of us were very happy, even though the children were confused by our behavior.

The last lunch in Tabriz on the side of the road away from traffic. Tabriz is about one hour from the border of Iran and Turkey. The last day of winter of 1984.

137

CHAPTER 8

Passing Khoy Border Guard

We were very close to the city of Khoy where we were to meet our human trafficker at 5:00 p.m. I told my family, "We will be at Khoy in about thirty minutes, and if you notice, the elevation is rising. We are actually going from East Azarbaijan to West Azarbaijan." Khoy was a city in which many Iranians ended up as a result of leaving the country through human trafficking. Many made it out, but many were also caught by the Islamic *pasdars* in the area. In fact, a big percentage of its two hundred thousand population were supporters of the Islamic Regime.

It was Friday afternoon around 3:30 p.m. when I noticed the Khoy city limits from a couple miles away. Without realizing, I said "*Khdaya-be-Omideh-to*" (which is Farsi for *God with all your wishes*).

"Is that the city of Khoy in front of us? Are we going to enter the city now?" my wife asked. She looked concerned. "We still have an hour and thirty minutes before our appointment at the post office."

"Honey, this is the first time I've driven from Tehran to Khoy." I replied. "Under our special circumstances, I have to drive some parts of the route faster and some slower. There's nothing we can do about it and it's better to be early than late. I'll call our relatives in Tehran, whom I'm sure are anxiously waiting to hear from us."

It took us exactly fifteen minutes to get to the post office, which was sooner than we expected. I parked the car on the street and walked to a row of telephone booths; six attached together. I walked up to the first one, opened its door, and put a coin in the telephone to make the call. I noticed a bearded young man in a blue Levi jacket and dark sunglasses walk by and go into the booth next to mine. He pretended to make a phone call. Without putting a coin into the telephone, he put the phone to his ear spoke into it. I knew something was not right, so I walked back to my car.

My wife had noticed the young man, too, and asked me, "Did you notice that guy go into the booth next to you right when you were about to make a phone call?"

"Yes, that's why I didn't make the call," I said. "There is something definitely fishy about him. He could have gone to another booth, but didn't. He also didn't put a coin in the telephone either, but started to talk. I think the whole thing was a trick to listen in on my telephone call. I'll wait another couple minutes and make another attempt. But this time, I am going to go to the last booth."

I waited a bit and walked to the last booth and went inside.

Same scenario. The young man walked to the booth next to me and pretended to make a phone call, again without putting a coin in the telephone. I walked back to the car and sat down. He came back out of the booth and walked to the same spot at which he was standing before.

I was losing my patience with his nonsense. I recalled there were many people who worked for the *Komiteh* as either messengers or stool pigeons, dressed in civilian clothing so they wouldn't be noticed. They especially monitored public places to observe the behaviors and actions of the citizens, keeping an eye out for new faces in their city. Khoy is one of the most significant cities because many escapees from all around Iran congregate there before fleeing the country. "I'm going to the first booth again," I told my wife, "and this time, I'm going to make my call no matter what." I got out of the car and noticed he was watching me. I stared at him with an angry look upon my face for a few seconds. I walked to the first booth and without paying any attention to the young man, finally made the phone call.

My brother-in-law picked up the phone on the other line after one ring. He had been nervously waiting by the telephone for my phone call. I greeted him and said "What a nice trip we've had so far. I'm sure it's going to be a very good *Nowruz* holiday. My wife and the kids are fine. Oh, by the way, I forgot to tell you. Please don't forget to water the flowers until I come back."

I could feel the happiness in his voice as soon as he heard the code. He quickly added, "Don't worry about a thing. I will take care of them for you. Goodbye."

I hung up the phone and walked to the car. The bearded young man was still watching me. I started the car. I turned to my wife and said, "We have exactly forty-five minutes until 5:00 p.m., our appointment time. I don't like this guy watching us and I don't feel comfortable with the situation at all. Let's drive someplace and buy ice cream for the kids."

She agreed. We found a big roundabout not too far away. I parked the car and we bought ice cream from a nearby shop, and then returned to the car. Still unaware of our plan, the children were happy with the ice cream. It was a good surprise for them. I tried to kill a few more minutes before heading back to the post office. I lifted the hood of the car and pretended that I was looking at some problem with the car. Within two minutes, many heads were looking at the engine and talking in Turkish. They were making comments about what they thought was wrong, rubbing their hands over the engine and other parts. I thanked everybody and closed the hood. They made for a very good diversion.

I started the car and very quietly drove back to the post office. I don't know what they had done to the car, but as soon as I tried to put it into second gear, it started backfiring as loudly as the sound of firing a shotgun. The first backfire caused all the people to turn and curiously look at us. I drove very slowly and tried to stay in first gear. I realized going straight from first gear to third gear with a little more speed would stop the backfiring so I began feverishly switching gears.

We had planned to enter the city very quietly so that nobody would notice our presence. The bearded guy at the post office had forced us to go driving for ice cream and now we had a car that sounded like it fired shotguns. Now everyone was aware of us.

Once we were back, I parked the car in the same spot I had parked earlier and noticed that the young bearded man was still standing in exactly the same spot he had been before. We had five minutes until our appointment. I anxiously waited for Saleh and Abdollah. I hoped they wouldn't be late.

At exactly 5:00 p.m. a Zamyad pickup truck very slowly passed by us. Saleh waved to me from the passenger side and said, "Follow me." Then the truck made a quick stop just ahead, and the bearded young man who had been watching us swiftly jumped into the extended cab seat and they sped away.

I was already perplexed by the young bearded man's actions back at the phone booth and now his presence in the truck was even more disturbing. Instantly a thousand negative thoughts crossed my mind. I even began to question the trustworthiness of Saleh and Abdollah knowing any betrayal by them could result in us ending up in the hands of the *Komiteh*. I turned to my wife and said, "I hope we won't be arrested by the *Komiteh* or *pasdars*. In the last meeting I had with Sadri, he mentioned that if I ever attempted to escape from the country and was caught, I would be shot on the spot. I never told you this because I was concerned you might change your mind about our escape altogether." Right then, I thought of Mr. Simani, who is a very good friend of the family. He himself had assured me of Saleh's and Abdollah's loyalty.

I started the car and pushed the pedal hard to pick up some speed. I changed gears from first to third to avoid the backfire and not get the attention of people. We drove about ten minutes until we finally stopped. Then Saleh rushed to our car and jumped into the back seat with the kids. He had a very happy smile on his face and said, "*Marhaba* (which is Farsi for *very good).*" He then added, "You made it on time. I have been anxiously waiting to see if you passed

141

the Khoy junction. With your look and the way your wife dresses, everybody should think you are a member of one of the Islamic revolutionary groups. Especially with the red Tasbih around your fingers on your left hand. It makes you a perfect Islamic Brother look-alike. You definitely have to tell me about your crossing the Khoy junction."

The Zamyad pickup truck continued and I followed it for another fifteen minutes, with Saleh in my backseat. Then suddenly Saleh asked me to pull over and park on the dirt part of the road. I did as he wished and waited for his instructions.

But instead, he walked a few steps from the car, got his praying stone out of his pocket, unwrapped it from a cloth, and then spread the cloth on the ground, right there on the side of the road. He then prayed as the cars speed by.

I was so shocked by his actions that I turned to my wife and said, "In these very serious and important minutes, instead of driving us to our destination, wherever that is, he takes time out to pray?" We had no choice but to wait until he finished. I looked at the sidewalk and noticed it sloped, and at the end of it was a village with many people wearing the uniforms of the *Komitehs* and *pasdars*. One of them climbed the slope and approached me to find out the reason of our stop.

Luckily, right then Saleh finished praying. He came up to the guy and said, "I had to do my ritual praying before it gets dark. We are on our way to Salmas." He then continued to humbly rub his right hand across his beard as a sign of respect and repeated over and over again *"Tashakour. Tashakour,"* which is Turkish for *Thank you. Thank you.*

Then we all got into the car and Saleh turned to me and said, "Push the gas pedal and go as fast as you can."

I started the car and immediately picked up speed, quickly going from first to third gear without stopping. Finally, after about ten minutes of silent driving, Saleh said, "Quick, stop on the shoulder of the road!"

I screeched to a halt and pulled over. A white sedan approached from the opposite direction, then stopped in front of my car. A young man and a young woman, their ages around twenty-five to thirty, and each carrying a small bag, got out of the car and rushed to ours. Saleh opened the car door and they jumped in. Saleh commanded, "Go, go! Don't stop until I tell you to!" This whole event hadn't taken more than thirty seconds from the moment I had stopped the car to when the new young passengers had jumped in and I had sped off.

My wife and I didn't have any idea about who these people were. Puzzled, my wife looked at me and mouthed, without speaking, "Who are these people?"

I shrugged my shoulders and very quietly replied, "I don't know."

Saleh noticed our concerned. "This is Sarah and this is Nader. They are brother and sister, and will be traveling with you to Turkey."

I had no choice but to drive the car at speeds close to seventy-five miles-per-hour, which I was not very happy about. I did not feel safe driving so fast on a highway that had only one lane in each direction. The traffic was heavy with buses and other heavy commercial trucks, and sometimes I had to cross onto the other lane to pass a slower vehicle in my lane.

After fifteen minutes Saleh finally said, "Slow down a little, and when you see the Zamyad pickup, pull over. We are going to transfer to the pickup as fast as we can."

I saw the pickup and pulled over. Saleh turned to my wife and said, "You and your kids go with Sarah. Go into the extended cab part of the pickup. Nader and you, *Agha,* (Farsi for *mister,* referring to me), jump into the back of the pickup." We all got out and Saleh took the car keys from me so he could open the trunk. He took out the two small suitcases and threw them into the back of the pickup.

I made sure Sarah, my wife, and the kids, safely got into the cab of the pickup and then jumped into the back, where I met eye-to-eye with the young, bearded man I'd seen at the post office. Everything happened so fast that the kids forgot the toy cars they had received as gifts a day earlier. I checked on my wife and kids by watching them through a small window into the extended cab. I put my hand on my wife's shoulder and said, "Honey, the real action starts *now*. We need all the help from almighty God that we can get. As we always say, *Khodah Bozergeh* (God is great)." By now my patience was running thin and I had no choice but to confront Saleh and question him regarding the identity of the young bearded man who had given my wife and I a big scare. He had caused us to briefly leave the post office in fear of our lives and experience a lot of anxiety as a result.

Saleh very calmly responded to my inquiry and said, "He is escaping with you. Sorry, this was a last-minute decision and I did not have a chance to let you know. But he knew that there was a family of four in our group of escapees. His behavior was not professional; therefore, I apologize on his behalf of his actions and any inconvenience he may have caused you or your wife.

From inside the pickup I watched our family car fade into the distance as we sped away. It was another piece of our household heritage that had been with us for a long time that we had to part with, and it was also the last time I would ever see that family car again.

Our pickup took off very fast from the shoulder of the road without paying much attention to the moving traffic, and entered the highway. I can safely say that for the first time in our journey, the lord was truly watching over us, because as soon as we pulled onto the highway, an eighteen-wheeler violently hit the brakes and abruptly stopped to avoid crashing into us. If he had hit us, we would've all been dead for sure.

Our driver sped away. Saleh, who was in the back of the pickup, looked at the truck driver and kept rubbing his right hand on his beard. He took his hat off as a sign of apology about the incident that had just occurred.

The truck driver continued to follow us for about a quarter of mile.

Suddenly our driver made a sharp ninety-degree right turn

144

onto the open field and raced toward the distant mountains.

The truck driver stopped at the spot at which our driver had left the road, stepped out of his truck, and watched us speed away. I knew something was wrong and said, "Saleh. Look. Look at the driver of the truck. He is out of his truck and he's watching us!"

"Never mind the truck driver. Don't you worry about anything. It's not important. It's not important."

About ten minutes later, we cruised over flat dirt lands and finally entered a village with narrow alleys. Our driver drove fast, but very cautiously, through those alleys. Sometimes I thought he was going to hit one of the houses, which were primitive. Surely a small tap from the pickup would crumble the entire clay hut. We went through many alleys and finally drew closer to the mountains.

At the start of the mountains, which were partly covered with snow, everybody got out and took shelter under a big rock that hung over like a canopy. I hugged and kissed my wife and kids. For the first time I explained what was going on to the kids. "We are going to ride horses and it is going to be a lot of fun. Within a few days, we are going to America. We didn't tell you this before because your mother and I wanted it to be a surprise for you. Now what we want from you is to listen to the people who are coming with us and stay as quiet as possible. There are *pasdars* who are not very friendly." I waited for a moment and then asked, "Remember those at school that made you hit yourselves on your heart?"

They nodded their heads.

"We don't want them to know that we are leaving the country."

The kids listened wide-eyed and very carefully. We made sure that they had their warm clothing on. I opened one of the suitcases and put some of the cotton balls we brought along under their sweaters and jackets to make sure the kids stayed warm. I checked their gloves and I noticed my younger son had left his gloves in the pickup and that the pickup had already left the scene. I got one on of my own gloves and put both his hands inside it and said, "This one is good for both your small hands and will keep them warm."

As the weather got dark and everybody got quiet. My wife

and I each held one of our kids in our arms and made them feel safe and warm while we all sat together. Minutes passed by very slowly until we finally heard the sound of a whistle. The sound became louder and louder. The whistle stopped and then we heard the sound of horse hooves getting closer. Six guys with six horses appeared. The leader looked at me and in Turkish yelled, "You come!" He grabbed the suitcases and put each one into a separate bag that he tied together and hung over the sides of the saddle. Then he told me to get on the horse and I refused.

"What?"

"My wife first should mount a horse, then my kids, and then finally me."

With no time to argue, he helped my wife onto a horse. One of the other horsemen got on another horse and put my older son in front of him. Then he looked at me with a smile and respectfully asked me to get onto the horse.

As soon as I got on, he took a small blanket I had around my son, pushed it under my saddle, and put my son in the blanket in front of me, almost on the neck of the horse. Then he asked me to hold my son with my left hand and use my right hand to guide the horse by the rein. However, the horse was not a horse at all. It was a mule. I looked at my wife and noticed she was frightened. It was the very first time she was on a horse and she was scared of how high she was from the ground.

I turned to her and said, "Don't worry. Somebody will guide your horse and walk in front of you. All you have to do is hold and balance yourself on top of the horse."

Everybody was on horses now. Our first horseback riding trip had finally started on a dark night, as we moved through cold, icy mountains covered in snow. The rider with my older son was the leader of the group. He rode in front of everyone else, then came Sarah, Nader, my wife, the bearded young man from the post office, whose name was Pahlavan, and finally my son and me on the mule. I noticed all the horses travelled in one single-file line, but my mule had a mind of its own and travelled to the side of the lane, which was frightening at times because it walked very close to the edge of the cliff. Also, the knot that held the two bags of suitcases together was awkward for me because it pressed upon my tailbone. To top everything off, the right foot stirrup of my saddle had already broken and my right leg was now dangling free, so that I had to curve it under the belly of the mule to keep myself and my son from falling off.

Although snow covered the mountains, the weather was clear with no clouds. The moonlight glowed and thousands of bright stars twinkled in the sky. Two of the six horsemen were scouts for the group. They moved ten minutes ahead of us to make sure there were no *pasdars* watching our trail. The only way they could identify themselves was with lit cigarettes in their hands. They climbed the rough terrain like mountain goats. Sometimes I could see (from the edge of the cliffs that my mule liked so very much) one hundred-meter-long waterfalls formed from the melted snow. It was so beautiful, and at the same time so scary for me.

One of the scouts was the man who was supposed to lead my wife's horse. At one point, she noticed he was gone and she had to lead the horse by herself. We came to the top of a mountain, which had a long flat plateau, and there were caves like those of train tunnels on the side. Suddenly, my wife's horse decided to run toward one of the tunnels. I heard my wife call out to me in a very scared voice. I just don't know how I did it, but I hit my mule hard and led it to where she was located. I caught up with her as she continued to speed away. I shouted, "Pull the rein hard!"

She did and her horse stopped.

I then shouted, "Pull the left rein to draw the horse to the left!" She gave her horse a left turn tug and he turned around. We slowly made our way back to the rest of our party, but before turning around I saw a beautiful collection of icicles, some as long as five feet in length, hanging from the cave's entrance, shining and gleaming bright in the moonlight.

When we got back, we rode for about three hours. Were supposed to be at Abdollah's house already, but it took so long because his house was in the last village of the Iranian border. I noticed the scouts returned and were talking with the leader of our group. I didn't understand anything they said because they spoke either Turkish or Kurdish, but from what I gathered from the tone in their voices, the news wasn't good. They consulted amongst themselves several minutes longer before finally deciding to backtrack roughly half an hour and then continue on another route from that point.

We rode horses for another two hours on the new route and by now everybody had gotten used to maneuvering their animals through the mountains. But the only thing on everybody's mind was finding a warm room and getting off those horses. Finally, after more than a total of six hours riding through the night, we heard dogs barking. In these deserted mountains we hadn't heard any sounds, but those of horse hooves (either in the snow or shallow water), or the splashing waterfalls coming from the melting snow. Hearing barking dogs was a good sign that we were getting closer to a village with homes and people inside them.

Soon we saw two-story houses and most of them had double wrought iron gates. Our leader approached one of those homes on horseback (with my older son also in the saddle) and knocked on the gate. Someone opened it, and our leader guided his horse in, with the rest of us following behind. But then suddenly his horse got scared of something and both he and my son were thrown out of the saddle onto the stony ground. My wife screamed, jumped off her horse and rushed to our son's side as he lay there on the ground. Everybody was amazed by how she swiftly leapt off her horse to get to our son, when before she was a timid rider.

Luckily, my son was fine. The leader apologized for the incident and took us all inside the house to the second floor. There they led us into a room with a woman and two children. In the middle of the room was a heater that used dry wood, cow, and sheep manure as fuel. The room was warm and cozy and carpeted with beautiful Persian rugs from Tabriz, as well as special assorted futons to sit on.

We took off our shoes and all huddled on one side of the room. I sat just a few feet from the entrance so I could watch everybody and everything going on inside the house, including the front door where somebody new might enter. The room was so hot that we had to take off some of our heavy clothing. They brought us hot tea in special Persian-style glass teacups and saucers. Although the tea was hot, everybody drank them fast. As soon as the glasses were empty, the servers filled them up again. The second glass was good, too, and was followed by a third and fourth. I noticed that when the host finished his second glass he turned it on its side. That was the sign to the servers that he had had enough. Then the servers brought us cigarettes, one pack per person, and placed them in front of us, even the kids. Bahman Cigarettes was a popular brand produced after the revolution. Nobody touched the cigarettes.

I told everyone to wrap up and go to sleep. I also let them know I would remain awake and keep watch until morning. While everyone slept, I glanced at the sleeping faces of my kids and my wife. They seemed very relaxed and comfortable and looked like angels. Their faces were blushing red from the heat of the room and the traumatic excitement of their journey. I rubbed my hand over their faces. My wife opened her eyes and said, "You should sleep, too. You haven't had any decent rest in the last two days."

"I'm fine," I said. "Just praying to God, so he brings us safe and sound to our destination"

We lost track of time, and while I sat I dozed off a few minutes and suddenly opened my eyes again to wake up. I saw daylight through the window. The weather was clear, but there was not a sign of the sun. I woke everybody up. As soon as I called the names of the members of our group, they woke up one by one, as though they were already awake. We didn't have to do very much, just put on our shoes and warm heavy clothing. I turned to my wife and said, "I'm going to leave the room and see where we are and what our situation is. We were supposed to spend the night at Abdollah's father's house, but had ended up here. I think the driver of that eighteen-wheeler truck reported our pickup to the border *pasdars* and they must have shut down the route our smugglers usually go through. That's why they changed direction and we ended up here."

I walked out of the room into the yard. The wrought iron gate was shut and locked. The stables were located right under the room we were staying in. That's where the host kept his cows, sheep, and goats. The toilet for the entire house was inside the stables, so that one had to sit in the presence of the animals to use it. The natural heat produced by the animal's bodies kept the stable warm, as well as the sitting area of the second floor.

I went back to the second floor to peek over the gate and the walls of the house. All I could see were mountains covered with white, undisturbed snow. I went back into the room where we had slept and asked the host for a bathroom break for the kids. He walked with me to the corner of one of the stables and said, "This is the place to take care of your business."

I couldn't believe what he had told me. I took my kids one at a time to the corner and stayed with them so they could take care of their toiletry business. Nobody else in our group wanted to use that sort of a bathroom, but the kids couldn't wait!

I looked at my watch and it was seven in the morning. Everybody gathered their bags and waited. By 7:30 a.m. the wrought iron gate opened and six horses entered the yard. We were asked to get onto the horses. I was happy that this time I had a horse and not a mule. We didn't even have a small breakfast or a plain glass of tea to warm us up.

As we exited the gate one could see fear in the eyes of everybody as they looked up at the tall snow-covered mountains around them. Sarah asked, "Where is this place? We are surrounded by tall mountains full of snow."

I could see Sarah was on the brink of losing it. "Don't worry," I replied. "These people live here. They know the way and the trails. They know every mountain and the passages around them." I took a moment and added, "Don't forget we are still in Iran and there are border *pasdars* all over the area." Then I looked at the group and said, "As we go on the trail, please don't make any noise and try to stay as quiet as possible, because any mistake from anyone is going to cost all of us, God forbid, our future and our lives."

Our leader started to go toward the valley between two mountains and everybody followed very quietly. As we got closer to the valley, he took a side trail and we followed him. I'm sure we were on one of the highest mountains in the area, because the trail had almost a thirty-degree slope downward. Our leader was not going straight down, but rather in a very steady, zigzag winding-style so that it would be easier for all of us.

I was within ten feet from my wife and asked her, "Honey, are you okay? You are riding that horse like someone with many hours of experience."

She replied with a smile, "Sure, sure. But you know I am not scared of riding anymore. I am positive we are going to get to our destination."

I kept talking to my younger son very quietly, telling him, "You are my assistant on this trip. I want you to look around and let me know if you see anything that I miss."

"If I what?" he asked.

"If you see anything. But more importantly, I want you to keep an eye on your mom."

By now we knew we were headed to Abdollah's house, but we had no idea how much further or how much longer it would take to get there. An hour passed and I finally asked one of the human traffickers, "How much longer to Abdollah's house?"

He replied, "*Do-saat* (Farsi for *two hours*)."

I really believe he didn't understand me. He just understood when I said "Abdollah."

We spent two more hours in the snow up and down the mountains. I asked the same guy the same question again and he gave me the same answer: "*Do-Saat.*" I turned to my younger son and said, "My assistant, please look at my watch and tell me what time it is."

He looked and said, "It is eleven."

"Thank you. You are a good assistant," I assured him.

So far, we had ridden four hours and had no idea when we were going to arrive at Abdollah's house. Everybody was tired and eager to get into a warm place to rest.

One more hour of riding horses finally delivered us to Abdollah's place.

As soon as Abdollah saw us he rushed to the leader and got my older son down off the horse, then rushed to me to grab the younger one, and then rushed to my wife to help her from her horse. I got down by myself and everybody went inside.

Abdollah led us through a big foyer to a large living room. In the middle of the living room there was a big *korsi* (special heater covered with blankets) and all around it were large futons to sit and recline upon. There was a skylight at the top of the dome in the ceiling. He invited everyone to take off their heavy clothing and slip under a blanket until lunchtime.

He approached me and said, "If you want to take the kids to the restroom, it is on your right-hand side. There is also hot water and soap to wash your hands and faces with." Everyone freshened up and lunch was served right on top of the *korsi*. It was a delicious hot stew with freshly baked bread Abdolla's mother had made. Lunch was followed by hot tea and within a few minutes everybody was so tired that they all quickly fell asleep.

After a while I woke up and looked at my watch. It was 3:30 p.m. We'd slept two hours. Abdollah came by and said, "We have to get ready. The horses are here. In an hour there is a shift change at the station of the border *pasdars*. This shift change is the best time to ride to the border and make our escape through the mountains that divide Iran and Turkey."

I woke up everybody and within thirty minutes they had freshened up and put on their heavy, warm clothing and stood waiting for further instructions from Abdollah.

The group of human traffickers had changed and now the new leader wore two rows of bandoleers crosswise on his chest with a Kalashnikov automatic rifle over his right shoulder. Abdollah placed my older son on the saddle in front of the new leader… next to the gun. As soon as my wife saw that our son was going to ride with the armed man, she requested very angrily to have my son brought down from that horse. Abdollah tried to reason with my wife, but she asked, "Why do we have to have an armed man?" Without waiting for an answer, she demanded to know, "If there is any danger, my son is going to be the first target, because he is riding with a man armed with a rifle."

I immediately went to the horse and retrieved my son. One by one, everybody got on a horse and Abdollah put my older son with one of the other human traffickers. I was the last one to get on a horse and my younger son sat in front of me with the same blanket, and the two bags containing the small suitcases.

At exactly 4:00 p.m. the gate of the home opened and our caravan of horses moved out. Abdollah's house was on top of a mountain and roughly fifteen minutes from the last Iranian village. Although the weather was cloudy, it was daytime and we could see villagers working as we continued.

Abdollah said to everyone, "When we pass through the village don't talk to and don't pay any attention to the villagers. Also, try to focus on the right shoulder, which is going to be the mountains. On the left side there is the last *pasdar* station and they have a good view of the route we will be travelling through. But you don't have to be concerned or afraid, because there will be many villagers returning to their homes at this time, plus the guards will be changing shifts."

I said to my younger son, "I am going to read a prayer and when I finish, you very quietly say, 'Amen.'" I read the verse, "Listen and understand Israel, that Hashem, who is our God, Hashem is the one and only."

When I finished, I heard my son quietly say, "Amen."

I held him with my left hand against my chest and said, "I love you, my angel."

The leader of the group rode in front of the caravan of horses and everybody followed him by a distance of about ten feet moving on one lane. We passed the village while the villagers got ready to retire for the day and occasionally their dogs followed our caravan barking at the horses. As we were instructed, nobody looked at the villagers or their dogs. All of us looked over our right shoulder towards the mountains. It took us exactly thirty minutes to get to the village and another fifteen minutes to pass through it. Our caravan moved along the snow-covered mountains and little by little, the leader headed further ahead to climb the mountain, once again in a zigzag, winding style.

I retrieved my camera from my jacket pocket and took a photo of our caravan ahead of me. As we climbed higher and higher, we noticed the snow on the ground became deeper and deeper until there wasn't any bare land. The weather got colder and colder, until when we finally made it to the top of the mountain. At the summit, there was a plateau the length of two football fields. At the beginning of the plateau, there was a column made from bricks about five to six feet in diameter and roughly twenty feet tall. One of the human traffickers said, "When you cross this column, you will be in Turkey."

I looked at my watch. The time was 6:00 p.m. It was Saturday, the first day of *Nowruz*, the Persian New Year. I looked back towards the snow-covered mountains of Iran with a bittersweet feeling and said, "Goodbye, my country. My birthplace. My land. The land of my ancestors for the past 2,700 years. Shame on those who have forced me to run away from you. God knows if I will ever get the chance to see you again."

My son turned around and stared at my face. "Papa? Are you happy or sad? Are you talking about our country, Iran? We're not coming back after we go to America?"

"I really don't know what is going to happen in the future," I admitted. "Our main concern now is to get to Istanbul and from there finally make our way to America." I waited for a moment and added, "You see this column that we passed? We just entered Turkey, and now we are out of the hands of the *Komitehs* and those no-good *pasdars* who caused us and other Iranian people so many problems. No more *Komitehs*. No more *pasdars*. And no more agony and hardship. Heaven knows how much I hated those people. It's unbelievable how fast they changed from being cultured Iranians to religious fanatics. In the name of Allah, they kill, steal, and they call themselves 'The followers of Allah.'"

As we rode I noticed our feet touched the snow and our horses couldn't move ahead anymore. Suddenly the weather had changed and it started to snow. Because hardly anybody ever travelled in the area of the plateau, the snow on the ground was very fresh and not compacted. We all left our horses and tried to walk on the snow, but with a single step we sank up to our hips. "Don't walk," I shouted. "Try to crawl on your knees and elbows to get the end of the plateau."

I had my younger son on my back and started to make my way to my wife and my older son. I noticed Pahlavan had my older son with him on his back and he turned to me and said, "Don't worry about your son. You take care of your wife and the other one." The snow fell quickly and became worse until it was a blizzard and we couldn't see more than ten feet ahead of us. But now we could talk to each other because there weren't any *pasdars* and they couldn't cross the Turkish border to get to us.

I heard Sarah having a good time talking and joking with one of the human traffickers who was leading her horse way ahead of us—so far ahead we couldn't see her. The rest of the group stayed very close together. I said to Nader, "Go get to your sister and tell her to not become too friendly with these people. No matter what, they are smugglers and we don't want to tempt them."

He said, "You are absolutely right. I have been telling her, but she thinks because she is three years older than I am she can do anything she wants." Nader got closer to his sister, and I could hear them talking in Armenian. Finally, he told her in Farsi what I had told him to warn her about.

She didn't like my opinion, either, and asked, "Who the hell does he think he is?" She waited a moment and then said, "He is not my father to order me around. Even my father can't order me around."

Again, Nader turned to her and said, "When you jeopardize his escape and endanger his family's life, it becomes his business."

Within minutes, they returned to the group and we finally were able to make our ways to the end of the plateau. The human traffickers brought the horses and as we walked in our wet clothing down from the mountainside on this very cold day, the blizzard abruptly stopped and everyone had a chance to huddle close together to wait and stay warm. I got blankets from the smugglers and covered the kids with them. I took my camera out of my pocket and snapped a photo. Then one of the smugglers took one with me in the picture. I wasn't sure the photos would turn out under those circumstances, but later when I developed them they turned out just fine and are tangible documents of the harsh and difficult realities we faced in our escape.

Per the suggestions of our leader, we had to wait and keep ourselves warm for an hour until the weather was completely dark enough so that we could go to Abdollah's father's house. It was located in the very first village of Turkey. Everybody waited anxiously looking forward to getting to a warm place to relax. Finally, the leader said, "Very quietly, walk down the mountain. We will bring your belongings with the horses."

The leader walked in front of us and we all followed him. We heard the sound of a whistle and there appeared a man holding a cigarette in his hand shaking it to the left and right as a sign that everything was okay. We got to the house. It had a wrought iron double gate very similar to the home we had just stayed in the night before in the last village of Iran. The gate opened and all of us rushed inside and made our way into the house.

There was a tall man standing in the doorway of the living room. He approached me and said, "You must be the man that my son Abdollah has told me so much about. I congratulate you and admire your bravery in taking your family and escaping with them from your country under such circumstances."

I shook hands with him and he offered us his best hospitality.

A woman approached us and ran to the kids and turned to

my wife and in Turkish said something, which was right away translated by Abdollah's father.

My wife said, "Let's get these kids out of their wet clothes and put some dry clothing on them." Her request was translated and the woman rushed to get dry clothing for the kids. "Thank you," said my wife. "I have more warm clothes for them in the small suitcase."

Two ladies started changing the kids and washed their faces with hot water and then joined the rest of us in the warm living room. Everybody freshened up and sat on futons on the floor next to the same sort of wood and manure burning heater we had experienced two nights before. Hot tea was served and half an hour later a hot dinner appeared, which included chicken kabob, rice, and stew with freshly baked bread.

I was amazed by the kid's well-mannered behavior. Especially when it came to the escape and the hardships of riding horses in the snowy mountains without making the smallest complaint or dropping the slightest tear. Our host noticed I was holding two of my right-hand fingers and rubbing them trying to warm them up. "What's wrong with your fingers?" he asked.

I replied, "These two fingers got frostbite many years ago when I was in the army and now I think they are really in bad shape. I have no feeling in them and I am worried about it."

He called his wife and said something in Turkish. Minutes later, she walked in with a bowl of water filled with a lot of ice. He turned to me and said, "Give me your hand, and don't try to get your fingers out of the bowl" He put my fingers in the very cold water. I tried to get them out of the cold water, but he was stronger than me and held it inside until I felt excruciating pain. He took my fingers out of the water and rubbed them with a special medicine, which was made up from different herbs, and then held them close to the heater. He then let my fingers go and said, "You will not have any more problems with these fingers."

And he was right.

There was a knock on the door and Abdollah walked into the

house. He approached me with a large smile and said, "I am so glad to see you here in my father's house. My father was very eager to meet you. I see you two have already met." He waited a moment and said, "This is actually my stepmother. She lives in Turkey and my other mother lives in Iran. My father has businesses in both Iran and Turkey. He stays a few weeks here in Turkey and then returns for a few weeks to the other house in Iran."

"Abdollah, you don't have to explain yourself to me about your father and your family," I reassured him.

"From the first moment I met you and your family in Tehran," he replied, "anytime I ever saw my father I talked about you and your family. My father and I feel very close to all of you."

I thanked him and said, "I congratulate your father for having a brave son like you."

He again offered us his hospitality and said, "Please, ask me or my family if you need anything. Anything at all. Now, please relax. I know you won't like the idea I proposed in Tehran, because of the kids, regarding if you go give yourselves up to the *askars* station, which is very close to us. Believe me it is going to be easier for you and your family. You are out of Iran now and they can't do anything to you. You are out of the danger-zone."

I thanked him and said, "The answer is still no."

My wife agreed with me by a nod of her head.

Abdollah smiled and added, "By the way, tomorrow is election day and our house is one of the voting stations for the area, therefore, please stay inside the entire day and relax, but don't make too much noise. The government representative will be here from 7:00 a.m. to 3:00 p.m. They will be in the back of the house in the open field. They are not allowed to enter our house. If they have to use a bathroom, there are plenty of open-field areas for them to take care of their business."

"You knew about the election date in advance?" I waited a moment and then asked, "How come you scheduled our escape for a day like tomorrow?"

He quickly replied, "You were scheduled the same day you left

Khoy. But unfortunately, our pickup driver made a big mistake by not paying attention to the traffic and almost caused a big accident when he entered the highway. Our scouts reported that the border *pasdars* had been notified by the driver of the eighteen-wheeler, so we had no choice but to take you to the other house, which put us behind. By the way, I fired that pickup driver. He is not going to work for us anymore."

"I did notice the eighteen-wheeler driver had stopped," I said. "I saw him step out of his truck. He watched our pickup as we headed towards the mountains. I even mentioned it to Saleh, so he was also aware of the situation."

"Well, don't worry about it," Adollah said. "All of you need some good rest and some of the good food that my stepmother is cooking for us. Enjoy, and spend a lazy day in the warm and cozy room so that you can get ready for two to three nights of riding."

Although we were in Abdollah's father's house, I did not know his name. I thought there was a special reason Abdollah hadn't mentioned his father's name to me, because I noticed that he called him only "sir." No use of the word "father," and no calling him by any given name. Therefore, I turned to Abdollah's father and said, "I feel bad that I don't know your name."

He said, "In Turkey, they call me Big Morteza. Everybody knows me around these villages and the nearby villages in Iran. In Iran, they call me Morteza Khan, and I am happy to be the very first host for you and your family. I also wish you all the success and happiness for all of you in your escape and in the future. I have many Jewish friends in both Turkey and Iran, and I have been doing business with them for years. Mr. Simani and I have been business partners for a long time in the import and export industry. This business of smuggling people from Iran to Turkey is a new venture for us."

It was getting late and the kids had fallen asleep. We joined them on the beds readied for us on the ground, which had been covered by camel wool blankets. I can say that the first night in Turkey was the best sleep I had had in a long time—since the first of the demonstrations against the Shah had begun five years earlier.

I woke up the next morning and the sun was shining. The weather was clear and bright and the glow of the sunshine on the snow-covered mountains made it seem like a picture painted by an artist. I pushed the window covering aside, which was made from a heavy expensive fabric, to get a better view. I could see up to two hundred yards from the house where people were already standing in line to place their votes. I looked at my watch and the time was 8:30 a.m.

Everybody woke up refreshed. There was warm water available in the very clean and real bathroom they had in the house. We had an all-natural breakfast, which included eggs, different goat cheeses, some with dry mint, honey, a special cream spread, which was similar to butter, tea, hot milk for the kids, and plenty of hot freshly baked bread. With a heavy breakfast like that, nobody wanted to walk around the house. As I remember, it was the laziest day of our escape.

It was about 11:00 a.m. when our kids approached us and complained about stomachaches. My wife prepared hot tea with crystal sugar she had packed with our clothing, specifically for such unexpected cases. Within half an hour, all the members of our group suddenly developed stomachaches, including my wife and me. Tea with crystal sugar was served to everybody, and by 2:00 p.m., per my wife's recommendation, her, the kids, and I only had yogurt and freshly baked bread for lunch. The rest of the group also decided to have the same for their lunch meals. My wife's suggestion took care of our stomachaches and everyone was happy.

Voting day ended on the property and we finally had a chance to walk in the front yard, which was surrounded by tall brick walls and a double wrought iron gate. The air was fresh. The sky was full of sunshine. It was all so beautiful. I turned to my wife and said, "We haven't seen a shiny and clear day like this back home for many years. During the rain and snow seasons when the weather was supposed to be healthy and clear, the cars, buses, and factories created so much smog that the whiteness of the snow turned gray."

At 5:30 p.m. Abdollah approached the group and said, "In half an hour, our caravan will hit the road and hopefully within three to four days we will arrive at our destination in the city of Van." I was surprised by his statement, because he had previously mentioned it would only take two to three days to arrive in Van. I decided not to say anything for the moment. I figured, what's two, three, or maybe even more extra days? At least we are out of Iran, and eventually we will be in Van and within a day or two after that, Istanbul.

Abdollah brought my briefcase and handed it to me. "Please look inside and you will notice that it hasn't been opened at all, and that everything is in order as you packed."

I thanked him for smuggling it out of the country for me when I had given it to him back in Iran to bring for me, because it would have been a sign of escape in case the *pasdars* at the Khoy junction had checked it. And then I would have been caught. "Do you remember in Iran when I told you that I might need some extra Turkish *lier?*"

"Yes, I remember."

From the briefcase, I took out $1,000.00 American dollars and asked for it to be exchanged to Turkish *lier.*

He was surprised that I had money in the briefcase and said, "I thought there would be passports and histories of medical papers for the kids like vaccination cards. I never thought you would have any money in there."

"Saleh told me that if I have any jewelry, money, or important papers, to just pack them in the briefcase and he will get them back to me in Van. He knew I had money in both Turkish *liers* and American dollars. He even knew the amount of each. I gave him a copy of a list of the items in the briefcase."

"I'm glad everything is in the briefcase," said Abdollah with a smile. "As for that $1,000.00, when I have the bus tickets ready for everybody I will hand you the Turkish *lier* for your $1,000.00 in Van"

At exactly 6:00 p.m. the gate opened and seven horses with six human traffickers rode in. A young man approximately six-feet-four inches tall, around two-hundred-fifty pounds, very well built, and who spoke in Turkish and Kurdish join our group. He thanked Abdollah for giving him a chance to ride with us. He also was assigned to hold my older son on his horse. Everybody was ready and Abdollah opened the gate.

Another night of our escape had started, but this time instead of Iranian *pasdars* we had to worry about the Turkish *askars*. We were refugees who had entered the country illegally and if they had caught us we would have to go through a formalities process and be placed in a refugee program, which had been decreed to the Turkish government through the refugee program of the United Nations.

We were told that it would take us six hours to get of the village and that we were going to spend the night there. There wasn't the smallest cloud in the sky, and the weather was still very cold. Some parts of our trail were covered with snow and some parts by small rivers that had formed from the melting snow. Our group was really happy and was in very good spirits, because we were getting closer and closer to our destination.

I turned to my wife and said, "Look up. For centuries, people gazed at the sky after the sunset. They always see thousands of vibrant, sparkling stars." I waited a moment and asked, "Have you ever viewed the moon and the Big Dipper as it appears now? So bright and close, as though you are a short distance from them?"

She replied, "You are right, and it's so beautiful. It's unbelievable." She waited a moment and asked, "Did you notice how healthy and strong the people who live in the wilderness are? All of that comes from good weather with no smog, plus eating all-natural food, such eggs, meat, milk. I'm sure all dairy foods products are homemade without a shred of antibiotics."

Six hours passed but we were still riding in the snow-covered mountains. I turned to one of the human traffickers and asked, "How many hours to our stop?"

Just like before he replied, "*Do-saat*" (two hours). I noticed the newcomer who had just joined our group (and was now responsible for my older son) walked with my son singing special lyrics in Kurdish. The area in which they were walking was flat. It was a road the villagers used to travel on from one village to another.

I got down from my horse and joined them. "Thank you for taking care of my son," I said to the man. "I hope someday I will be able to repay your hospitality. I am Hakimi, and he is my son."

"My name is Ghasem. It is my pleasure to be able to help your son. I also want to thank you for not refusing me to join your group. Abdollah was very concerned about it. He told me that if the group becomes larger than six or seven people that there could be consequences."

"In your case there would not be any concerns or consequences, because you speak both Turkish and Kurdish. You can be a great help to our group." I then asked, "How did you get out of the country? Did you escape by yourself, or were you brought out of the borders by a human trafficker?"

Ghasem replied, "I escaped by myself and in a big hurry because the *Komiteh* and the no-good *pasdars* came by in the morning to my house and asked for me. My mother and my fiancé told them that I wasn't home. The *pasdars* asked where I was, and my mother told them that I had gone shopping and would be back in two hours. I knew right then that they had come to arrest me, because I was part of a Kurdish group fighting the Islamic Republic. I had time to only take just a few, small things and some food. I even forgot to change my shoes or to put on socks. As you can see, my shoes are in pretty bad shape. As soon as we get to the village I will have to buy new socks and shoes." His shoes were a mess.

And then he added, "I must let you know that the reason I am walking with your son is because he was cold and was falling asleep. I decided to walk with him and sing to him and ask him to jump up and down with me so that he would stay warm and alert and not freeze. You should get your younger son down from his horse and make him walk, too. It would be good for him."

He was right. I got my younger son down from his horse and followed Ghasem's footsteps down the trail.

One of the scouts approached our group and spoke with the leader of the human traffickers. Ghasem understood their language and said, "We should take cover because an *askar* jeep is headed our way and the leader of the human traffickers has warned everybody to very quietly follow him and move to the side of the road among the trees covered with snow." Everybody followed him to the trees and tried to hide amongst them. The human traffickers brought the horses and hid them between the trees. We waited a few minutes until we saw a jeep with four *askars* headed in the opposite direction. The leader made sure the *askars* had left the scene when he finally said, "Everybody get on your horses so we can continue our escape." He decided to go through the forest and not continue on the snow-covered road because it would probably be safer that way.

We rode a few hours longer and then we heard the barking of dogs in the distance. To our surprise we passed through a village with no sign of a stop in sight, and then got back onto the road. I turned to Ghasem and said, "Please ask one of the human traffickers how much longer we have to go before we stop."

He spoke with one of them and returned to tell me that the reason we didn't stop was because the house we were supposed to stay in had unexpectedly become occupied by another group of escapees. The leader of our group didn't want to jeopardize our escape by putting the two groups together. So, on we went.

We rode for another hour until the sound of dogs barking could once again be heard in the distance.

We arrived at a shack with a stable attached next to it. The leader of our group said, "Very quietly, everybody get down from your horses and go inside.

We entered, and to the right of the door was an open space. We sat down, but then I stood up to see what was in the adjacent room, because it smelled of sheep and cows. As I returned, I stepped in something and my right foot sank in a hole up to my waist. I swiftly jumped out of the hole and examined my leg to see if I was hurt. Luckily, everything was okay. The hole was actually the shack's ground oven used to bake bread. It had been left uncovered.

A man came by with a tray of cups and saucers to give us some tea. Suddenly, one of the horses outside charged in from the opening and headed towards us. My wife jumped, attacked, and screamed at the horse to defend the kids from being run over, shouting so loud that the horse speedily turned around and charged back to the outside. The horse knocked over the man carrying the tray of cups and saucers so that we never received any tea for the night. All of us started clapping our hands for my wife's bravery and gave her compliments regardless. Although it could have been a disaster, it instead made everybody laugh for a few minutes and gave us a boost of energy.

The leader of the group came in and said, "It's time to get on our horses and continue. Please be very quiet." Within a few minutes our group had once again mounted our horses and I was happy that Ghasem had also joined us. I was also glad he was part of our group because he looked after my older son and I knew I could count on him.

Everybody was very cold and tired. We rode another two hours and again the sound of barking dogs was the best music to everybody's ears. My younger son asked, "Papa, can you hear the barking of the dogs? You said before, it's good news, isn't it? Why is it good news?"

"It's a sign that we are getting close to a village and most probably we will be stopping soon at a nice warm house to rest and sleep."

We entered a village and were welcomed by the local dogs. We stopped near the village end, by a two-story house with a double wooden gate in the front. As soon as the horses stopped someone opened the gate and said, "Hurry! Come in!" He placed a finger on his lips giving us a sign to be quiet. After everybody entered, they closed the gate and we were led to the front of the house where we dismounted our horses and headed inside to the second floor.

We took off our heavy clothing items and shoes and entered a big warm room with a wood-and-manure-burning heater next to a wall. The owners of the home were a husband and wife with three beautiful daughters who all wore beautiful colorful clothing. They looked at the kids and the wife approached my wife and said, "Bring the kids close to the heater." Then she started to rub both kid's hands in turns.

The girls curiously kept looking at my boys as though they could not believe their eyes. One of them made a comment to the others, "These boys are so small and innocent. How come their father took them on such a dangerous and harsh trip in snowy weather?"

Ghasem translated the comment for me. I thought to myself that they see what they see. They don't know the real story behind it. And they can never know how difficult it was for me and my wife to make that decision.

One of the girls brought us a tray full of cups and saucers along with a large pot of tea. Everybody enjoyed at least three if not four cups of the tea as they spoke with each other. Although we hadn't had dinner yet and the last lunch had only been plain yogurt and fresh baked bread, everybody was so tired from our riding that we immediately fell asleep. I looked at my watch before I fell asleep and the time was 3:30 a.m.

I woke up and noticed that all the members of our group were still asleep and it was about ten o'clock in the morning. I looked around and saw that our host family members were sitting at the same spot at the end of the room as though they hadn't moved or slept at all. I realized that the room we were sleeping in was the only room in the house. The owner and his family could not sleep because our group had practically taken it over.

I said, "Good morning." At the same time, I gestured to the father with a sign of hello. He stood up and spoke in Turkish, but also signaled to me to come out of the room and head outside. Ghasem was awake and translated for me. "He wants you to go out of the room with him."

I walked outside of the room onto a balcony. Ghasem joined us. "I think I have to be here with you to translate," he said.

I thanked him and the three of us headed downstairs. He took us to the stables, which practically made up the first floor of the house and pointed at a corner that had been cleaned for use by our group and said, "Try to use this area as a restroom and don't worry about cleaning up after yourselves."

I looked at Ghasem and started laughing. "Anybody who wants to use the bathroom is going to have a lot of spectators watching him."

The man turned to Ghasem and asked, "Why is your friend laughing and what did he say that was so funny?"

Ghasem translated to the host with a large smile on his face and the host started to laugh when he realized my joke.

When we returned upstairs, my wife and the kids were ready and waiting for me. My wife said, "I knew where you were and I am so happy that we have a friend and a translator like Ghasem with us now. The kids and I are ready to go wash up." Ghasem and I started laughing. My wife was surprised and asked, "What's the matter? Did I say something funny?"

Ghasem and I looked at each other smiling and I turned to her and said, "Please, bring the kids and come with me." We headed to the stables downstairs. As we walked into the stable, all the animals kept looking at us as though they realized strangers had entered their personal area. The host had given me a vase filled with water to wash up with and some papers for cleanup when we had finished taking care of our businesses in the corner. I took the kids with me and they took care of their business while I stood between the animals of the stable and my sons.

Eventually, every member of the group used the restroom with the cows, sheep, goats and a couple of donkeys as spectators.

We were ready for a good meal because everybody was very hungry and our bodies were still in pain from riding for so many hours. Our host spread a sheet of colorful fabric on the floor and asked everybody to sit around it. Hot milk was served for the children and hot tea for the grownups. Fresh baked bread and goat cheese, which had dry mint in it, was also part of our breakfast and lunch. The same water vase (filled with water) was the centerpiece on the fabric for anybody who wanted something to drink. Everybody enjoyed the bread and cheese better than they would have a shish-kebab or chicken kebab and crashed right there in the same room to rest until we were asked to get ready.

At exactly 6:00 a.m. the wooden gate opened and seven horses with six human traffickers entered the yard. Everybody was ready and with the same setup as before the group mounted on their horses. Every new village we stayed in, six new human traffickers replaced the ones from before which, of course, one of them had been appointed as the leader. I turned to Ghasem and said, "Please ask them how many hours it will take us to get to Van. Abdollah told me it would take three or four nights to get to Van. Tonight, is the fourth night of our escape to our destination."

Ghasem left and returned and said, "He doesn't know how long, but he told me that we are going to be riding for another five or six hours until we get to the next village."

I got a feeling that it was going to be more than four nights of riding.

The weather was cold and the sky was clear without even the smallest patch of clouds. We travelled on a road with snow, but the trails of the tires of motor vehicles that had recently passed could also be seen. Both sides of the road were forest grounds with tall trees covered by the snow. We rode about an hour and then the leader headed to the right of the road and entered the forest. The snow was so clean I am sure we were the first group riding over it. The route we travelled wasn't flat. Sometimes we had to go down the mountains and sometimes climb them. By now every member of our group had gotten a good grip on riding their horses. Everybody rode like a professional rider. Sometimes the slope was so deep that we had to dismount and walk behind the horses while holding to the tail of the horse.

Little by little the nightfall took over and the moon and the stars appeared in the sky. Although everyone had had enough of riding and looked forward to getting to our final destination, they enjoyed the minimum freedom they had. Just thinking about being out of the areas controlled by the *Komitehs* and *pasdars* was a great feeling. I rode close to my wife and said, "Honey. How are you doing? I am sure you know that this is not the last night of our riding, but at least the weather is not that bad. In about two or three more nights, we will get to our destination."

Then she smiled and said, "What good news you have just told me."

The leader asked everybody to mount, and we were on the road again. Ghasem approached me and told me that the leader had told him the reason we had to go through a forest was to pass by an *askar* station without them seeing us. He also told me that now we didn't have to ride through the forest anymore, because in two hours we were going to be in our designated village. The word of getting close to our destination village quickly got around to everybody. I turned to my younger son who was riding with me and said, "Listen very carefully and as soon as you hear the barking of the dogs, tell me." I kept talking to my son during the ride and tried to keep him awake. I didn't want him falling asleep in the cold weather. Also, Ghasem was constantly talking to my older son and sometimes I heard him sing revolutionary Kurdish songs to keep him from falling asleep.

My younger son said, "Papa, I can hear the dogs. Listen, listen, I can hear them."

I said, "You are right. I can hear them, too. Good work, my assistant"

We got to the beginning of the village and the leader said, "Everybody get off your horses and go to the house on your left-hand side."

The human traffickers assisted us down from our horses and led us through a door inside of a very large room. The room was carpeted throughout. At the end of the room there were about ten to twelve men and women. There were two big heaters in the room. We took our shoes off and got close to the heater.

They watched our group with curious eyes especially when looking at the kids. I could see they were surprised by the presence of my kids. The owner of the house approached us and brought us a sheet of fabric, which he spread on the ground. Plenty of fresh hot baked bread was served, so fresh that one could see the steam still rising from it, along with more mint goat cheese and hot tea.

I took the kids to the bathroom, which at least was better than the previous village, because it was in a part of the stable that was completely away from the animals. At least one could take care of their business without an audience of different animals watching them. My wife and I spread one of the blankets we had brought with us under the kids as a mattress and another on top of the kids as a blanket. Within a couple minutes, they were asleep.

Ghasem talked to the other people and even got friendly with them. He also arm-wrestled with them. He won every single match. One of them said, "You are the strongest man here and you beat all of us."

He then asked, "What do you want us to do for you?"

Ghasem replied, "I just need a pair of good shoes and a warm pair of socks, because I don't have any socks and my shoes are all torn up. The host went to another room and returned with a set of handmade wool socks, especially made for the cold, and a pair of shoes. Finally, Ghasem got to wear some decent socks and shoes.

Everybody was so tired and beat that one by one they fell asleep very quickly close to one another. Ghasem approached me and said "Agha-ye Hakimi (Farsi for *Mister Hakimi*). I heard they have been talking about moving us to another house because there has been a mix up between our group and another group escaping from Iran. The other group has complained and wants our group to leave this house as soon as possible. The owner of the house got upset about their request and said to them, 'It's not fair. They have small kids. Have a heart. It's very cold outside and they rode horses for about eight hours and have nothing to do with you. They will leave in the morning to another house.'"

The other leader objected to our presence and told the host, "Get rid of them immediately."

Finally, the host approached Ghasem and said, "I am so sorry, but I can't reason with this guy. You better ask your group to get ready and leave our house before the night is over and the sky has turned bright. There is another house scheduled for you and they are waiting for you right now. I have sent somebody to tell them you are coming and they are awaiting your arrival."

Ghasem and I woke everybody up and asked them to get ready to leave. Ghasem carried my older son on his back and I held my wife's hand while I carried my younger son on my back. Somebody else was carried our belongings to the new house. There were no horses and no human traffickers anymore. They had gone back to their village. We had to walk through the village to almost the other end to get to this new house, which was our resting stop for the next day.

We approached a one-story home, and when the owner opened the gate everybody rushed into a very warm and cozy room. The heater was burning and one could see the flames of the burning wood and dry manure. As soon as we got inside, my wife and I made sure everything was safe and made a bed for the kids with our own blankets and within a very short time we all fell asleep.

Later I woke up and noticed the sky was bright and the mountains around us were covered with a new layer of snow. It was a beautiful day. The sun was shining and the beauty of the village and location were very peaceful. The host rushed to me with excitement and said something in Turkish, which I couldn't understand.

I woke up Ghasem and said, "Our host is telling me something in Turkish. Please ask him why he is so excited."

Ghasem spoke with him, turned to me and said, "He wants us to leave his house, because one of his neighbors who has a quarrel with him has found out about our group and reported us to the *askars*, asking them to come to arrest us. He told me he has been working for Abdollah and he is afraid about us being arrested by the *askars* and losing his business with Abdollah."

It was amazing. Within fifteen minutes everybody had mounted the readied horses, which had been brought for us a few minutes earlier and we were once again on our way. In fact, this was the first time we travelled during the day in Turkey. The leader quickly headed to the forest and we followed right after him. I have to say that I never thought my kids would be so understanding and go along with our crazy situation, but they did. I was riding very close to my wife and talking to my younger son the entire time. Ghasem was responsible for my older son so I didn't have to worry about him, because he was in good hands.

We rode through the forest and mountains for roughly three hours. Finally, we were out of the forest and riding from mountain to mountain until we came to a valley between three very tall mountains. The snow was fresh and was not compacted. There hadn't been any traffic by anyone or any animals. In the middle of the valley, there was a small shack made of bricks without any doors or windows. The leader headed towards the shack but approximately one hundred yards before the shack the horses started sinking into the fresh snow and we had to dismount and crawl our way to the shack. I turned to my wife and jokingly said, "At least we can see each other on a very bright and sunny day. It's not like the plateau between Iran and Turkey with a blizzard around us."

It took us about half an hour but finally we were in the shack. I asked one of the human traffickers, "Why is there a shack in the middle of nowhere like this?"

He must have understood me because he asked Ghasem to translate the answer. Ghasem said, "This is a safety house for shepherds in case they ever get stuck in a blizzard. They take refuge in here to be safe until the weather is good enough to continue home."

I looked at my wife and said "It's amazing how these mountain people live in contrast to our luxury of living in large, developed, sophisticated cities. Maybe it was meant for us to learn to appreciate our lives and the opportunities we have, so that we don't take them for granted."

With a smile my wife said, "Please try not to be a philosopher and find out what program is next for us."

Ghasem by now had become my translator and everybody in the group listened to me as the decision-maker. It just evolved that way. I was older and more experienced. And on several key occasions my suggestions were vital to our escape, such as crawling over the snow on the plateau to avoid sinking into the drifts and finding our way out of a frozen lake. Eventually they all respected as a leader.

I asked Ghasem to find out what was going on and how much longer we were going to stay at the shepherd house.

Ghasem returned and said, "They are aware that we left in a hurry and didn't have breakfast and so far, no lunch. One of the human traffickers has gone to the nearest village to bring us food and fresh horses because one of the horses is pregnant and injured and can't carry anybody. By nightfall we will be at the next village, which is about two to three hours from here."

We tried to stay warm and everybody bundled up together. I put the suitcases on the floor and sat my kids down upon them. Then I then wrapped the kids with the blankets we had brought.

My wife cuddled up on one side of our kids and I did the same on the other side. I did my best to keep them warm. Two hours passed and nothing happened. Another two hours passed and finally we noticed someone approaching the safe house with two horses. He came in with some food, but to our surprise, they started to eat all of it. They didn't even offer us any. I said to Ghasem, "Ask for some bread." He got some bread from them. My wife had six cans of Tuna Fish in the suitcases. I got the cans out and with a knife, our strong man Ghasem opened them, and we all had some tuna fish with bread. I turned to our group and said, "Let's thank my wife because she insisted on bringing the tuna fish cans along even though I had been against the idea." I have to confess that women's intuition is sometimes unbelievable. I thanked my wife for a very healthy meal in the middle of nowhere.

The weather was getting dark and per the request of our human trafficker we left the safe house and walked to get out of the valley. Everyone looked forward to mounting their horses and heading out of the area. Two hours passed and we could see the moon and sky was full of stars. Finally, after five hours of riding in the mountains we arrived at a flat plateau. It was so nice to ride on a flat area without having to climb up and down the mountains. I turned to Ghasem and said, "I think they are lost and we are going around in circles."

"How do you know that?"

"By looking up at the stars and constellations. I learned this during the time I was in the army."

Ghasem approached the human traffickers and participated in a conversation with them. He returned and said, "You are right. They don't know which direction to go. That is the reason they are arguing."

I rode close to them and asked Ghasem to translate for me. I turned to one of the human traffickers and asked, "Which direction do we have to go to, north, south, west, or east?"

The leader of the human traffickers replied, "We have to go west."

I showed them the direction and it was between two mountains. Everybody agreed and we headed towards the valley between the two mountains. We rode for another hour until we heard some other riders coming towards us. Three riders approached and one of them was a very sophisticated-looking man with elegant clothing and a sheepskin hat who rode on a special saddle and advanced towards the human traffickers shouting at the leader and his crew. He then approached me and in very perfect English said, "I am so sorry about the delay. I was expecting you two hours ago. I noticed your group was late and I knew something must have gone wrong. That's why I decided to come find you." He noticed my son on my horse and the bags of suitcases. He dismounted and asked me to switch onto his horse. He walked in front of our caravan holding unto my horse by the rein for the next hour until we arrived at his house.

A double-door gate opened and several men and women rushed to help us get inside. They even helped us take off our shoes and warm heavy clothing. We found ourselves inside of a beautiful house, carpeted throughout with futons to sit on and relax. The heater was on. The host approached me and said, "There is a bathroom for your use with hot water. I am sure your wife and you want to take care of your children and then we will have a warm dinner and tea ready for you."

I thought it was a blessing. We took care of the kids and freshened up. They gave hot tea to the grownups, while the kids got hot milk.

The wife of the host brought a big colorful fabric and spread it on the floor and put hot stew in bowls with freshly baked bread on the side. The hot food and warm room with great hospitality, especially after such a long trip, was like a gift from heaven.

The host approached me and asked, "I heard you found the way out of that frozen lake?"

I was shocked and asked "Frozen Lake? You mean the plateau on which we went around in circles two or three times? That was a frozen lake?" I waited a moment and then said, "I had a feeling something was wrong and that they had lost their way and direction"

He replied, "I was really worried about you and your group. Unfortunately, we have had accidents there before and the ice broke under the horses and people lost their lives. I am so happy that it didn't happen to you guys. Also, I am so glad that you were able to show them the right direction."

I couldn't believe what I had heard and without even thinking, I raised my hands up to the sky and said, "Thank you God, Thank you!" That was the last thing I could imagine after escaping the *Komitehs* and the *pasdars*. To have been able to cross and escape the *pasdars* of Iran at the border, as well as the Turkish *askars*, and not get caught, but then suddenly end up sinking and drowning in a frozen lake? That would've been too much. I looked up at the sky one more time in prayer and said, "You are everywhere and watching over us," referring to the lord.

Our host said, "Believe me, from the moment I headed towards you I was praying and asked Allah many times to help me find you and your group safe and sound. I even made a promise to myself to sacrifice a sheep for the well-being of all of you."

I wondered about our host and exactly why he had such a great command of English if he was only a human trafficker. I looked him straight in the eyes and asked, "I have to be honest with you, from the first moment I saw you, it has been a question for me. A man of your character and knowledge of English and now I see this beautiful house. I don't know how to express myself. What are you doing in this part of the world and mountains?"

He smiled and replied, "I am a big man around here. I have a lot of properties and in every nearby village I have a lot of cattle, sheep, goats, and their products are sold within the city of Van and the other surrounding cities. I have a very dependable truck and I travel to the nearby cities all the time. Sometimes I am here with my wife and my kids. My family and I like to live in nature. My wife grew up in one of the villages around here and wants our kids to feel nature and to also get to know the mountains and the snow; experience how people live in villages. When we're here she makes them live the life of one of my workers. They are very good at milking and collecting wood and manure for the cooking and heater fires. Many times, before, I told her to take it easy with the kids, but she believes they should learn and appreciate the luxury of the life I have provided for them in the city. Therefore, I never argue with her."

That was one of the biggest experiences of the trip; to see a man who had been educated at one of the best universities of Turkey, has a good knowledge of the English language, and runs a very successful business, to come to such isolated mountains with his family and spend time in the snow and the wilderness around it. He likes the natural environment, especially because his wife wants their children to appreciate their lives in the big city where they have all their amenities almost always available.

I turned to him and said, "You know, I am your guest. You have given me, my family, and the group travelling with me, shelter, warmth, and a cozy room as well as food to eat. We are all very thankful for your kindness and hospitality" I waited a moment and cordially asked, "You know my name, but I don't know what the name of my gracious host might be."

He very humbly replied, "My name is Haydar, but everybody around here calls me *Afendu-Haydar*." (*Afendu* is Turkish for *master* or *boss*.) We shook hands again and he then said, "I am very happy to have this opportunity to meet you too. I heard about you and your family from Abdollah in Van. I was very eager to meet a man who is so courageous as to take his family with two small kids on an escape like this, especially during the snowy season."

I held my head in my hands and said, "I am not so courageous. Believe me I am not a political man. I am a simple man with a simple family. Like most other people, I had a job, and I loved living in my country. But that dammed revolution took everything away from my family, me, and the rest of the Iranian people. Plus, I'm Jewish living in a Muslim country. There weren't any issues for minorities during the Shah's regime. In fact, many minorities had very responsible and highly-paid positions and were amongst the best of the citizens of Iran."

Afendu-Haydar was shocked by my story and I noticed his wife was getting very frustrated.

"I am sorry, but it seems that your wife has become upset by my story. I can see that she understands English very well. I better stop and talk about something else."

Afendu-Haydar's wife said, "Please, don't stop."

I noticed my kids had fallen asleep and my wife was listening to me. The rest of the group, except Ghasem, had fallen asleep.

Ghasem turned to me and in Farsi asked "Mister Parviz. I don't speak or understand English. Is it possible that you can explain some parts of your story in Farsi, too, so that I can understand it, please?"

In Farsi, I replied, "I will try to tell the story in both English and Farsi." I had an urge to speak. Maybe it was because such a long time had passed since my country had been hijacked by a bunch of thieves and enemies in the name of Allah and religion. But I remembered how it all started and what resulted from it. I talked about everything including the demonstrations and the burning down of the government buildings in all the major cities. I also spoke about the invasions of people's homes and the confiscations of their livelihoods as well as the killing or arresting of some of them in the name of Allah. I spoke about how the Islamic Republic had deprived the Iranian people of their businesses and had taken over everything while accusing them of being against their so-called revolution. Usually, a revolution comes from the heart of the people and not from outside of the country. It was obvious that the so-called Islamic Revolution of 1979 was an imported revolution, arranged by the countries that didn't want Iran to get out of underdeveloped status and become part of the developed twentieth century, as the Shah wished. The timing was perfect. The Shah of Iran had cancer and his top advisors, one after another, disappeared completely from the picture. It broke my heart.

Afendu-Haydar asked, "What is your opinion of the Shah and the way he ran the country? Do you think he should have fought for the country and the people, or not?"

I paused to gather my thoughts before answering, because I knew it was an answer that most of the world had never heard. "There are many people in Iran who represent the silent majority. These people are not the hoodlums that demonstrate in the streets, attack businesses, burn down buildings, harass civilians, or create any sort of chaos. They are everyday people who trusted the Shah, because they knew he wouldn't go along with past agreements that took advantage of Iran and all of her natural resources.

And then along comes Khomeini, who was no angel. His one wish was to topple the Shah's dynasty, and change modern-day Iranian back to a way of life experienced fourteen hundred years ago. As soon as Khomeini took charge, he executed hundreds of thousands of top army and police officers without due process. More Iranians were killed in the first few months of Khomeini's takeover than during the entire time of the Shah dynasty, and that bloodshed tricked down to us—the silent majority. We were caught in the middle, and feared for our lives. But the Shah would not fight the revolutionaries because he wanted to avoid further bloodshed. So, he left the country.

Yes, I believe that the Shah should have stayed and fought even if that meant he would have been killed and dragged through the streets. At least he would have died as a hero and not a refugee. But politics is the dirtiest game in the world. Because he didn't fight back, a manufactured, imported revolution took over. In the last five years, Iran has regressed and because of that, many of the silent majority, like me, had to leave the country, some legally, some illegally, in order to survive."

It must have taken me about an hour and a half to finish explaining. Then I said, "You see, as they say, when push comes to shove, one doesn't have much of a choice in making difficult decisions. Abdollah warned me that it would be very hard during the snowy, cold weather. We hadn't planned on coming at a time like this. Our original plan was to leave two months from now, but we were forced to leave earlier than originally planned." I paused and then added, "I guess the real plan is in the hands of God, or Allah."

My hosts and Ghasem looked at me as though they couldn't believe their ears regarding what they had heard. Afendu-Haydar took my hands into his and said, "All I can say is that I am happy you and your family are out of that miserable country and the Islamic Republic, who has taken over your beautiful country. I have traveled to Iran many times during the Shah's regime and I still have many good Iranian friends in Iran. But since the takeover by the religious fanatics, I haven't been there and believe me, I have no interest in returning to Iran under any circumstances."

Ghasem held his head between both hands and in Farsi said, "Mister Parviz. I thought we had a hard time in Kurdistan, but I see that all Iranian people, no matter if they are Jewish, Christian, Bahaie, Kurd, Baluch, and so on, are in trouble in Iran. I make a promise to you. You don't have to worry about your older son until we get on the bus to go to Istanbul. I will help you as much as I can."

I turned to him and said, "Ghasem, you have been a great help to all of the members of the group, especially my son. On behalf of the group and me, we thank you." It was getting late and we were getting sleepy. My wife and I lay down with the kids between the two of us and we all fell asleep.

I woke up and noticed it was almost 3.00 p.m. and then woke my wife and the kids. We freshened up and the rest of our group's members had awaken up by then, too. Everybody had a nice and relaxing sleep. Our hosts were waiting for us to serve our lunch meals. In most of the homes we stayed, the same breakfast was served; hot-baked bread, mint goat cheese, yogurt, and hot tea. I turned to Afendu-Haydar and pondered, "It's interesting for me, but in most of the homes we've stayed we consistently have a breakfast of mint goat cheese, yogurt, and hot tea. There must be a reason behind it. Am I right?"

He answered with a smile and said, "Yes, you're right. You will be travelling by horse and sometimes riding six, seven or more hours in the wilderness and the mountains. This sort of meal is meant to prevent the urge to use the bathroom while riding and at the same time it is very wholesome food."

"So far, I have really discovered many new things of the wilderness life, whereas in the city I wouldn't have had the slightest idea about them. Live and learn. Thank you."

Everybody ate well. I was amazed by my kids, who hadn't so far uttered even the smallest complaint, and enjoyed their lunches.

As usual, around 6.30 p.m. the horses arrived and by 7.00 p.m. we said our goodbyes to our hosts and continued on our escape. The two hours of the trip consisted of riding on a road that had a lot of uphill and downhill sloping. It was dark and the sky was clear and we could see the moon and the stars. The mountains around us were covered with white snow. One could see the beauty of the snow-covered mountains in the moonlight. The leader of the human traffickers decided to get far away from the road and continue to lead the group by riding on the side of a nearby mountain. We had experienced this before and we knew that we must have arrived near an *askar* station. We finally got back on the road.

We rode for another hour and then I noticed that each of the human traffickers suddenly positioned themselves behind their horse and held their horses tails little-by-little trying to get all the horses very close together and in a single file line. My wife rode in front of me while Ghasem and my older son rode behind us. Pahlavan rode behind Ghasem, and the brother and sister were at the end of our line. I looked towards my wife and said, "Something is going on. Hold onto the reins very tightly and be very careful because they are planning something that they don't want us to know about. A few minutes passed and then suddenly the human traffickers jumped on their horses and within a second every one of them quickly hit their horses and started to speed away fast. They took over the reins and said, "Hold onto the saddle and try not to fall. If you fall, we are going to continue without you!" In just two or three minutes all our horses charged forward fast on a flat road with the sound of sirens and floodlights suddenly shining on us. I held onto my son following the trail of our group. In a split-second, I looked towards my left and saw a big *askar* station and *askars* turning on the search floodlights. They quickly opened the gate to come catch us. I looked towards my right and on the snow-covered side of a nearby mountain, I saw the shadows of our horses and their riders. We were riding very fast. It took only a few minutes after that chaotic episode before the trail of our group broke up and went in different directions.

Ghasem with my son and me with my other son headed towards a small hill. We all arrived at the top of the hill together. I turned to Ghasem and said, "I have no idea where my wife is. I just saw that the human trafficker who was responsible for her jumped on her horse and held the rein and charged in an unknown direction. I hope she's fine, because only those who had a responsible human trafficker knew where they were going. Only you and I got lost and ended up here."

Then I noticed that the saddle of my horse had gotten loose. I turned to my son and said, "Hold on to the saddle, because we're going to fall off the horse." I held my son to my chest and with the saddle and everything else on top of the horse we fell onto the snowy ground. I tried to fall on my right side with my son on my stomach. We were lucky. The fresh snow acted like a soft cushion for our landing and we didn't feel the impact of our fall.

Ghasem jumped off his horse and brought my older son down and came to help us. Luckily, my horse hadn't moved at all or tried to escape. I started to laugh and turned to my kids and asked, "Remember? I told you we are going to ride horses and have a lot of fun. Isn't it fun?"

Ghasem and I put the broken saddle back on the horse and fixed it. Then I got on and he put the bags with the suitcases back on my saddle and finally sat my son down in front of me. He put my older son on his horse and then he got on himself. We had no idea in which direction to go. I turned to Ghasem and said, "We travelled from the east heading towards the west. I think we should go down the hill and when we get to the bottom we should make a right turn and continue from there."

Ghasem said, "Anything you decide is okay with me. I'm sure you will be able to find the right direction by looking at the stars because you were the one who found the way out of that frozen lake for our other human traffickers." We headed down hill and then we made a right turn and rode about an hour. We rode close together and looked for any sign of a village.

Finally, my son said, "Papa. Listen, listen. Can you hear the dogs barking?" I listened carefully for a few seconds. I could hear dogs barking in the distance.

I then replied, "Good work. Yes, I can hear the dogs barking"

Ghasem said, "We can hear them too. You were right again, we are getting close to a village."

The entire time my thoughts were with my wife, her whereabouts, and her safety. But somehow I managed to remain hopeful that I would find her in the village safe and well.

As we entered the village. the door to the very first house on my left opened and I heard my wife ask, "Parviz? Parviz, Is that you?"

I replied, "Yes! It's me! The kids, Ghasem, and I are all fine. I am so glad to hear your voice!" I then asked, "Are you okay?"

She replied, "Yes, thank God. The rest of us are okay." Two of the human traffickers stepped out and helped us dismount our horses and led us inside to a room. Everybody in the room was happy to see us. It was a large room with two heaters, and everyone there was sitting close to the first one. My wife, kids, and I hugged and kissed each other. We took our shoes off and sat close to the heater. I looked at our group and luckily everybody was accounted for.

I turned to my wife and asked, "How did you get here?"

She replied, "When you told me something is about to happen, my guide jumped on my horse and took the reins from me and quietly repeated, 'Okay,' three or four times before starting a fast getaway as quickly as he could from the *askar* station. We headed towards the road and I started to plead with him. I thought he was going to take me away from you and our group and I was paranoid. I pleaded to him and said, *'afendu, afendue. gugukhlary, gugukhlary,'* which is Turkish, for "mister, mister, little kids, little kids. "Then I started to cry. I even thought about doing something to the horse that would cause me to fall off. It was then I noticed that Nader had fallen off his horse and had somehow managed to grab the horse by its tail and running after it. He finally got a chance to remount his horse and follow us. It was then I realized we were going in the right direction. When I got to the room, I first called out your name hoping you were already here, but then I noticed that there were a bunch of men and women at the end of the room. A few minutes later, Nader arrived and then Pahlavan and Sara. There was no sign of you, the kids and Ghasem, because your horses went in another direction. I thought the four of you had been caught by the *askars*. I thought if you didn't arrive within the hour, I would ask somebody to bring me close to the station to give myself up to the *askars*."

It's amazing how everybody could become so happy after a great episode occurred. We were happy because we were still together. It would have been a disaster if any of us had been caught. The leader of the human traffickers turned to Ghasem and said, "We knew we were getting close to the *askar* station and that there was no other trail for us to take. We had to pass in front of the *askar* station and we knew they would see us. That was the reason we got on our horses and took over and started to ride as fast as we could to pass the station. If any of the escapees happen to fall from their horse, we usually leave them behind and get out of the area. If the *askars* catch an escapee, they would take care of them and with some paperwork bring them to the city of Van. But if they catch a human trafficker, there is a chance he would be executed by a firing squad. Nader was lucky because he held the horse's tail and was able to get back onto his horse.

Everybody was very tired after all that and just wanted to sleep. Ghasem approached me and said, "Mister Parviz. They want us to leave the house because this is not the house we were supposed to stay in."

I spoke to everybody about the situation and then we hit the road. It was about a fifteen-minute walk before we arrived at the house we should have come to in the first place. The human traffickers had decided to initially take us to the first house as a decoy to protect us. The owner was already expecting us. Our group got inside and there was a man, his wife, and two daughters. We simply said 'hello' and sat down by the warm heater. I went to search for a bathroom or a stable where our group could go take care of their toiletry businesses, but I couldn't find any. I turned to Ghasem and said, "Please ask them about a bathroom or a stable that we can use."

He returned with a smile on his face and replied, "You won't believe what I'm about to tell you. There is no bathroom or stable. You have to go outside behind the trees and find a place or maybe on top of the roof. They clean it later."

I really couldn't believe what I had heard. We got some papers and walked to the roof. It was very cold and the breeze of the snow made it impossible to be on top of the roof. I chose the roof because

I wasn't sure how safe it would be in the trees from any sort of wild animals or even dogs. We had no choice but to go outside in the middle of trees. I found a spot and brought the kids to use that area as their bathroom as I stood guard. Every one of us washed their hands and came back into the room. I looked at my watch, it was almost 5:30 a.m. Within half an hour, all of us were asleep.

After a bit I woke up and noticed the owner of the house, who was an older man, along with his wife and daughters, were sitting in the same spot staring at us.

I said, "Hello" and called my wife to wake her up.

"I am awake," she said. "I woke up an hour ago. I noticed you were in a deep sleep and decided to stay quiet."

My wife and I decided to wake the kids up and freshened up. The rest of our group's members also woke up and by 3:00 p.m. we had breakfast, lunch, or dinner, I'm not sure which it was because the same menu of fresh baked bread, mint goat cheese, yogurt, and hot tea was ready for a bunch of hungry people to enjoy. I should emphasize that although it wasn't the greatest menu one could ask for, when you're hungry and stuck in the mountains and wilderness that simple menu is as good as the best steak or kebab.

I remembered how Abdollah at the beginning had told me two or three nights of riding will take you to Van. Later on, it became three to four nights. I really hoped this would be the last night of our escape, because the group was really getting tired. And on top of everything else, I was coming down with a cold and running fever.

My wife looked at me and said, "Your face is red and you look very tired." Then she asked, "Are you feeling alright?"

I replied, "I'm fine. If my face is red, it's because I was close to the heater. I am fine."

She put her hand on my forehead and said, "You are burning hot. You are running a fever." She then sarcastically asked, "You tell me you were close to the heater?" She opened the first-aid kit, which she brought along, gave me a couple pills from inside, and made a large glass of hot tea with crystal sugar and dried mint from the host. She forced me to drink it. We had two hours' time to kill before we again hit the trail. Amazingly, I felt much better. She repeated her formula of two pills and a tall glass of hot tea with crystal sugar and mint. I had no choice but to listen and do what she said.

Ghasem approached me and said, "Mister Parviz, good news. I just heard from the host, tonight is our last night of riding. We are going to ride on mostly road from now no, and within four to five hours there will be cars waiting to take us to Van. From there we will get on the bus that will take us to Istanbul."

I looked at him and said, "Having you with our group is a blessing. Thank you for the good news." I passed on the news to group, and that gave everyone a boost of energy and spirit. I could feel my throat getting dry and thought to myself there is no time for a cold right now.

As we waited for our horses to arrive I played with my *tasbih*. As the host looked at my *tasbih, he* said something in Turkish to Ghasem with the word of *tasbih* in it.

I turned to Ghasem and asked, "Is he asking for my *tasbih?*"

Ghasem replied, "Yes. He said he reads his prayer five times a day and wants it for his prayer."

I approached him and handed him the *tasbih.* He was very happy and thanked me for it. I said, "The mission of this *tasbih* with me ends here. It really served its purpose, especially at the junction of Khoy. I also thank my brother-in-law in my thoughts who had given it to me my very last night in Tehran."

The horses arrived at about 6:45 p.m. and our group mounted their horses with a lot of energy and in good spirits. As we started the last night of our escape, I turned to my younger son and said, "Very soon we are going to get into cars and go to Van. We will relax for a few hours and then ride a beautiful bus on our way to Istanbul until we fly to America.

On this leg of our journey, some parts we traveled by road, and sometimes through the forest and the surrounding mountains. After approximately five hours of riding, I turned to Ghasem and asked, "Who is our translator now? Please ask them how many more hours before we get to the cars?"

I wasn't surprised when Ghasem returned with the answer of "two hours."

Another two hours passed and the same exact question got the same exact answer.

We could see that the sky was getting bright. That this was the first time we had been on our horses for more than ten hours without any breaks. The leader of the human traffickers showed us the headlights of three cars in the distance and said, "There they are. Very soon we will get to them and you all will be in a warm, soft car on your ways to Van."

Our eyes were focused on the lights of the cars making their ways in the winding roads of the mountains. At some points, they drove behind the mountains and we couldn't see them and then we could see their headlights come into view again. We were just like a bunch of kids excited about getting a lollypop we'd been waiting for. It took us more than two and a half hours to get to the cars. When we saw the cars within a few feet from us we wanted to dismount, but we were so exhausted we couldn't. Each one of us was carried by two human traffickers to a car. My wife and the kids, along with Sara, sat in the backseat of the first car, and the driver and I sat in the front. The seats were soft and the heater warm. After the long horse trips, that car was so very pleasant!

It took nearly two hours of driving to get to Van. The backseat passengers were asleep and my head kept dozing off, even though I tried very hard to keep myself awake.

We finally arrived in the city of Van, which is the first major city from the Turkish border. All the cars stopped at a house and everybody quickly went inside. We were happy that we were finally out of the wilderness. We were in a city with houses, shops, electricity, and people on the streets going to work. We could see life as we had known it all our lives. I looked at my wife and kids. I hugged and kissed them. I was so happy that I constantly repeated to myself the words, "Thank God. Thank God. We are here at Van. We are here at Van."

Eight members of the group sat in a small storage room with

some furniture and chairs stacked up inside it. Everybody got themselves a chair or a sofa to sit on. I opened the suitcases and brought out my suit, a clean dress for my wife, and clothes for the kids. We hung the wrinkled clothing outside on a string in the very cool, but sunny, day.

A car stopped by the house and Abdollah walked in with plenty of bread and hot, freshly made *kabab*. He greeted everybody and borrowed a table from the owner of the house. He then invited everyone to have lunch and handed them their bus tickets from Van to Istanbul. I received four tickets for my family and me, and each member of the group got a ticket. Abdollah approached me and in my ear quietly whispered, "Your Turkish lira is in Van with my partner and when we get there I will give them to you."

I nodded my head as a sign of approval. Then to everyone he said, "I am glad that all of you are well and made it here. From here on, it's going to be a very easy and comfortable trip once you get onto the bus to Istanbul. You now have about two hours' time before we leave. I will come back and take you via automobile to the bus station in Van. It will take about thirty-six hours from Van to Istanbul. The buses are very modern with soft seats. The bus will stop at different restaurants along the way for breakfast, lunch, and dinner. This part of the trip will make up for the hardship and cold nights you endured and spent in the mountains and wilderness." I made a little place for my wife and the kids on one of the sofas so they could relax and sleep and sat on a chair next to them. The warm room and the heavy kebab meal with bread and cold Coca-Cola after the longest ride we had caused everyone to fall asleep quickly.

Riding to climb the last mountain between Iran and Turkey. We had to climb zig-zag to get to the top of one of the tallest mountains which lasted almost two hours. There is a flat area almost two length of football field. when one crosses the field. enters in Turkey.

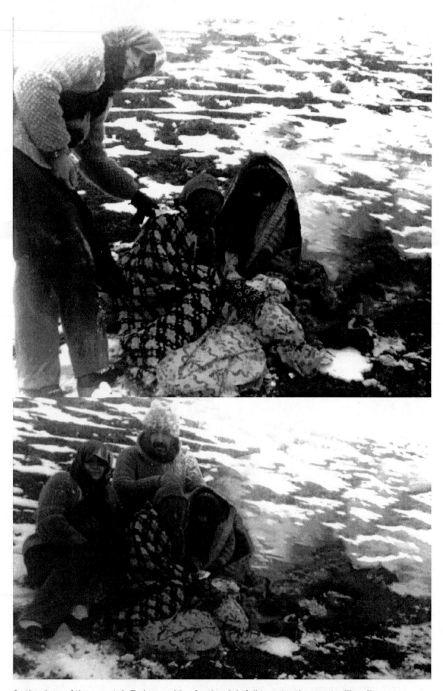

On the slope of the mountain Turkey, waiting for the nightfall to enter the country illegally

CHAPTER 9

Arriving to the City of Van

We were awakened by the owner of the house who said, "Time to wake up. Abdollah is going to be here in half an hour."

We all woke up. I brought our clothing in from the outside of the house. The wrinkles were gone, but the clothes were still very cold. I held them next to the heater so they would warm up. We all got ready and sat next to our suitcases waiting for Abdollah to arrive.

Twenty minutes later he showed up. "Please get in the cars outside in the same order you were in when you came from the mountains to this house."

After my family, Sara, and I got into the first car, the driver quickly drove us away from the area. The second and third cars followed suit. Abdollah was in a Jeep that hurried passed us. It took one hour to get to our first destination.

When the cars stopped, we got out and someone was waiting for us. We were on a very busy street. Cars were driving fast on both sides and pedestrians were everywhere. I searched for Abdollah, because I wanted to ask him about the one thousand dollars in Turkish lira he was supposed to deliver to me. I asked his friend, but he didn't know anything about it.

I turned to the group and said, "Hide your bags under the bushes by the side yard, and stay in small groups so that nobody notices us as newcomers." The group split into smaller groups of two and I stayed with my family. I saw the bus approach, and as it was about to stop a police van suddenly made a rapid U-turn in front of the bus and stopped right in front of our group.

An *askar* got out of the van and ordered the bus to stop just behind the bus station line. He then approached every member of our group and asked us to show our identification cards or passports. In English the *askar* said, "You are new in my city. You must have arrived this afternoon, because this is the first time I've seen you. I know who all the newcomers in my city are and so I have to arrest you and take you to the police station."

Without delay, he ordered the bus driver to drive away. "These people are not going to go with you," he told the driver in a bossy tone.

The bus left. Very politely, while pointing at me, the officer said, "Please get in the van with your family and then everyone else get in the van after them without any arguments."

We did as we were told. I noticed the kid's faces blush red from the excitement of being arrested. I hugged them. "Don't worry. It isn't anything important," I downplayed. "We are in the city so look at the shops and restaurants. We will go to a nice hotel and enjoy ourselves until they give us an entry visa to go to Istanbul legally." My little encouragement speech gave them some peace of mind.

The police van arrived at their station and we walked to the second floor. The officer said, "Put all your suitcases and bags on the ground and stand to the side." He looked at me. "We are going to start with you. Are they your family?"

"Yes, they are," I replied. "This is my wife and these are my two sons."

"Do you have any proof that they are your wife and your sons?"

"I have a passport with their pictures and their names on it."

"Where? Give it to me."

"Do I have your permission to open my briefcase?"

He was impressed I asked. With a small smile upon his face, he replied, "Go ahead. I can see you are an educated and polite human being and I appreciate your behavior under these circumstances."

I retrieved the passport from the briefcase and handed it to him.

He looked at it. "This is a good and valid Islamic Republic of Iran passport." With a curious expression on his face he then asked, "Why did you take your family out of the country through the mountains, especially with the snow and on horses, if this is a valid passport?"

"That is a very good question," I admitted, not sure how much to share. "But it's a really long story. Being a minority in the Khomeini regime is not easy. Each *ayatollah* is like a big boss for only themselves. The country is in chaos right now. The people are in trouble and life has become very miserable, even for many Iranian Muslims. Therefore, people will leave everything to get out anyway they can and as soon as they can. Although we have a valid passport, we couldn't get permission to leave. So, my wife and I decided to take the kids, which are most precious to us, and get out of the country as quickly as we could."

He seemed genuinely concerned and sympathetic to our situation. "When I saw your kids and imagined bringing them through the mountains, no offense to you, but I thought you must have been either crazy or a real big hot-shot in your country to take such a risk."

"No," I replied. "I am not a big hot-shot. I am not a politician, nor am I wealthy. I am a very simple man, a university graduate who loves his country and wanted very much to have a healthy and happy life there."

"Where did you learn English?"

"In America. I went to college there and then worked for fourteen years at the Iranian Oil Company."

Fortunately, the officer was a man of understanding. It took us about half an hour to go through the suitcases, which by now didn't contain much, because we left our dirty clothes in the first place we stayed. But I had some Turkish lira along with some American dollars, and an old passport, which I had forged and put my picture on, and another old passport, which I had brought out of the country for someone. All this could have been a disaster for me. A foreign passport in Turkey is like a commodity. It can be sold on the black market, and if caught with one, it's as bad as if someone was caught smuggling drugs. However, I had no idea about that at the time.

As I spoke to the officer, I discretely transferred my briefcase to where the other bags and suitcases that had already been inspected had been placed. Neither the officer nor the two other *askars* in the room noticed me do that. My little talk with him really made a good impression about us. He was not very strict with us after that. "How much money do you all have in your pockets? Empty your pockets of your money and hand it all to me. I have to make a list of your money to keep it in the police safe box."

Thank God he didn't ask about the briefcase. I hand him all of my Turkish lira. He made a note about it on a pad. The other officers signed the paper as witnesses and watched as he placed the money in a separate envelope for each one of us.

"Why are you taking all of our money?" I asked. "Are we going to prison?"

"No. You're going to a hotel. If I give you all of your money you might find a way to travel to Istanbul tonight through smugglers. We want all of you back in the morning for questioning."

Suddenly, a door opened and a lady colonel walked in. She must have heard the entirety of our conversation, because she looked at me and in English said, "I wanted to take a look at you, the gentleman with kids who has come from the mountains." She paused before adding, "Be honest, do you think it was worth it?"

I looked at her and confidently replied, "Colonel, we are here, aren't we? We went through horrible, dark nights in the wilderness, didn't we? Believe me, sometimes I felt God so close to my family that I thought I could touch him." I had her attention, so I continued, "You all saw my family and my kids. I have to feed them. Now that we are here, after five years of harassment in my own country, I want them to be able to enjoy our freedom in your country and give sincere thanks to the Almighty for all his kindness and help. Tonight, I want to celebrate all that with a good dinner. You might not understand the meaning of a night like this as much as we appreciate it."

She turned to the officer and said, "Release as much of their money they need from their money envelopes." Then she turned to me. "Go and enjoy your night and celebrate your freedom with your family and friends. But don't forget, all of you have to be here for questioning tomorrow morning by 10:30 a.m."

A civilian walked into the office and the officer introduced him to us. "This is Oscar. He is the owner of the Oscar Hotel. He will take you there. You don't have to pay him for your stay. You only have to pay for your food."

We thanked the colonel and the officer and followed Oscar to his hotel.

We walked through streets filled with restaurants, coffee shops, shoe stores, appliance shops, confectionaries with all types of Baklavas, cakes, freshly baked pastries, cream caramels, chocolate puddings, and many other appetizing goodies. Although we had seen shops like these in different cities of Iran, it was interesting for all of us to see them here. Maybe because we had spent the last few days in the snow-covered mountains and wilderness away from civilization, where the barking of dogs was a happy sound to our ears. We followed Oscar and enjoyed the walk through the city.

Finally, we arrived at a big bazaar (central market) filled with many delivery trucks. Oscar looked at us and said, "There are all kinds of shops for your everyday needs; butcher, fruit shops, vegetable stores, bakeries with freshly baked *barbari* (Turkish bread). Everything is wholesale prices. Very cheap, and many people from different parts of the city come to purchase their necessities here." He pointed at a wagon filled with small fish not much longer than twelve inches. "You can't find this kind of fish anywhere else in the world. This is a special fish from Van Lake, and it is very delicious."

We continued through the bazaar and at the end of it was a four-story building. "Welcome to Oscar Hotel," he said proudly. "Please come on in." He called one of his bellhops over and asked him to take us to the second floor. We had the biggest room in the hotel, with a window that looked out onto the bazar. One room had also been set aside for Pahlavan and Ghasem, while another had been readied for Sara and Nader. All the rooms were on second floor and attached to one another. Each room had a sink for washing our hands, but the bathroom was at the end of the hall.

Although we had planned and endured the hardships and tortures of riding horses at night and taking refuge in different homes to escape from the *askars*, we had finally been caught. Everybody washed up and came to our room. "First of all," I addressed everyone, "we should all be thankful to the Almighty for getting us to Van safely without a drop of our blood spilled. Secondly, we are in a city away from all the harassments of the Islamic Revolutionary peoples. We might get to Istanbul with a delay of a few days, but eventually we are going to get there legally. The Turkish government is responsible for the well-being of every refugee and they want to make sure everybody has the proper papers when they go to Istanbul. They will ask us a lot of questions in the upcoming days, many of them the same, therefore we have to be prepared to answer exactly the same way each time. The most important question they will ask is how we got out of the country and what the name of our human trafficker is. All we have to tell them is that we don't know their real names. We'll say we can't recognize them because we escaped from Iran at night and entered Turkey at night and our traffickers changed so many times. Then tell them that when we arrived at the border, a man approached us and told us that he could take us to Istanbul within two days. I will tell them that because of my wife and kids, I decided to go along with his offer. I will tell them that I told him I don't have very much money to pay, but that when we get to Istanbul a friend of mine will send me money to pay. If they insist on knowing his name, which they will, I will tell them that others call him Rajab.

I will tell them that he took most of my money as part of the deal until we get to Istanbul. I will tell them I don't have any address or telephone number for him, nothing at all. I will tell them that he told me not to worry and that he would find us in Istanbul and that he handed us the tickets for the bus before we were arrested." I recommended the group keep to the same story so that we would all back each other up.

Everyone approved of my suggestion.

"Now that we've freshened up and are ready, let's go out for dinner and enjoy our stay in Van."

The group locked the doors of their rooms and headed to the lobby where Oscar sat behind the reception desk. He was happy to have us in his hotel. "Are you going out for dinner? Do you want me to recommend a restaurant?"

"When we were walking here, I noticed a restaurant that had a covered patio, three *shwarma* stands, and many tables. People were enjoying their meals. I think we are going to check out that one first. If everyone agrees, then we will have our dinner at that restaurant."

"Actually, I had that place in mind for you. It's about a ten-minute walk from here."

We thanked him and left the hotel.

Most of the shops in the bazaar were already closed, because they normally open at 3:00 a.m. when the delivery trucks arrive so the merchants can have everything ready for the mostly mom-and-pop shops.

The restaurant was quite warm and cozy. As we walked in, the owner approached us with a warm greeting, and then added, "I should tell you that since you have small children inside will be warmer. But it's up to you."

Ghasem translated and we decided to stay inside close to the clay oven. The owner fixed us a big table and quickly brought menus and a bottle of lemonade with eight glasses. My kids decided to have the *shwarma* plate when they saw the big piece of meat being carved from on a long skewer as it turned on its wheel. Everyone

197

else followed suit. Then we raised our glasses high. "Let's drink in the name of freedom," I said. And that's exactly what we all did.

Within ten minutes our table was covered with dishes of soup, salad, big plates of *shwarma*, and two baskets of hot, freshly baked bread covered by a cotton cover in which one could see the steam still rising from the bread. The owner came over and Ghasem asked him about other escapees that might have passed through their town.

"During the last five years, we have seen many Iranian refugees. But to be honest, this is the first time we've seen a family with small kids coming from those mountains in the winter. That is why you immediately looked out of place when the police officer saw you."

As we ate, anyone could see the calm and happiness in all our faces. Every once in a while, people curiously stared at us. To them I raised my glass of lemonade with a sign of cheers and then drank from it. This gesture seemed to make them happy, as they responded back with a smile and their own congratulation toast.

After dinner I felt so grateful. "Please allow me to pay for tonight's dinner." I said to our group. They refused and insisted on paying for their own meals. I guess they felt grateful, too.

As we said our goodbyes to the restaurant owner and wait staff, many of the customers clapped their hands for us. It was a bittersweet moment that warmed my heart. Here we were, finally free. Escaping from my birth country to take refuge in another country is a saddening situation and emotionally I could not feel any worse. At the same time, the people of our host country were already accustomed to refugees from Iran. I could see genuine sympathy in their faces. Those expressions showed in their kindness towards us, especially when it came to our two small boys.

After dinner we ended up in a confectionary shop to enjoy Turkish coffee. Inside, we noticed a big television on a tall cabinet, situated in such a way that every customer could see it. An American movie with the very popular actor Charles Bronson was on TV. As we entered the shop, the owner moved some of the customers to make a table for all eight of us in the middle of the shop. He then rewound the movie so we could see it from the beginning. Their hospitality was unbelievable. We watched the movie as we enjoyed our Turkish coffees with fresh baklava pasties while the kids had their favorite, cream caramel pudding. The kids couldn't stay awake after desert and quickly fell asleep in their chairs. Ghasem carried my older son on his back and I carried my younger one on mine when we left and headed back to our hotel.

Although it was a few minutes past 11:00 p.m., the streets were full of lights and the restaurants were packed with customers, which seemed strange for such a small city. We arrived at our hotel, put the kids to bed with my wife on one side of them, me on the other. We all had a very good four-hour sleep.

We were awakened up by the sound of delivery trucks bringing their goods from the nearby farmlands to the different shops. I looked from the window and was delighted to see the excitement of the bazaar. But even so, I went back to bed and slept for another three hours when we all finally woke up together.

At breakfast, I said to our group, "We might have to stay here for weeks before they sort things out. To be honest, it hasn't been bad so far. With what we went through since we left Tehran, I wouldn't mind relaxing here and taking it easy for a while simply because time will take care of everything on its own."

We made it back to the police station by ten in the morning, as they had asked. On the second floor and the same officer was already waiting for us. We all said, "Good morning!" to him and were then led to a room as a group. Each one of us had to fill out a questionnaire, which only took about a half hour. Then they handed each of us a folder and said, "You have to go to a hospital for x-rays and blood tests."

Then the lady colonel walked into the room and the three officers stood up with army salutes to her in attention. "Take them to the hospital by van and then they can have the rest of the day to themselves," she commanded. "Tomorrow we will see them here again at the same time for more questioning."

The scare of the summon to the police station for questioning as compared to how we were actually treated by the staff on the first day was not as bad as we had imagined. In fact, it gave us the feeling that we were not going to be hunted by the authorities. They were just doing their jobs.

It was beginning to become like a vacation. When we arrived at the hospital, the officer there with a kind, and large smile said, "Enjoy your stay in Van. There are legal formalities we have to observe. The United Nations Refugee Program requires us to take care of you as refugees and they want to make sure you are healthy and have no illnesses. After everything is clear and checks out, they will send you by bus to Istanbul where you can then legally go from Turkey to your destination anywhere in the world."

These words coming from an officer were like music to our ears. The fear of being summoned by the authorities for entering the country illegally had created a great deal of anxiety in everyone's minds. But his nice words immediately took all that away. We all thanked him personally and congratulated each other on the good news.

We entered the hospital and the lady behind the information desk approached. As though she recognized us, she led our group into a separate doctor's office but allowed my wife and I to stay with our kids. Within a minute, a doctor came by and examined us all, and then a nurse walked in and drew blood from each of us. Another nurse then led us to the x-ray room. Urine tests rounded out the examination. The entire process happened so fast and efficiently that all of us were out of the hospital within an hour. The X-ray and blood tests went smoothly, and the children showed no fear of getting their blood tests done. We were very impressed by the treatment of the police officer and the kindness of the hospital staff. Then we left.

"Do you have your bus tickets with you?" I asked our group.

"Yes," they all nodded in agreement.

"Let's go to the bus station. I have an idea. Ghasem and I will go in, but the rest of you stay outside."

We arrived, and Ghasem and I walked to the reservation

counter and in English I said, "I would like to see the manager."

"No manager," he replied.

"What do you mean no manager? I would like to talk to the manager." I spread our group's eight bus tickets across the top of the counter in front of him.

"No good. No good," he said and then pushed the tickets back to me.

A distinguished man in a suit and tie approached us and said, "I am the manager. How can I help you?"

I introduced myself and then got down to business. "These are eight tickets for yesterday. When we got to the bus station and before getting on the bus, we were arrested. The police made the bus leave without us. These tickets were purchased with our own money and they have not been used. We have to stay in Van for a few days, so we wish to return these tickets and get our money back."

He looked at me with surprise and said, "They are not valid anymore. Please leave the building."

"The bus left for Istanbul with eight empty seats that we paid for. We are under the protection of the police so I am going to have to report that you will not honor our tickets."

His tone suddenly changed. "You don't have to get the police involved with such a simple matter. I am sure we can come to some agreement. I will refund fifty percent of the cost of each ticket. You will be happy, and I will be happy. Right?" He had both his hands on the counter as though the problem had been solved.

"No. You are happy, but I am not." Then I looked at Ghasem and in English said, "Let's go. I have no other choice but to report him to the police."

"No, no! Come back, come back. I will give you seventy-five percent."

I shook my head in dismay. "One hundred percent."

"You drive a very hard bargain. One hundred percent it is." He asked the cashier to refund the full amount paid for the eight bus tickets and we all ended up with some extra cash in our hands. Everybody walked away with large happy smiles on their faces.

"I have a suggestion." I turned to the group. "How about we buy a portable butane gas stove, plates, silverware, a table cloth, and a couple pots of fresh fish from the bazaar for dinner, along with some alcoholic beverages, and we celebrate tonight!"

Everybody replied with a hearty "YES!".

When we entered our hotel, Oscar was surprised to see our shopping bags. I asked him for a tape recorder and within five minutes it was in our room. My wife was responsible for the cooking, because she was the expert. Sara volunteered with her brother to wash the dishes. Pahlavan and Ghasem had been responsible for carrying the purchased goods to the hotel and also for the cleanup after the meal. The sound of Persian music filtered throughout the building. Everyone was so happy and without worry, even though the questioning by the police officers had not even started yet. Deep in my heart I had a very good feeling and said to the group, as the old saying in Farsi goes, "The spring promises a good year ahead of us," which means we had a lot to look forward to. I took the bus ticket deal as a good sign for our success in our mission.

I said to my wife, "I am going to the coffee shop next door to ask around and see if I can find out about Abdollah." He still owed me a good sum of Turkish lira and I was hoping to hear from him soon. I know he saw our group getting arrested as he sat in his jeep across the street.

As I entered the coffee shop and took a seat, a man brought me a glass of tea with his head nodding towards another man. I had no idea who this man was. But he approached me and said, "Mister Hakimi, Abdollah will be here in an hour. He wants to see you. He sent me here because he knew you are staying at the Oscar Hotel. I have been sitting and waiting here for you about two hours, hoping I might see you." Apparently, Abdollah followed us to Oscar hotel, but did not let Oscar see him. He planted this man here to wait for me to eventually come in.

"I am happy that you came by to bring me a message from Abdollah," I said. "Please don't forget to ask him about my Turkish lira."

"Actually, he plans to bring you your money," he replied.

The man left and I returned to our hotel room to share the good news with my wife. Pahlavan, Sara, and Nader also came by and told me that they had the same dilemma. They had also given Abdollah money to be exchanged into Turkish lira. They were happy to hear that there was still a chance of recovering their money.

Within an hour I went back to the coffee shop. Abdollah entered five minutes later wearing a heavy coat with his head down. "I was across the street in my car and watched you and your group when the police arrested you by the bus station," he admitted. "But I couldn't do anything to help. About the Turkish lira I owe you, I was going to deliver it to you at the last bus stop in Van. The bus driver is a good friend of mine and we already made the arrangements."

I showed Abdollah the list of people to whom he owed money and he handed me an envelope that contained everyone's share. We shook hands and he thanked me. I thanked him for all his help and his expertise. He walked out of the coffee shop and from that moment I've never seen nor heard from Abdollah again. Over the years, I've thought of him often, and I always wish him good luck and success in the endeavors of his life. I always remember Abdollah as a major facet that helped us gain our freedom.

I returned to the hotel to face a bunch of people anxiously waiting to hear the good news. I handed each one of them their money and handed my wife our share. She was surprised when she heard I had given Abdollah the thousand dollars to be exchanged to Turkish lira. One could see that everybody was quite happy, because we honestly thought the money was gone, never to return. But I had a good feeling about Abdollah. I believed him about our arrangement. I turned to our group and said, "Today we have had a good money-making day. First, we cashed in our bus tickets and now our Turkish lira has been recovered. I think it's time we take a nap and around 7:00 p.m. get ready for dinner.

That evening I decided to get rid of my beard after almost four full months of growing it. I took a nice shower and then shaved. I was ready to help my wife with the fish and the rest of the cooking. She noticed my clean-shaven face and said, "Thank God. Now you look like the man I married seven years ago. I didn't know when you would be able to shave that awful thing from your face, but I didn't say anything."

Everyone was surprised when they saw me without the beard. The group gathered in our room for dinner and we spread the cloth we had purchased on the bed and sat around it. There was plenty of fish, rice, vegetables, olives, pickled cucumbers, beers, and vodka for everyone, as well as soft drinks for the kids. We thanked the Almighty for our successful escape and began to eat. I must say, that was one of the greatest nights and dinners that I have had and I will never forget it the rest of my life. The classic Persian music playing gave a special meaning to our dinner. The kids were sleepy and got to their beds soon after dinner was over. My wife sat close to the kids as she spoke with Sara. I sat on the edge of the bed while the others brought some chairs and sat in front of me.

Ghasem kept drinking the vodka. He almost finished two-thirds of the bottle by himself. I had a feeling something was bothering him badly. Then he looked at me and said, "I have many things my mind. I left my mother, fiancée, brother, and all my relatives behind when I escaped. My fiancée and I were engaged only three months and were planning to get married in two weeks. Who knows when we will get the chance to see each other again? The whole family insisted that I leave the country to save my life. In the last two months, three of my relatives were arrested and the next day they were executed by the firing squad by the brutal Islamic Republic of Iran. That was the reason I had to leave my life behind. Sometimes I am ashamed and can only blame myself if anything happens to them." Ghasem, who was almost six and a half feet tall and very strong in character, suddenly became very emotional. The sound of the music encouraged his thoughts and anger to burst open. He wept quietly like a baby.

I told him, "Go ahead and cry. Now we are all like a family. We have traveled together under very hard and troubling conditions. You are like a brother to me and besides, I am a Kurd, too. I was born In Sanandaj of Kurdistan."

"No wonder you look after everybody and are kind to all of us. It's because you are a Kurd and I am very proud to be part of your escape group." This made Ghasem feel a little better. He washed his face and in a few minutes went back to his room and slept.

I turned to everyone and said, "Don't forget we have to arrive at the police station at 10:00 a.m. for the results of our tests and further questioning." We went to bed after a relaxing night.

The next morning, we arrived at the police station fifteen minutes early, and an officer brought us to the same room that we had sat in the day before. The same officers and gentleman in civilian suits and ties from the day before entered., "Mister Hakimi," called one of the officers. "Are you the leader of this group?"

"What do you mean by *the leader*?" I asked.

"Did you organize this group from Iran and escape through human smugglers?"

"No," I replied truthfully. "I didn't know any one of them before this trip. I met them in Turkey when we met the man who offered to bring us all to Istanbul if we paid him."

"How did you meet that man, and what was his name?"

"He introduced himself as Rajab," I said, hoping this didn't go much further.

"You mean, you're telling me you trusted a man, just like that? As simple as that?"

"Yes, just like that."

He looked at me as if I were hiding something. "That's very questionable to me."

Another officer looked at me with surprise and said, "Mister Hakimi, in the last five years we have experienced many groups of people like yours escaping from their countries with different crews of human traffickers. Your group is not the first and is not going to be the last. We know very well what is going on in your country. We are aware of the way the Islamic Republic of Iran has taken the

Iranian people hostage in a big prison called *Iran*. I know that the minorities are in the worst situation. Therefore, I want to warn you to please think about what you say. Please don't try to make a fool out of us with ridiculous statements."

I waited a few more seconds to reply and finally said, "Do I have permission to speak?"

He nodded his head and said, "Go ahead."

"Because of this manufactured revolution, my family and I were in danger. I left a house, a good job, our friends and family. A life. We fled because we can't do anything safely anymore. We can't even buy food. My neighborhood grocer knew my family since the day he opened. We supported his business all those years and he respected us very much. But because of this so-called revolution, he suddenly saw us as Jewish instead of Iranian. Now he's had a change of heart and doesn't want our business anymore. I had to drive to other parts of the city further away from our house where the grocers didn't know me as a Jew so that I could purchase my necessities.

Everyone was gripped by what I was saying. Then the lady colonel walked into the room. All the officers and the civilian gentleman quickly stood up at attention. Our group was confused by about standing up or not, so they looked at me for guidance. Out of respect for the colonel that I stood.

"Please sit down and continue with your comments," said the colonel. "You don't have to stand when I enter the room."

I sat down and waited.

She looked at the officers who were at attention and said, "As you were." She took a seat and said some words to the officers in Turkish and all of them smiled. She then turned to me and said, "You answer a simple question with a lot of detail. Do you think my officers have time to listen to your stories?"

I didn't reply.

"When anybody asks you a question, answer it with a 'yes' or a 'no.' Then we can all get to our own businesses."

I did as I was told. After two to three hours of questioning the lady colonel said to us "That's enough for today. You are excused. Enjoy the rest of your day in our city." She then slyly added. "I understand you have been to the shwarma restaurant already and had a good desert at the famous confectionary. And let's not forget the breakfast with fresh cooked eggs, milk, butter, honey. You are making my merchants happy."

I was surprised and asked, "Remember the first day I asked for some of my money?" I waited a moment and said, "I told you I have come to freedom and I want my family and I to have the best of everything on our stay in your city, which I will remember my entire lifetime."

She smiled and said, "I'm going to tell you of a very nice family-type restaurant and coffee shop which is very famous and is located in Van. It's called Kim Restaurant. I am sure all of you will really enjoy it."

The group thanked the colonel, the officers, and the man in the civilian suit, who had become sort of puzzle for me, because the entire time, just as the day before, he didn't say one word. He just sat there.

We left the police station when we were finished. As we exited the building, I took a deep breath and turned to our group and said, "Thank God, I thought it wasn't going to finish until 4:00 p.m. today."

Ghasem, Nader, and Sara didn't have an idea what the questions and answers were about, but Pahlavan, who had a good command in English and was going to a university in the United States before returning to Iran due to his father's passing, had overheard my answers and understood the content of the meeting. The reason he was with our group was because the Iranian authorities had confiscated his passport. He had no other choice but to escape across the border to get back to America so he could continue his education.

Ghasem, who was very excited, turned to me and asked, "Mister Hakimi, please tell me just a little bit about what happened at the meeting. I'm afraid they will return us, or perhaps just me, back to Iran."

I looked at him and said, "Don't worry at all. Anything I discuss with them is for all of us. I will try my best to talk for all of us. There's not a chance that they will return us to Iran. We are worth too much. The government of Turkey is responsible for each one of us, and they get paid from the United Nations for each one of us."

I continued to assure them and said, "Let's go to the Kim Restaurant to have lunch and a good time."

As we were trying to find our way to the Kim Restaurant, one of the officers rushed towards us from the police station and said, "Come back tomorrow morning at the same time. But only men." I thought it was good news. At least the women and kids could stay back at the hotel. The colonel must have seen the kids sleeping on the chairs. After all, I'm sure she was a mother herself. She must have thought it useless to tucker out the women and the children with all that questioning. It only took us twenty minutes until we arrived at the Kim Restaurant. "You must be the new group of Iranian escapees who came to Van a couple days ago," said the owner.

I smiled and said, "It seems as though everybody in Van has heard about us and our presence in your city. I don't know if it's good or bad news."

As we ate our lunches, many families entered the restaurant with their own kids. We also met some young Iranians who approached our group and introduced themselves. I asked them about their stories of how they got here. One of the young men said, "I have been here almost seven months and my file is still not complete. I can't speak English or Turkish very well and I have nobody in Turkey at all. There are some businesses owned by Iranian people who came to Van three or four decades ago. I asked one of them to translate for me but that didn't help."

I then asked, "Are there any other Iranians here that you know of?"

He replied, "There are about twenty to twenty-five, most of them are young people."

"Do you know how long they have been here?"

"Most of them arrived in Van between two to seven months ago."

I noticed he was really happy to see a family with kids, but what mostly impress him was that we were a group that stuck together.

As we left the restaurant after we ate, I asked the owner to break some change so I could make a telephone call to my brother in Israel and let my other relatives know about our well-being in Van. At around 8:00 p.m. Pahlavan and I entered the telephone station, and saw people waiting in line to use the phones. It took us a few minutes until we were able to get to a telephone booth. Pahlavan fed the coins into the telephone as I dialed my brother's home telephone number in Israel.

My brother picked up the receiver and I said "Hello. It's me Parviz, calling from Van. We are all fine and waiting for our files to be sent to Ankara for approval of entry visas. Please write my name, my wife and the kids' names, and these two other names that I will spell for you. They are my wife's cousins and they are brother and sister. Please call the Israel embassy in Turkey and let them know that we are here so that they can accelerate the process of our files, which will allow us to get to Istanbul quicker. And call our relatives in America and Iran. Tell them we are doing well and having a great time here." Although making a call to my brother had come with a two-day delay, it was still very important that I had called him.

I knew that Nader and Sara had introduced themselves as Jewish to us, but from the first moment we had heard their accents my wife and I could tell that they were Armenians. The Armenians were not welcome into Turkey and have not been since an incident when there was a genocide carried out of the Armenians by the Ottoman authority. The Armenian Genocide, as it has come to be called, began on April 24, 1915, in the historic homeland of the Ottoman, which now lies within the present-day Republic of Turkey. However, it actually started with the deportation of 235 to 270 Armenian intellectuals and community leaders from

Constantinople to Ankara and eventually led to the systematic extermination of about 1.5 million of its minority Armenian subjects. Which is why Nader and Sara decided to call themselves Jewish and got fictitious names so that no one would find out they were Armenians. Nader and Sara were not really their names, but their last name happened to be similar to my wife's cousin's last name. I decided as long as we escaped together as a group, this is the one way I could help them while they were in Turkey. With their permission I included their names on the list and asked my brother to give their information to the responsible department for Jewish escapees and refugees at the Israeli embassy.

Later, as we were all about to leave the hotel together for dinner, both of the kids turned to their mother and said, "Mom, please don't forget to wear your scarf and the Islamic dress. We are afraid that the *pasdars* will stop us and create problems."

I looked at them and could see the fright and anxiety in their faces. I knelt down and while I held them said, "Please, don't be afraid and don't worry. We are out of Iran now, and there aren't any *pasdars* or anybody else here to harm us. They are all in Iran and we are now in a different country. They can't and won't cause any problems for us anymore. We had many hard nights riding horses through the cold snow-covered mountains and stayed in different homes for shelter because we were running away from the *pasdars.*"

I then added, "Remember the man who made you hit your chests over your hearts very hard because you were Jewish?" I waited a moment and they seemed to understand and then I said, "We're in Turkey now, and the people here are very nice and hospitable. We have to stay for a few days until we go to one of the most beautiful cities in the world, which is called Istanbul. As you can see, we go to different restaurants, coffee shops, and confectionaries, and have a good time. So, don't the two of you worry about anything. If you need something, anything at all, just ask me or your mom and we will get it for you."

My kids listened and then my older son asked, "Papa, why have we been going to the police station and why do they keep asking you questions? Have we done something wrong?"

I pulled both of them towards me and pressed them to my chest and replied, "They are our friends. They want to get visas for us to go to Istanbul."

The younger one then asked, "What is a Visa?"

I replied, "We entered their country without their permission. The permission we need is called visa. Now they are trying to get us permission to go to Istanbul." I didn't know that the kids were afraid of being at the police station and watching me being questioned. Apparently, it had been traumatizing for them to see their father being questioned by the police, but nobody else.

I turned to my wife and said, "You don't know how happy and grateful I am that the lady colonel said the women and kids don't have to come in for questioning anymore." Then I turned to the kids and asked, "Where do you guys want to have dinner? You two tell us where you want to go, and what you want to eat."

They looked at each other and replied, "Anywhere that everybody else decides is okay with us. But for desert, we want to go to the confectionary for some cream caramel and chocolate pudding."

I kissed both of them and said, "You got it."

Ghasem joined us for dinner, but I noticed his face was very sad and tears fell from his eyes without him even realizing it. "Ghasem, my friend. Please take my older son and walk with him."

He looked back at me and said, "When you were talking to your kids, I remembered my nephew. When I left Iran, I had to say goodbye to my family. I kissed my nephew and looked in his face, which seemed confused about the commotion until he finally realized that I was going away and then he started to cry."

I looked Ghasem in the eye and said, "Life is full of surprises. I am sure someday you will see all your family and your nephew again. Time will take care of everything. Our group is like a family now and we will all leave together to Istanbul. Believe me, I will talk to anybody, any organization, and not for just our group, but also for all the other Iranians who have been here for many months so that they can get to their destinations, as well. I promise you."

The next morning our group of four men walked to the police station and the exact scenario occurred again, where we entered into the same room and then were followed by the officers and the gentleman in a civilian suits and ties. One of the officers turned to Ghasem and said something in Turkish. They carried on a Turkish conversation for roughly ten minutes. I noticed that Ghasem was getting frustrated and his answers, along with his tone, grew louder and louder. Although I didn't understand Turkish, I noticed that Ghasem's face was now covered with small dewdrops of sweat. Pahlavan and Nader were also becoming nervous.

The colonel walked in and the officers stood at attention. I stood up as well, and finally the rest of our group stood up. The colonel took a seat and everybody sat down after her. She looked at the four of us and said, "We know that there are different groups of human traffickers. We know the names of some of them. We don't care who brought you out of Iran, but we want to know about the ones who brought you from the border to my city of Van. Which one of you, except Mister Hakimi, would like to answer my question?"

Ghasem and Nader didn't exactly understand what she was talking about, but Pahlavan understood well and said, "If you allow me, I will tell you my escape from Iran."

The colonel nodded her head in agreement and said, "Go ahead, tell us."

Pahlavan said, "I am a sophomore at Los Angeles State University in California. Unfortunately, I was notified that my father was in the hospital and that he didn't have very much time left to live. My mother asked me to come back home for a last visit with my father before he passed away. I did, and fortunately I was able to speak with my father for about two hours before he was gone."

Pahlavan was visibly shaken by this memory. He then said, "After that, I tried to return to the United States to continue my education, however the Islamic Republic of Iran confiscated my passport and wanted to draft me into their army. My family and I decided that I should leave the country as soon as possible. We had some relatives in Khoy and I spoke with them and eventually my mother and I made a trip there to meet them. They knew a *pasdar* at the border who for a sum of money ended up bringing me into Turkey. It was there that I met the group. When I noticed Mr. Hakimi negotiating with a man called Rajab, I decided to go along with him and his family." Pahlavan drank some of the water in the glass in front of him and continued. "Rajab told me that it would only be two nights to get to Van. He brought our horses and a group of people with him and at night we all headed to our destination of Van. I should tell you that our group was very happy when Ghasem joined us because none of the human traffickers knew a single word in either English or Farsi." His face was red and sweating.

The colonel looked at Ghasem and Nader, and in English asked, "What about you two?" Both of them didn't understand a word. I raised my hand to ask permission to speak.

The colonel looked at me and asked, "Do you have a question? What is it?"

I replied, "Yes, thank you. Ghasem and Nader don't speak a word of English. Ghasem speaks Turkish. If you allow me to translate the question for them in Farsi, I will be more than happy to, or you can speak to Ghasem in Turkish if you like."

She allowed me to translate the question for both of them.

The colonel turned to Ghasem and in Turkish asked, "What is your story? Why did you have to escape? You are Muslim. The Islamic Republic of Iran is not against the Muslims. Were you a political man? Were you against the regime?"

Ghasem explained his story in Turkish. All I could understand from what he said was the word Sunni, and nothing else. The Sunni are a denomination of the Muslim religion and Iranian Muslims are mostly Shiite.

When Ghasem finished explaining, the colonel and the officers looked at each other and the colonel finally turned to me and said,

"I think we have to question you as the leader of the group."

I looked at the colonel and said, "I am the leader of my family because I am the head of my family. But any decision we make is always made between me and my wife." As for this group, we met each other under very severe and difficult situations. As the old saying goes 'We are all in the same boat.' Therefore, if there is a danger, it can affect all of us. So, I tried to give them some good words of advice. If any one of them made a mistake, it would affect all of us. Plus, I am the oldest among this group, so maybe they respect my age."

Acknowledging the whole room, the colonel said, "They chose a smart man as their leader. I know that you are interested in knowing about the progress of your case. We sent your documents to Ankara and we have to wait for their final decision. To make you feel better, we have put in good words for you with them."

I thanked the colonel and then asked, "Only for me and my family? Or all eight members of our group?"

She replied, "I knew you were going to ask me this specific question. In fact, I would have been disappointed if you hadn't. The answer is all eight of you."

Pahlavan and I were very happy hearing the good news since we understood English, and right away I translated the information to the other two in our group and I saw that both of them were very happy about it too.

We were dismissed and before leaving the police station one of the officers turned to me and said, "Don't forget to bring the group to President Street tomorrow at 10:00 a.m. There will be a parade and I think it will especially be interesting for your kids. The participants in the parade are going to be all the high school students, both boys and girls. And I will be there with my fellow police officers and we want to recognize your kids and let them know that we are their friends and we want to make them feel better about us."

We left the police station and headed to the Kim Restaurant. When we arrived at the restaurant and I noticed a young man, who our group had met before, sitting with my family and Sara. They were having Turkish coffee and sweets. As soon as my family saw us, my kids left the table and their ice creams and rushed right to me. I hugged and kissed them both.

We walked back to the table and sat down. I explained the agenda of our meeting in detail to my family and Sara, regarding the colonel and the other officers. Then I shared the good news about our documents, which were now in Ankara, and that the colonel had already put in good words for all the members of our group. All we had to do was wait and see how fast the documents were reviewed by the authorities in Ankara.

As soon as the young man heard my comments, he shook his head and said, "Those were the exact words that they told me months ago."

I turned to him and asked, "You mean to tell me, you heard the same news from the colonel, yourself?"

With a little hesitation he replied, "One of the merchants who translated for me told me so."

I got a feeling that the person who had translated to him didn't give him all the necessary information and he was not sure where his case was exactly, and what was going on with his situation. I turned to the group and said, "Let's enjoy our coffee, because we have no other choice but to wait."

We left the restaurant with the young man, got onto a bus and headed to Lake Van, the largest lake in Turkey. It is a saline lake, which receives water from many small rivers descending from the surrounding mountains. The railway connecting Turkey to Iran was built in 1970 and led to the shores of Lake Van. The goods transferred to ferries and were then delivered to Tavan City, which is located at the western side of Lake Van. Lake Van occasionally hosts several water sports, as well as sailing and inshore powerboat racing.

I have to confess that it wasn't until we were at Lake Van, and I had the chance to study an article about the lake, that I first realized what a dangerous escape we had just put behind us. I turned to my wife and said, "The more I study the city of Van and its surroundings, the more I get anxious and even scared about the successful escape we just completed. With only the help of the Almighty, in the first place, and hardworking human smugglers who brought us out alive to this beautiful place. No wonder all the people from 'Mrs. Colonel' to her officers, and all the other merchants in the city, look at us with shock every time they see us. They really must think that we had gone out of our minds to do such a dangerous escape during a cold season, and travel through such tall snow-covered mountains."

We spent the rest of the afternoon with our young friend, who finally introduced himself as Mehdi.

In the later afternoon, we all boarded a bus and headed back to the city of Van. I noticed that Mehdi didn't seem to have any plans and just wanted to hang out with us, therefore I invited him to spend the rest of the day with our group.

The next day, everybody woke up at 7:00 a.m. and by 8:00 a.m. we were at the same coffee shop for breakfast where our table was already set waiting for us. We enjoyed our breakfast and because it was merely minutes to President Street we didn't have to feel rushed to get there and could take our time. We stayed at the coffee shop until 9:30 a.m. before we finally left to the parade. The parade started exactly at 10:00 a.m. with many colorful uniforms of different high schools with their music bands and banners, and at the very end the police and army members marched on the street in their uniforms as army marching songs played. The Turkish people had gathered on both sides of the street waving flags of Turkey, as well as large portraits of Ataturk. This parade was one of the best and most interesting events that the kids enjoyed. When the colonel and police marched by, they noticed us, and the police officers that knew us made funny faces at the kids to make them happy.

The entire parade took about an hour to complete and while we were there we met other Iranian escapees who had also gathered in Van. Among them was a pregnant woman who approached us and asked, "Are you Mr. Hakimi?"

I replied, "Yes. How do you know my name?"

She quickly answered, "I heard about you from other Iranians who are waiting for their Visas and they told me that you have been speaking to the police colonel about your case."

"How come you have come to me?" I asked. "What can I do for you?"

"I am nine months pregnant," she replied, "and I am expecting a child any day. My husband has been arrested by the *askars* and has been in Van jail for the past three days."

"What is wrong with your husband that he ended up in jail?"

She started to cry. "Many years ago, my husband had Maoist ideas in Iran and the government found out and tried to arrest him. Although he realized his Maoist thoughts were wrong and he changed, they still wanted to arrest him now. I asked him to leave the country without me and he told me that either we all leave together while I'm pregnant, or we stay and see what happens. Therefore, we decided to escape Iran with the help of human traffickers. When we were halfway to Van, we were arrested by the *askars*.

"Although I thought I was going to deliver my baby at any moment, we made it through three days and nights before finally being arrested. My husband had a small gun with him for protection and when the *askars* found it they put handcuffs on him and separated us from each other. The *askars* brought me to Van and delivered me to the colonel and officers who know about my case, Last I heard, my husband is still in jail in the city of Van. Please go to the colonel and the officers, especially because you know English and can speak to them, and please ask for his release. Please explain to them that we are not dangerous people and that the gun was only for the protection of his family, and nothing else. From Turkey, we are planning to leave to my husband's brother's house in Germany. He is a prominent and successful businessman and has promised that he will take care of us under the condition that no political agenda will ever arise in the future."

When I saw her crying and her large pregnant belly, I couldn't help but feel sympathy for her.

My wife approached and hugged her, and then said, "I promise my husband will do anything possible to help you and your husband." Then my wife asked her to join us for the rest of the day, and because we had an appointment the next morning at the police station to answer more questions, my wife told her she could join us then, too.

The next morning, we had our usual breakfast at the coffee shop and while our group of four men left to go to the police station, the women and kids did more window-shopping and walked around. By the time we got to the police station, the pregnant lady was there waiting for us. I greeted her and asked her to remain outside, because I first wanted to speak to the colonel regarding the matter, and then if the colonel approved it, someone could come outside and get her.

Our group went to our usual interrogation room. A few minutes later, the colonel walked in and the officers stood up at attention, as well as our group. The colonel looked at me and asked, "Tell me, did your family, especially the kids, enjoy yesterday's parade?"

I replied, "A small city right on the border, and yet, with so much civilization and development."

The colonel and the officers nodded their heads in agreement.

I said, "Our group of four men is here to answer any questions that you might have."

"Thank you for coming in," the colonel replied. "But we don't have any questions for you today, because we have to wait to hear from Ankara regarding your entrance visas to make you legal in this country. All you have to do is come in every morning at 10:00am for a few minutes and say, 'hello' and if we have any news we will let you know. We want to make sure that you are still in Van."

Then I raised my hand to get a permission to speak. The colonel nodded her head to me. I said, "As you know, there are approximately twenty-eight to thirty-five Iranian escapees in your town. Some of them are Muslim, some Christian, some Jewish. Each one of them has their own story. As I understand, most of them can barely speak Turkish or English. And the word has spread amongst them that I am here with my family in your town and am answering interrogation questions for you in English. I have been approached by one of them and she want me to explain her situation to you. She is a pregnant lady whose husband is in jail because he had a small gun with him when he entered your country with his wife. The wife explained that her husband is in jail in Van right now, downstairs, and would like to see you to explain everything to you herself in Farsi so that I can translate it for you.

I waited a moment and then asked, "Do I have your permission to ask her to come up?"

The colonel didn't seem happy about the idea, but as a sign of respect for me she sent one of the officers down to fetch the pregnant lady. Five minutes later, the pregnant lady and officer entered the room. I asked her to put her right hand on her heart and tell the truth because I am sticking my head out for her.

She carried out the gesture and said, "Believe me, I will tell the truth."

The colonel allowed me to ask the pregnant lady their questions and I translated the answers into English for them.

The colonel said, "First of all, I would like to let you know that your husband is doing well in our Van jail. Secondly, we have already sent his case to Ankara and we have to wait to get permission for his release from the security police of Ankara. Entering a country illegally is a crime by itself. Having a firearm makes it more difficult for the refugee or escapee. Mr. Hakimi must have believed in you that he has taken up this task of helping you. I am a mother myself and I can sympathize with a pregnant woman who had to escape on horseback to find her freedom in a foreign country. But at the same time, we have an obligation to our own people to make sure that there is no danger that comes with any of these illegal groups."

The pregnant lady sobbed some more and then slowly said, "Believe me, we are not terrorists. We are simple everyday Iranian people who have lost everything, including our freedom in our own country. And my husband's brother asked us to leave Iran and stay with him. He will offer my husband a job."

The colonel asked for all the information they had on the brother-in-law.

The pregnant lady took a piece of paper out of her purse and handed it to me. I read the name in Farsi and wrote it down in English along with the phone number on a separate piece of paper. I handed the English version to the colonel and the other paper back to the pregnant lady.

The colonel looked at it, turned to the pregnant lady, and said, "This can help your husband's case very much. I am going to contact your brother-in-law myself. I can speak German."

The pregnant lady was happy and wanted to know if the colonel would allow her to see her husband.

The colonel turned to me and said, "If Mr. Hakimi accepts and takes the responsibility of coming with you, I can send you with a police van to see your husband right away."

I said, "As long as my presence can be of any help, I will be more than happy to come along with her because, as you can see, she is pregnant and will have a baby soon. At least her husband's mind may be put to ease."

The session was dismissed. One of the officers escorted the pregnant lady and me with a police van to the jail in Van. The rest of our group went to the Kim Restaurant to meet back up with the women and kids and to let them know what was going on. I would meet them later.

It took about twenty minutes to arrive at the jail in Van. We were escorted on foot to where the pregnant lady's husband was being held with several other inmates. We waited in the waiting room until the husband was brought in five minutes later. He had shackles around his hands and ankles.

The officer turned to me and said, "Go ahead and speak to him in Farsi. I trust you. You have proven to be a good human being."

The husband approached us and hugged his wife and both of them started to cry. The pregnant lady told her husband that I was there voluntarily to help them out however I could. We spent about ten minutes talking and I told him that the colonel was soon going to contact his brother in Germany and that this could be a very good sign that he would be getting out of jail soon.

By the time the pregnant lady and I got back to the police station the colonel was standing outside waiting for us. The colonel looked at me with a big smile on her face. "While you were gone, I contacted the brother in Germany. He was very excited about the situation and asked for the security police phone number in Ankara so that he may contact them and assure them that his brother is clean and that he has a job waiting for him as soon as he gets to Germany."

That was the best news that the pregnant lady could hear. For the first time, out of respect I approached the colonel and extended my hand to shake hers. She shook hands with me and said, "The kind of person that I know you are, I'm sure every day you're going to come here with a new case and try to help each one of them. I appreciate that. Because of your knowledge in English, you are a great help to me and you make my task easier. In the future I hope all the Istanbul escapees get to their final destinations. With all the escapee stories I have been heard, I have come to appreciate my own freedoms in my own country."

The pregnant woman and I walked toward the Kim Restaurant. The entire way to she cried and was very excited about the good news. When we arrived, I told everybody in our group the good news. Everybody had lunch and then the pregnant lady left to go to her hotel because she was tired and wanted to rest.

Our group headed back to our own hotel but stopped on the way at a shop that sold dried nuts and berries, including sunflower seeds, pistachios, cashews, and of course, dried figs, which are quite popular in Turkey. The owner happened to be an Iranian who has been in Van for many years. As soon as we entered, he began to play Iranian music for us. We purchased some of the goodies we needed and headed to our hotel. It was now nearly a week we had been in Van and pretty much knew all the places in the city.

As usual, the group came to my room to listen to Persian music. Pahlavan said, "Mr. Hakimi, it's time that the members of our group pay for their share of expenses. As we agreed, you would pay, and at the end of the week, everyone else then pays for their share of the cost. Please tell us how much each of us owes."

I brought all the receipts I had kept in a small cardboard box in the closet. Pahlavan and Ghasem added all the other receipts that they wanted to divide amongst the total of six paying people, not counting the kids. I objected to the idea of excluding the kids and suggested that eight persons be considered instead of six.

Ghasem said, "Both kids combined don't even eat as much as half a grownup. It's not fair to pay for each one of them at full price. Please accept our suggestion."

I got the total and divided it by eight and said, "If you want me to continue to be responsible for the expenses, then you have to agree with my proposal. I want my family and me to feel free to eat together whenever we want, so please don't argue with me."

They finally agreed with me, paid their shares, and headed back to their rooms to sleep for the night.

Two more days passed and we hadn't seen the pregnant woman around. We asked the other Iranians who were staying at the same hotel as her and learned that her husband had been released and that as soon as he had arrived at her hotel room, they had to take her to the hospital where she delivered a baby boy. It was very good news for all of us. We paid a visit to her in the hospital where our group finally got the chance to meet her husband. He approached me and thanked me for helping them with his release from the jail. I was just happy to see them reunited, along with their little son, as well.

Every day for the next few days, the four men from our group paid visits to the police station, but only for a few minutes each time, and almost every time I had another Iranian escapee with me who needed my assistance. There were new escapees arriving in Van on a weekly basis. Among them was a family of four, which included a husband, his wife, and a daughter and a son around ten to eleven years old. Another escapee party of two, a mother and her ten-year-old son, also arrived. The colonel was happy to see me

222

bring in the escapees, because I translated all the information for the police and made their jobs much easier for them.

Meanwhile, the newborn and his mother were released from the hospital and returned to their hotel with the father. One of the Iranian women approached my wife and said, "The mother of the newborn doesn't know how to give a bath to the baby and since their release from the hospital the baby hasn't been bathed."

As soon as my wife heard this, she quickly went to their hotel and washed the baby boy for them and taught the mother, along with the help of the father, how to give a bath to the baby boy. My wife went there a few times more in the days that followed, until they really didn't need her help anymore.

Days passed and there was still no news from Ankara regarding our visas. I had to call my brother again to let him know about our situation. My brother also contacted the responsible Israeli council in the matter. Our stay in Van had become tiresome and we were looking forward to going to Istanbul as early as possible. There was almost a parade every three to four days in Van, which kept our minds occupied.

I realized that my older son's birthday was coming up soon. My wife and I decided to have a gathering for all the Iranian escapees at the Kim Restaurant. We spread the word to all to come and reserved one of the rooms in the restaurant. The owner made a beautiful fresh fruit desert from watermelons and other fruits as a gift for our son. He had hollowed out the inside of a large watermelon, cut the rind into a flower-pattern and put a lit candle inside it. It was used as the centerpiece for our table.

Persian music and dancing by the guests took some of the pressure off the minds of everybody. My wife and I knew that in a few days we would be celebrating the coming of Passover, one of the most important Jewish holidays. I called my brother and asked him the exact date so at least we would have a small ceremony for ourselves. I knew the approximate date and could remember the years we observed Passover with all my family members in our homeland, but now this Passover we would be in Van with no relatives at all, just friends.

I thought to myself that the Almighty must have a big purpose for us to be all here together. I didn't know back then that very soon after I'd get my answer.

On one of the days our group went to the police station, I saw the colonel outside and greeted her. I then asked her if she heard anything from Ankara about our case.

She waited a few seconds, and replied, "No. Nothing yet."

I looked at her and said, "I brought my family out of Iran to save them from the hands of the *pasdars* and *Komitehs* of Khomeini. We went through a lot of trouble to get here and for what? To be stuck here? It's not fair."

The colonel didn't understand exactly what I had said, but she got furious with me about hearing the name of the Ayatollah Khomeini. She turned to Ghasem and in Turkish asked, "What did he say about Khomeini?"

Ghasem tried to explain to the colonel that I want to take my family to America as soon as possible and that I am worried about the health of my children. The colonel went into her office and shut the door behind her. The other officers approached me and told me that the colonel hates to hear the name of the Ayatollah Khomeini, because she thinks he is a devil and not only hurts Iran and the Iranians, but also the whole world.

Our group left the police station. It seemed to me that we were wasting our time. I didn't know what to think anymore and couldn't figure out another way around the visas. Perhaps I was tired and didn't realize it but we had no other choice but to wait and hope to get a positive answer from Ankara.

We walked to the Kim Restaurant and as usual the owner greeted us. Everybody sat down but nobody, including the kids, was in the mood to order anything.

Suddenly, I felt that all the problems of the world were back on my shoulders again. My wife noticed that I seemed disappointed and very quiet. She then turned to me and said, "I am the witness for the last five years of how much you have confronted different issues in your life since the beginning of this so-called 'revolution' and dealing with the responsibilities of taking care of your mother and grandmother. And then regarding our own passport issues. Also, what you had to go through with Sadri. And all this, while at the same time watching the country that all of us love, and still love, go to ruin. I understand your anger and disappointment. We knew that we would be here for three to four weeks, so it's not late yet. You have helped so many people here whom you didn't know. Everybody looks up to you and they really count on you. Therefore, please cheer up and smile. Because everybody is already disappointed and when they see you like this they think something is really wrong."

I took her hand and said, "Thanks. You have always been there for me, and I am such a lucky man to have a partner like you."

I went to the restroom and washed up with cold water and returned to the group with a big smile on my face. When I came back to the table, the owner of the Kim Restaurant, who had become a friend of sorts by now, was happy about my change of mood. He came by and said, "Please order anything you like. Today, you are my guest. I am going to sit down with you to have coffee." We spent almost three hours there before we finally headed back to our hotel.

As we passed by the fish market at the bazaar, the members of our group decided to have oven-cooked fish for dinner. Sara and Nader volunteered to clean the fish. Ghasem took it upon himself to bring the readied fish to the bakery to be cooked in the oven. And Pahlavan decided to make the salad and said, "Speaking for our group, we would like Mr. and Mrs. Hakimi to rest tonight. We will serve them their dinners." Pahlavan then turned to me and said, "Since the first minute that I saw you, back at the Khoy post office, I had a very good feeling about you. During our escape and with the many days and nights that we spent together, I am very glad that you were there for me, and for the rest of our group. I should also mention that since the time we've been in Van, we have all noticed that you always try to defend us and answer for us. On behalf of the group and me, we want to thank you for all you have done for

225

both us and the other Iranian escapees you've met in Van."

I thanked everybody and said, "It's been my pleasure to be with you and I will never forget all the help and assistance that I received from you guys." We bought the fish and the other goods we needed for our dinner.

Sara turned to my wife and asked, "Mrs. Hakimi, can I ask you to help me in cooking the caviar?" Before my wife answered, Sara added, "Because I am afraid that I won't cook them as deliciously as you did before."

My wife turned to her and replied, "Don't worry. I will cook them myself and you can watch and learn. It would be my pleasure."

We had a very relaxing night with a good dinner, beer, soft drinks, and Persian music with a special guest; Oscar, the owner of our hotel also joined us.

A new day started. We walked to the coffee shop for breakfast as usual and then walked to the police station. I didn't want to go into the police station, so my wife and the kids walked to the second floor and met the officers. The colonel walked out of her office and talked to my wife regarding my absence.

My wife turned to her and said, "My husband was trying on shoes when we noticed that we have to be at the police station at 10:00 a.m. I rushed to meet you and the officers. My husband will be here very soon."

The colonel said, "I love your husband, and I love your family. I want to get you on your way to Istanbul as soon as possible. I will wait another day or two and if I don't get an answer, I will fly to Ankara myself. I have thirty-six cases there, mostly thanks to your husband's assistance with each one of them. I want to see every escapee get to their families and their destinations."

My wife and the kids walked out of the police station and I could see she had a happy face. She shared the good news with me and the group. To kill time, we decided to go to the confectionary to have some coffee and sweets and keep our minds busy by watching a movie or two while there.

Time passed and the Passover holiday was around the corner.

My wife had planned to have a small Passover Night (Seder) for our group, when the time came. She said, "We have to buy some potatoes, eggs, vegetables, and fish. Try to keep the first night as Kosher as possible."

I reassured her and said, "One can be excused from observing the Passover ritual under our circumstances." Regardless, I promised her that I would make her Passover request come true.

The next day our group headed to the coffee shop for our usual breakfast. We spent almost two hours at the coffee shop and then went to the police station. I walked up to the second floor and saw one of the officers waiting for my arrival. Jokingly, I turned to him and said, "Here I am. My family and the rest of the group are outside. As you can see, we haven't left from Van yet." I then asked, "May I also say good morning to the colonel?"

"The colonel is not in Van," he replied. "She flew to Ankara yesterday afternoon. She will be there for about a week. She took a list of all the names of all of the Iranian escapees and wanted to make sure that there is not a problem for any one of them. As usual, come every morning to see me, because any day we might get a message from her."

I was happy about the news. I thanked him and headed down to the street to join our group and let them know about the colonel being in Ankara. Every bit of news was very encouraging for us. I was already looking forward to returning to the police station the next day to find out if the officer had heard anything from Ankara regarding our cases.

Two days passed and there was no news from the colonel.

Finally, Passover came, and we got ready to celebrate. We had breakfast at our usual coffee shop and then headed to the police station. I rushed upstairs to the second floor and met one of the officers. He was very happy to see me. He said, "I just had a telephone call from the colonel, and she is going to telex the names of the people whose visas have been issued." He waited a moment and then asked, "Where is your family and the rest of the group?" He then said, "Go get them and come to the third floor where the telex machine is located."

I quickly rushed downstairs back to our group and said, "Come on everybody let's go to the third floor. We are about to receive our visas via telex from Ankara."

We got to the third floor and the officer approached our group and said, "Please be seated." He then asked me to stand next to him by the telex machine. We waited and the telex machine started printing the names. The very first name was my name, followed by my wife's name, and then the names of my two kids. I read each one out loud as it was printed. Our group was the first eight names that arrived through telex. The rest of the people that we knew had their names printed, as well, and the only names that were not on the list were those of the husband and wife with their little newborn baby boy, which was very disappointing for me.

We got out of the police station and went directly to the confectionary. I bought three different flavored cakes, boxes of cookies and soft drinks and brought them all to the police station and thanked them for the good news. Although I was happy for our visas, my mind was concerned for the other three people who hadn't gotten their visas yet. I talked privately to the officer regarding their case and he assured me that they would be leaving to Istanbul within the next two weeks. He told me that they would have to wait until the brother from Germany sends the required documents to Ankara.

I turned to my wife and said, "Honey, this is the miracle of Passover for us. The first night and we already have our visas, and hopefully very soon we will be on our way to Istanbul." The other Iranian escapees were notified by Ghasem and Pahlavan about the news of their visas.

We prepared our dinner table and my wife cooked the fish. It was around 8:00 p.m. when we started the first night of our Passover ceremony. I explained to our group why we celebrate the Passover and why we have to eat Matzos instead of bread. I said, "It is about the miracle of freedom of the Jewish people from the bondage of slavery in the land of Egypt." The group had questions and answers so we had a discussion for a while. I had no idea then that talking about Passover would eventually provide a future miracle for the brother and sister in our group, Sara and Nader.

The following morning and when we were already at the police station, I saw the colonel with a very happy face. I approached her and shook hands with her. I thanked her for taking the time and trouble of travelling to Ankara for our visas. She also thanked me for helping her with the translations and the information about the so-called "revolution." She said, "It will be five or six days until the police can get all the documents of the escapees in order and make arrangements with the bus company, as well as for a hotel stay in Istanbul"

As we left the police station I saw the husband and wife with their newborn baby boy watching me. They approached us and the husband said "We want to thank you for all you have done for us. We need one last favor from you. Please talk to the colonel and let us know when we will be able to leave for Istanbul."

The colonel was on her way out of the police station and she saw them. She turned to me and asked, "Are they here to see me?"

I replied, "Yes. They want to know about their case. Please tell me the information so that I can translate it for them."

The colonel looked at the baby boy and said, "Tell them that in a maximum of two weeks, they will be on their way to Istanbul. Also, tell them that they don't have to worry about anything. Their case is already complete and their visas have been issued. We're just waiting for a letter from his brother in Germany to finalize everything."

We got back to our hotel and Pahlavan and Ghasem requested to observe the second night of Passover. Sara and Nader also wanted to join the group for the ceremony. When we sat for the second night, I questioned them about the reason we eat Matzos and celebrate it. It seemed that they all had listened very well everything that I had told them before. Celebrating Passover in a small city such as Van, far away from our families and relatives while listening to Persian music, with not really even a half-decent

Seder, had its own merit.

Oscar approached us and said, "The officer from the police station just called and asked that all the men from your group come to the police station at 10:00 a.m. tomorrow."

One moment, we were on top of the world and now suddenly our minds were occupied by a thousand thoughts. I tried to stay calm, although I was disappointed.

My wife said, "You were summoned there before. Besides, we all saw the list of the visas and therefore there shouldn't be anything you should be concerned about."

I looked at the group and said, "They might think that all the members of our group are not either Jewish or Muslim. They might have some questions about Passover as a test." I turned to Nader and added, "You better remember the Passover ceremony and if you have any questions about it, ask me now. I'm sure it must be about religion that they have summoned us."

The next day the four men of our group walked into the police station at 10:00 a.m. The officer asked us to go to the same interrogation room as usual for questioning. We sat down and one of the officers, along with the gentleman in a civilian suit, walked into the room after us. The man in the civilian suit looked at us and said, "Nader and I will leave the room and wait outside in the hallway." I was amazed by his command of English. This whole time he had been in the room with us during the entire course of our interrogations, he had not said a word in English to anyone and had shown no signs that he understood our questions and answers.

Nader and I walked out of the room and sat on the chairs they had placed for us in the hallway. I turned to Nader and said, "I'm sure it's about religion. Remember, if he asks you about Judaism or Passover or anything related, explain as much as you can remember from the last two night's ceremonies." I even went further and asked him if he had ever been circumcised.

"Yes," he replied. "I was circumcised about a year ago when we were just thinking about escaping." That was when he finally disclosed to me that he was an Armenian. We waited for about fifteen minutes until Pahlavan and Ghasem finally stepped out of the room. Their faces were red and they seemed nervous. The gentleman in the civilian suit was an undercover police officer. He asked the uniformed officer to send one of the two 'Jewish guys' in the hallway back into the room. I stood up and volunteered to go in first. The officer opened the door for me and asked me to walk inside.

The undercover officer offered me a seat and said, "Mr. Hakimi, please sit down." He waited a moment and then continued. "I listened to you during the course of the interrogations and believe me, at times I wanted to personally ask you questions because you seemed to explain everything in detail and I like how you defended your family and your new friends who have now become a part of your group. You stated before that you are Jewish. That your wife is Jewish and, of course, that your kids are Jewish. Is this correct?"

I replied, "Yes. I was born Jewish. I lived a Jewish life and will die as a Jew as well. This is the main reason I left my country."

He looked straight into my eyes and asked, "What is happening in the Jewish religion these days?"

"You mean Passover?"

"Yes, please explain to me this Passover that you have just mentioned."

I went over the entire story of Passover with him in detail.

He then asked, "Have you been observing Passover all your life?"

"Yes. But this time, our Passover table wasn't as complete as always. However, the law of the Jewish religion explains that under special circumstances, one may be excused from observing it. My wife cooked everything for us herself and the last two nights we had homemade fish, potatoes instead of Matzos, hardboiled eggs, and salads."

"You explained everything so well and so completely," he confirmed. "I really learned a lot from our meeting." He then asked, "But, what about the other guy in the lobby? Is he Jewish too?"

I replied, "He is my wife's cousin. Of course, he is Jewish."

He stood up and shook hands with me and said, "Good luck to you and your family. Go to America, it's a beautiful country. All of you can go to your hotel and in the next two days, you along with many others are going to be on your way to Istanbul.

I walked out of the room and looked at the others and said, "Let's go to our hotel." I looked at Nader's face. His face was as pale as a white wall. On the way, I told them about my interrogation and asked about how each of theirs had been.

Ghasem said, "The interrogator asked me if I am a Muslim and I answered yes. Then, he continued and handed me a Koran and asked me to read from it. I told him that I was not very religious and couldn't read Arabic and that is the reason that I had left the country because I didn't believe in their system."

Pahlavan told me a similar story. The interrogator had spoken to Ghasem in Turkish and in English to Pahlavan. I turned to both and asked, "What happened at the very end of the interrogation?"

They both told me that they had been physically examined to make sure that they had been circumcised. Even though it was an embarrassing situation for both of them, it was funny enough that all of us started to laugh at the matter.

When we arrived back at our hotel, the women and the kids were anxiously waiting for us. They noticed our happy faces and knew that we had good news. I explained the interrogation procedure we had endured and about the gentleman in the civilian suite who was really an undercover security police officer and who conducted the questions that we had to answer. I never forgot the happiness of that day although during the interrogations, we did have stressful moments. We celebrated that night with a good dinner and desert, along with Persian music.

The next day, which was a Wednesday, we went to the police station to find out about the time and date of our departure to Istanbul. The colonel entered the room and with a very large smile and happy face approached me and asked, "Mr. Hakimi, have you and your group packed your suitcases yet? Are you ready to be on your way to Istanbul, tomorrow morning at 10:00 a.m.?"

I looked at her and the officers and replied, "Yes, Madam Colonel." I then turned to the officers and said, "On behalf of my group and all the others who are going to Istanbul, I would like to thank all of you for all your hard work and your cooperation."

The undercover security police officer looked at all of us and said, "You all had to go through a lot of hard times and endure pains and hardships to get here and we are very happy to see that you are all getting your wishes and freedoms, which is very important to every human being. Go and may Allah be with all of you."

On the way to the hotel, we purchased some fruits and cookies to take along for our trip. We were notified that our trip would take about thirty-six hours and to expect stops for lunch, dinner, and finally the next day's breakfast. The bus will travel constantly with three drivers who will change shifts every four hours.

The building on the right is our hotel which located in the Central Market.

CHAPTER 10

The Trip to Istanbul

It was Thursday morning and we were all at the coffee shop 7:00 a.m. sharp for our last breakfast in our usual favorite coffee shop. We had the heartiest breakfast that we could eat and when I went to pay our bill, the owner refused to accept our money. He turned to Ghasem and in Turkish said, "Please tell Mr. Hakimi and the others that it's been a pleasure to have them in our city and that I want them to be my guest this one last time. Tell them I will miss them all, especially the kids whom my own children got to know when you came in for breakfast."

I insisted on paying the bill, but finally accepted his hospitality. We shook hands and left his coffee shop to pick up our suitcases and go to the bus stop, which was about five minutes from the hotel.

When we arrived at the bus station, I couldn't believe my eyes. There was a big crowd gathered to see us off. I saw the three officers with whom we were in contact at the police station during our interrogations. Most of the merchants were also there, including the owner of the Kim Restaurant, the owner of the Shwarma restaurant, the owner of the confectionary (who always rewound the movie to the beginning for us), the dried foods vendor (whom as soon as we walked into his shop played Persian music for us), the owner of the liquor store (where we bought our vodka, cognac, and beers), and last but not least, the husband and wife with their newborn baby boy had come to say their last farewells. Everybody cheered and rushed towards us and helped with the new suitcases we had purchased full of new clothing we had recently purchased in Van. The husband and wife approached us and the husband hugged me and kissed my cheeks as a Persian custom. He thanked me again for all my help in getting him out of jail in time for his newborn baby boy's arrival. The wife approached my wife and handed her son to my wife to hold and thanked her for all the assistance and teaching that she provided about taking care of the baby.

One-by-one, the merchants approached and handed me cakes, boxes of baklava, dried fruits, a big box of oranges, and finally, a bottle of Hennessey cognac, one bottle of vodka, and a box of beer. Although we had already said goodbye to Oscar, the hotel owner, he had made it to the bus stop to see us off. Everyone wished us a very good trip and cheered, "Bon-Voyage" over and over again. All the passengers got onto the bus, and then our group boarded, including my wife and kids, and I was the very last passenger on. I stepped onto the steps leading into the bus and turned to the people and said, *"Tashakour, tashakour."* (Turkish/Farsi for *Thank you, thank you.*)

As I stepped into the bus, I subconsciously noticed tears running down my cheeks in regard to the hospitality of the good people of the city of Van. The last passengers were two police officers who were in civilian suits and ties, with all of our documents in their hands. They were escorting us to Istanbul to a designated hotel. I should mention that the cost of the hotel in Van, as well as the bus fare and being checked by doctors (including all necessary medical tests) were paid by the government of Turkey out of the agreement per escapee from the United Nations Refugee Program.

Exactly at 10:00 a.m. the bus left the station and we rode through the streets of the city, which technically had become one of the most important stops of our escape. Getting to Van was always a big wish for any escapee. Upon our arrival to the city of

Van, being arrested by the police was very disappointing, but we had tried to make the best of our stay. Maybe it was meant in our lifetimes to experience the hospitalities and affections of the people of a small border city. Maybe our presence was meant to help the other escapees that had been stuck there for many months, but now were heading to Istanbul on the same bus with us. Although our kids had their own seats, my wife and I placed them on our laps for the first two hours and talked to them about the good times we would be having in Istanbul.

My older son asked, "Is Istanbul as beautiful as Van? And are the people there as friendly as they are here?"

I then replied, "Istanbul is much more beautiful and the people are as friendly as the people of Van." Feeling safe and looking forward to the better days to come caused our kids to quickly fall asleep on our laps.

Traveling on the highway through beautiful mountains in a very comfortable, warm, and modern bus, that had running hot water bathrooms, was quite different than riding horses at night through the snow. Every hour the host of the bus brought us warm wet towels soaked in fresh lemon juice to wipe our faces and hands. We all indulged in all the wonderful goods that the merchants and good people of Van had given us to take on our trip.

According to the drivers, we would arrive in Istanbul the next day in the afternoon around 3:00 or 4:00 p.m. We passed through small cities and sometimes tiny mountain villages, which reminded us when we were looking forward to barking dogs in the middle of the night as a sign of being able to soon rest and get off those horses. Our kids slept on their own seats and many other passengers enjoyed a nap along with the relaxing humming sound of the engine of the bus. My wife and I spoke with each other the entire time. She had already decided that as soon as we were in Istanbul and had checked into our hotel, we would get a taxi and go to the Jewish district of Shoshone where the big synagogue and the Jewish shops were located. I promised her that we would do that.

Ghasem approached us and asked, "Is there anything you need?

I noticed that this entire time, you were talking and not resting."

We thanked him and I replied, "We are just planning our schedule for when we arrive at Istanbul."

He was such an appreciative person and every once in a while came to us and thanked us for being there for him during the course of our escape.

It was 8:00 p.m. when we arrived at a restaurant. Our group sat together and ordered their dinner. I looked everyone and said, "I want you all to know that it has been a pleasure for my wife and me to spend the last four to five weeks with you. I learned a lot from you and our escape. I think we have found new friends that will be in our hearts forever. Therefore, I want the honor of inviting you all for dinner tonight as a formal farewell, even though we will be still together in Istanbul at times." I insisted on the offer and the group finally accepted it.

As we returned to our bus and got seated, I handed one of the Persian tapes to the driver and said, "Please play this tape on the loudspeaker. I am sure everyone will enjoy it." He played the tape. There wasn't any other noise, but the sound of the bus engine trying to climb the uphill road mingled with the vocal sounds of "Hayedeh," a legendary Persian singer and one of the best female singers in Iran. The song was about someone leaving for a trip, but had no hope of a return. Ghasem and Pahlavan served the passengers soft drinks and alcoholic beverages. The tape was emotionally moving and I had to translate the lyrics for the undercover police officers and the driver. The melody itself was so emotionally gripping that the driver played it over and over again. We were all in a good, bittersweet mood when Pahlavan approached me and asked, "Mr. Hakimi, would you sing some Iranian classic music for us? And do I have your permission to announce it to everybody?"

I looked at my wife and she said, "Please sing for us. It's been a long time since you've sung anything. This is a special occasion and I'm sure the kids would also enjoy it. You used to sing for them all the time." Then my wife turned to Pahlavan and said, "Go ahead, and announce it. He will sing for us."

Pahlavan started announcing first in Farsi and then in English. I had a good feeling and was in the mood to sing. I started a song and on some parts I asked the passengers to join in. Everyone was now also in a good mood, so I sang some classic songs. One of them told the story of escapees.

We sang until everyone was tired and fell asleep.

Soon after that it was time to change bus drivers. The bus stopped at a small coffee shop for about five minutes while most of the passengers were still asleep. I looked at my watch and saw it was 2:00 a.m.

I stared at the lights of the houses far away among the trees. Some were still covered with snow and then I turned to my wife and said, "Honey, look at the beautiful view. People are in their homes sleeping, and all they hear is the sound of cars and buses passing by, but nobody knows what is going on in every bus or car." There was a time not that long ago we were in warm comfortable beds. All we could hear were the car and bus noises, too. We never thought that there would be a day when we found ourselves in the circumstances we are in right now. Unless one goes through unexpected surprises in their lifetime, they can't realize that every car or bus has its own story.

We brought the kids from their seats to our own and held them in our laps hugging them until all of us fell asleep. The bus stopped and the driver made and announcement on the loudspeaker. "Attention, ladies and gentlemen. Please wake up and get ready to have breakfast."

From this point on, there wasn't a lot of distance between cities and as we progressed we noticed the activities of each city with their cars, taxis, buses, and people walking the streets, shopping or going to their jobs. We could see life in the big cities again. Every city had its own beauty and character. They all had old homes, newer homes, shops, restaurants, parks where children could play football and other sports, as well as long tree-lined streets. Although it had been only a month since we had left the big city life in Tehran, having gone through the snow-covered mountains and riding horses to finally arrive in a large city and watch life again had a special meaning and sentimental value for us. We were acting like a bunch of prisoners who had just been recently released, feeling freedom and liberty with our hearts.

As we got closer to our destination, we became more impatient and anxious to arrive. We still had our kids on our laps, and they were also eager to get to Istanbul. In their own small way, they knew that Istanbul was going to be the launching pad of our trip. They looked at the view of the mountains, the hustle and bustle of the towns we passed through and asked many questions along the way. My wife and I felt they wanted to be on our laps for the rest of the way, because maybe they thought that being closer to us was safer than sitting in their own seats. Or perhaps the anxiety and the exhaustive trauma from the trip played on their minds.

I turned to my wife and said, "I think now our kids finally feel the full gravity of our escape. They are occupied by the excitement of the trip and they hadn't seen a live horse before except for in the movies. But then suddenly they come across a situation that forces them to ride horses through the fearful darkness of night and climb snow-covered mountains with cold fast winds upon their faces, which was a harsh experience. At least they did their best and cooperated with whatever we asked them to do. I won't forget the nights my younger son, who rode with me, cried very quietly and didn't want me to hear him weeping. Whenever I heard him, I pressed him harder to my chest and heart and tried to comfort him. I never thought the escape was going to be so hard, especially for the kids."

My wife and I kissed them and spoke to them motivationally about the future. We told them about how there would be a day when they would be successful grownups and when they'd remember these days escaping, they would be proud of themselves and cherish the value of being a free human being. What we had been through was simply and only for the pursuit of our freedom, which had been brutally and viciously robbed from us by a bunch of Godforsaken persons in the name of religion.

The driver cut the music and made another announcement. "Ladies and gentlemen, on behalf of the crew of the bus and the government of Turkey, I would like to welcome you to one of the most beautiful cities, not only in Turkey, but the world; the city of Istanbul."

I could see happiness in the faces of everyone. The last five years of my life flashed before my eyes like a movie and now we were at the point where it would be one of the highlights of our escape. In a few minutes, we will be on the Bo-ghazi Bridge, one of the tallest and longest bridges in the entire world. A masterpiece of engineering that connects Asia to the European continent.

Finally, we had arrived at Istanbul, which was one of the most important key locations of our escape. Istanbul was the city where all the refugees and escapees of the time had a chance to go to any other country. It was the gateway to the world. There were private organizations, along with Turkish government institutions, to assist them.

As we approached the Bo-ghazi Bridge, the driver again made another announcement. "Ladies and gentlemen, what you see ahead is the Bo-ghazi Bridge and I'm going to drive slowly so that all of you can have a good look at it as well, as the beautiful views of the city, the sea, and the hills around it, and the city with its beautiful homes." The driver was so excited about the Bo-ghazi Bridge, one would think it was the first time saw it, too. He kept repeating, "Yes sir, yes sir. This is the famous Bo-ghazi Bridge." And as promised, he drove as slowly as possible so we could see the bridge, the colorful hills with the beautiful homes, and the sea with its smaller boats and cruise ships coasting. I think it was a very nice gesture for the driver to make it so exciting and memorable for his passengers. He knew everyone aboard (except the two undercover police officers) were escapee refugees. I should mention that by now we had acquired a new title of escapee refugees, but to respect us they simply called us refugees.

One of the officers stood up and said, "Your presence in Turkey is now legal. We are going to take you to a hotel. From now on, you will be responsible for your own expenses while you remain in Turkey."

It was approximately 4:00 p.m. when we arrived in a hotel, which already had our names and a room reserved for us. We thanked the drivers and the officers who had brought us into the hotel and gave us our room keys.

Once in our room, my wife refused to open any of the suitcases. "We are not tired or hungry. Therefore, let's get a taxi and go to the Shoshone area where the synagogue and the Jewish deli markets are located and buy some Matzos and kosher cold cuts. Or perhaps, some readied hot food for our Shabbat dinner. Also look for a hotel close to the synagogue."

I said, "Honey, let's just change our clothing. You wear your new dress, which is appropriate for Shabbat and put new clothes on the kids. I would like to wear the new suit I bought in Van for the Shabbat night of Passover to celebrate our first Shabbat services since freedom after five years."

She agreed. And off we went to the Shoshone area.

When we arrived at the synagogue, it wasn't opened yet. I rang the bell and the caretaker came to the door. "The services will begin at 7:30 p.m.," he said.

I asked, "Where can I find a Jewish deli market?"

He replied, "You are late. They are closed for Shabbat. But they are all on the same street near us so you can't miss them on Sunday or Monday."

We were very disappointed, but decided to look for a hotel within walking distance to the synagogue. We walked about two blocks and found one called Yeshiladah Hotel. I spoke with the manager and he said, "Bring your suitcases inside and I will give you the key."

"Our suitcases are not here with us. I have to go and get them. I will need an hour."

"No problem," he said. "I will save the room for you."

We rushed to get a taxi and got back to our assigned hotel. And within an hour we were back at the Yeshiladah Hotel. We paid for our room and then the manager said, "I need your passports."

I got my passport out, which was not a legal one, along with a legal Islamic Republic passport for my wife and the kids. I handed all of them to him.

He looked at the passport for my wife and kids and said, "This one is good." He then turned to me, and said, "But yours is not good, so I can't give you the room." We were shocked. The manager turned around and left. I followed him and said, *"Afendu, afendu!"* (Turkish for *Mister, mister!*) He stopped and I reached into my pocket and gave him three extra nights of hotel fare to keep for himself. He counted the money and there was suddenly a large smile upon his face. He returned to the front desk and gave me the key.

My wife must have seen me giving him the extra money and by a nod of her head and a smile, I knew that she approved of my bribe to get the room for us.

We carried our suitcases to the main building, but the bellhop said, "Your room is on the other side." We followed him to a small bungalow at the end of the yard. He opened the door and turned on the lights. It was cold and smelled damp and had two beds in one room and one bathroom. It must have been the room the custodian used to stay in. I was furious. We walked to the manager and complained.

He said, "You were late and I thought you were not coming, so I had to rent out my last room. I will have a room on the second floor with a window towards the street and in a very good location. It will be available in a couple of days." My wife was very anxious to get to the synagogue for Shabbat and agreed to the room we had. After that we were on our way to the synagogue.

We were never as disappointed by any synagogue or rabbi as we were that night. We expected as was the costume in synagogues all over the world that when there is a guest in any synagogue the rabbi would invite them to the sanctuary, so that they could pray and do the ritual services together. The Shabbat services started, but nobody, not even one member of the management, asked us to join them in praying.

I didn't want to impose ourselves upon anybody so we sat on the chairs by the door of the entrance to the sanctuary until *Arvit* (Hebrew for *night prayer*) was finished. When the congregation in their Shabbat suits and dresses were leaving the synagogue, they all looked at us as though they had just seen ghosts, or beggars waiting for some charity.

Finally, the rabbi approached us, and asked, "Can I help you? What are you doing here?"

I looked at him with anger and said, "We are Jewish and escaped from Iran. We just arrived in Istanbul a few hours ago. My wife and I tried very hard to observe our Passover ritual since the holiday began even though we were on the road. We came to the Shoshone area to purchase Matzos and some kosher food for Shabbat, but unfortunately all the Jewish shops had closed before we got to them. All we want is some Matzos and kosher food, if you have any to spare in your synagogue. Of course, I will be more than happy to pay for them."

The rabbi went to the pantry and brought a box of Matzos and handed it to me.

I had money ready in my hands, and said "Please rabbi, tell me how much it is."

He looked at me and said, "Oh no, no, no money. It's Shabbat, don't touch the money." He refused to let me pay him for the Matzos and without any further action or word, he left the synagogue.

I put some money in the donation box and we left the synagogue. I was very ashamed of the rabbi's behavior, as well as the behavior of the rest of the congregation. I was even ashamed to look at my wife's face under the circumstances. The behavior of the rabbi and the congregation was neither Jewish, nor kosher. It is every Jew's duty to invite newcomers as guests into their homes, especially on Shabbat. A Shabbat of Passover would be one of the most important Shabbats.

I turned to my wife and said, "Honey, I know you try to do the best as a Jewish person, but I am sorry for what happened. It seems these people live on another planet."

She looked into my eyes and said, "I thank you for all of your efforts for making everything possible for us."

I waited a moment, and replied, "I remember that anytime we saw a stranger in our town, especially if they came to our synagogue, that many members of our congregation would invite them into their homes to have dinner with them, especially when it was a Shabbat, let alone a Passover Shabbat. Such a duty is one of the 613 commandments in Jewish Law."

My wife noticed that I was really hurt emotionally. "As you said at the beginning of Passover, we are technically excused from having to observe the holiday because we are in a foreign land under special circumstances. We'll try our best until a day in the future when we will have the chance to observe it completely."

Regardless, I couldn't keep my anger hidden from my wife regarding the ill treatment we had received from the rabbi and his congregation.

The next morning, we freshened up and headed to Taksim Square, where the statues of Ata Turk with some of his dignitary cabinet members make up the centerpiece of the park. A young Iranian man approached us because he had overheard us speaking in Farsi and asked, "You see that statue in the front row?" He pointed his finger towards the statue and we looked. "It is a statue of Reza Shah. Reza Shah and Ata Turk ruled their countries at the same time. Both of them were nationalists for their countries and shared development programs and ideas for both Iran and Turkey."

I have no idea if the statue actually contains Reza Shah or not. I thanked him for his information and then we went to a street filled with restaurants, confectionaries, boutiques, and other various shops. The kids chose a nice restaurant at which to eat. We had a hearty and healthy breakfast with American coffee, as well as milk for the kids. We walked out of the restaurant and headed towards the sea. It was a good half an hour walk and we enjoyed it very much.

On our way, we passed the synagogue and noticed the Shabbat

service attendees arriving, either walking on foot or driving. My wife looked at me and asked, "Do you want to go inside for the Shabbat services?"

I turned to her and replied, "I don't want to ruin my first Shabbat in Istanbul because I know I will end up saying something unpleasant to the rabbi regarding his consideration for Jewish newcomers into the city who have come to spend a Shabbat service with their community. Therefore, not only will I not do a Mitzvot, but since it could turn out a blameworthy act if I did go inside, I won't."

We arrived at the Mediterranean Sea where fishermen already had their early catches in their boats and customers were standing in lines on the shore waiting to buy from them. People ordered the fish and the fishermen cleaned and put them into plastic bags and threw them to the customers fresh from their boats. Then the customer handed over the money to a person standing next to them on the shore. It was very interesting to watch, especially for the kids. There were ships that would take passengers (for a very small fare) from one side of the sea to the other—from the Asian section to the European district.

It was a very pleasant day, sunny, but still a little cold. We decided to go on one of the ship rides from one side of the sea to the other. It was a twenty-minute ride. Employees of the ship made their ways around with trays of hot tea for the customers for a small additional charge. We relaxed in the fresh open air.

When we arrived at the other side, we walked on the sidewalk next to the sea. There were many families who had come to enjoy their weekends there, picnicking amongst the big rocks that had accumulated on the shore. Some were barbequing steaks or making kebab while others were stood on the rocks and enjoyed fishing. There were different types of musicians who played live music and made an already beautiful weekend day more enjoyable for the seaside attendees. Passersby placed money into the baskets of the musicians. We enjoyed watching the view of homes built directly on the slope of the hills with colorful flowers around them. One could see large numbers of tourists from all around the world walking around, taking in and enjoying the beauty of Istanbul.

There were many sightseeing areas close to where we were. One of them was a large mosque with tall minarets around it. The front area of the mosque had benches and many people sat and relaxed, enjoying hot tea delivered to them on trays. Hundreds of pigeons flew around and walked by in the area for the people to feed them something. There were shops where one could buy different sorts of birds to keep as pets with cages. Looking at the colorful birds in cages was also pretty interesting for the kids.

We walked to a confectionary and bought ice cream although the weather was still a little cold, but it was very enjoyable nonetheless. We took a bus and went through the city. Finally, we returned to Taksim Square, where all kinds of restaurants were located. We wanted our kids to feel included, so we left the choice of what restaurant to eat at to them. They looked at the colorful pictures of the different meal dishes displayed on the windows of the restaurants and finally compromised with each other to choose one place. We honored their decision and followed them to the second floor of a modern restaurant that had a view of the main street filled with passersby.

We had a very good time at the restaurant and met some American tourists while there. A young man approached me and asked, "Are you here from America for a tour in Istanbul?" I replied "No. But I have been in America before, many years ago. My family and I are on our way to America now, with plans to stay in there in the future." Then I asked, "How come you asked me about America?"

He then replied, "Well, I saw your ring and recognized it. When somebody graduates from a university in America, they receive a ring that looks like yours." The young man and his family were touring Europe, and Turkey was to be their last stop. I wasn't very surprised by the presence of the young man and his family, because there were plenty of tourists from all over the world in Istanbul.

It's important to mention that the tourist industry of Turkey has always been one of the most profitable income sources for its government, and therefore the Turkish people respect tourists very much, they bring in a lot of business for the local economy.

We walked all the way to the end of the street, enjoying the weather, as well as window shopping, and listening to the different musicians who played performed not only in Turkish, but in languages from other countries, too.

We also paid a visit to the previous hotel where the rest of the group was staying in Istanbul, to say hello to them. We saw Pahlavan with his mother, who had arrived from Iran two days before Pahlavan's arrival. He introduced my family to his mother and we were very happy to meet her. Ghasem had not been at the hotel since we arrived in Istanbul, and nobody had seen or heard anything from him. Nader and Sara came by to the lobby where we were sitting and said hello to our group. There was talk amongst everybody that we all needed to get stamps on our passports to show that we had entered Turkey. Nader approached me and said, "I have a friend in Aksaray, and he has connections. Sara and I have given our passports to him to have them stamped. If you would like, I can take your passports to him. He charges $100.00 per person, which in your case will be $400.00 to cover your family. I might be able to get a $100.00 discount for you."

I then turned to him and said, "That's very expensive for me right now. One hundred dollars per person is too much. Let me think about it."

I eventually spoke with other people who had the same sort of passport stamping issue. A young man whom I had helped regarding his escapee case in Van approached me and said, "Mr. Hakimi, you helped me in Van, and now it's my turn to return the favor. Go to Aksaray, to the Happy Coffee Shop, and ask for Alireza. He charges only $50.00 per passport. It is going to be only $100.00 total for your entire family. If you try to bargain with him, he might even be able to give you some sort of a discount. Don't listen to Nader. He should be ashamed of himself. With all the help he received from you, he is still trying to make money off you instead of returning the favor. You helped him so much and this is the way he returns your favor. Shame on him."

I thanked him and my family and I left the hotel. We headed to our hotel to pick up our passports. Once we got to our hotel, I spoke to the manager in the lobby regarding our room change and he said, "Tomorrow. The room on the second floor will be ready for you then. I promise you that the room is going to be kept for you." At least that was a bit of good news for us.

We headed to Aksaray with our passports to meet Alireza. We found the coffee shop and entered. I asked for Alireza. A man came out and inquired, "Who is asking for Alireza?"

I turned to him and replied, "I have a message from one of his friends."

He waited for a moment and then said, "I am Alireza. What can I do for you?"

I shook hands with him and told him about our mutual friend and exactly why I was there with my family.

He walked to a table in the corner of the coffee shop and asked, "Do you have your passports with you?"

I looked around to make sure nobody was watching us or could overhear, and replied, "Yes. I have them in my pocket." I then asked, "Do you want me to get them out for you?"

He then suspiciously looked around as well and finally replied, "Go ahead. Bring them out and hand them to me under the table."

I handed him the passports and he examined both of them and said, "It usually costs $100.00 for both of these, but our mutual friend called me and told me that you helped him out very much in the past and that I should give you a descent discount. I will charge you only $75.00 for them. I have expenses too. I have to pay half of that to another guy, anyways."

I looked at him and then said, "Thank you."

As we were about to leave, he said, "It will take between two to three days until they are ready. Please don't say anything about what I charged you to anybody else because I gave you a very special deal."

I assured him and we left the coffee shop to browse in the nearby areas looking at the different shops. There were very beautiful and high-quality fabrics in one of the shops and my wife decided to buy some items from them to ship back to her sisters in Iran. The fabrics were very well priced compared to their costs in Iran. She bought fabric items for many of her relatives and then we headed back.

When we arrived back to our hotel, we were all very tired and exhausted. In the lobby I approached the manger and asked, "Where is the bathroom and shower?"

He walked us through the lobby where a couple people were watching television and then opened a door and said, "This is the bath. Most guests use the Turkish baths outside of the hotel, but you can use this one because you have children and it is difficult for you to go outside of the hotel." We rushed to our room and brought all our fresh clean clothing items to the shower. I gave our older son a good bath first, then did the same for my second son. After that I finally had the chance to take a shower myself. The kids and I sat and watched television while my wife took a shower. We returned to our room feeling very fresh and had dinner which included cold cuts and soft drinks.

The next day we had breakfast at one of the restaurants our kids had chosen for us and went to the old hotel to thank my friend for his help. I explained to him about the discount Alireza had given us because of his telephone call. Nader approached me and asked, "Have you decided about your passports?" He added, "This guy can take care of it for only another week."

I turned to him with a very cold and disappointed look and replied, "Thank you very much for being so considerate. I found another guy with a much cheaper price than your friends. If it is not too late for you, let me take you to him and he'll also do it for you less than the half price." I noticed he got my disappointed message. After all that I had done for him and his sister, whom we later found out were not related to each other at all (they had passed themselves off as brother and sister with fictitious names). That was the last time we saw Nader and Sara. We heard that they eventually went to Germany and from a specific station there smuggled themselves into East Berlin to join their friends who had the same political ideas.

We left the hotel and had plenty of time to kill. We went to a fair ground that had different games, and the kids had a lot of fun. For dinner, we returned to Taksim Square and walked around and met some of our friends who had come to Istanbul on the same bus from Van. We spoke for a few minutes and one of them complained about two members of our group, the so-called brother and sister. One of the friends said, "Everybody in the hotel was upset when they heard about Nader trying to take advantage of you."

I stopped him and said, "Forget about them. I helped and will continue to help anyone who escapes from Iran, as much as I can. They don't have the same political ideas as I do, but they were escaping the same Islamic Republic of Iran. There is an old saying, 'The enemy of my enemy is my friend.' Regardless, I'm glad everyone is here and that they can all finally go to their destinations."

On Monday morning, we had breakfast and headed to the ICMC (International Catholic Migration Commission), a Christian organization run by a Duke and Duchess from Switzerland. They donated their lives to taking care of refugees from different countries by helping them reunite with their families or relatives in the countries of their choice. The ICMC was within walking distance of Taksim Square.

When we got there, we walked into a room that was filled with refugees from Iran, Afghanistan, and other countries. I approached the desk and spoke to the receptionist. "Good morning. My family and I escaped from Iran and we are on our way to America to join the rest of my family. I was told that your organization can help us. That's why we are here today."

I noticed a man and a woman from two different rooms suddenly rush towards me and the woman said, "You speak English! We are very happy to see you." She invited my family and me into a conference room and offered us seats. After that she introduced herself, and the man as her husband, and then asked for my name. I introduced my wife, the kids, and myself. "You are from Iran, aren't you?" she asked.

I replied, "Yes."

Then the husband looked at me, and said, "We overheard you speaking English with the receptionist. Of course, we will try our very best to help you, but meanwhile we'd like your help with the many other Iranian escapees here who don't speak English or Turkish. Would you be willing to help us?"

My wife and I looked at each other with a smile, and I turned to her and whispered, "Here we go again." I saw some of the people whom had been with us in Van and whom I had helped with completing their documents sitting in the waiting room. I said, "I will help you as much as you need, but at the same time I hope you help me to get to America as soon as possible, too. I will only be helping you as a humanitarian gesture."

She shook hands with me and my wife, and then said, "We have devoted our lives to helping refugees and we appreciate all the assistance you can provide, as well." They made an appointment for us to return the next day at 9:00 a.m. sharp.

We walked out of ICMC and headed to an address I had on a piece of paper to meet a man who had received a suitcase from Iran through a friend of mine and also had $10,000.00 American dollars of my money. We arrived at his office and I knocked on his door. A young lady opened the door. "Can I help you?"

I showed him the name and address, which was written on the piece of paper. She looked at it and invited us into the office. A gentleman walked into the room a few moments later and greeted us. He then looked at me, and said, "I was worried. I expected you here three weeks ago. Our mutual friend called me many times and asked about you. I am very happy to see you. Let me call him and you can talk to him and give him the good news about your arrival." He used a punch-button telephone (which happened to be one of the most advanced telephones of the time) and handed me the receiver.

My friend picked up the line on the other side and without hesitation I said "Mohsen! My friend! Finally, I am here with our mutual friend. I want to thank you for all your help when I was in Iran. We arrived in Istanbul three days ago and I hope I will see you someday in person again, so that I can tell you what we had to go through just to get here."

He was very excited to hear from me and I could overhear him choking back tears as he spoke.

Our mutual friend then took the receiver and spoke to him over the phone. "Are you happy now? How many times have I told you that I'm sure they would eventually arrive?" He then calmly added, "Now my friend, relax. By the way, I have his money and the suitcase right here with me, and I will give them to him."

We spent an hour with the mutual friend and when we left his office I turned to my wife, and said, "Honey. It's amazing that two Armenians who escaped with us were so unappreciative at the end and even tried to cheat us, but this new friend is also an Armenian, and even thought we'd never even met him before, he had all our money and the unlocked suitcase with him. And it hasn't been touched at all. Good and bad can be found among all kinds of people." I had a special belt that had a zipper inside the belly. I put the money inside the belt and then wore the belt on my pants covered by my jacket.

The day had been a very good day. First we went to ICMC and made good connections with them in agreeing to help each other, and then we got our suitcase back safely along with the money so we could be sure that we wouldn't come up short. We visited the large park close to Taksim Square, where one of the top European bands played and entertained a large crowd. Attendees of the festival, both young and old, danced and had a very good time. By the edge of the park, Turkish women wearing beautiful and colorful local dresses sold large baskets of flowers. I picked up a bouquet of flowers and handed it to my wife. "Honey, I hope someday I can buy you flowers in America, in our own house."

She was very moved by the gesture and replied, "Thank you.

As they say, 'From your mouth to God ears.' I'm sure there will be a day when we will have our own home in America."

The next morning, we had breakfast and headed to ICMC. My wife and the kids went to stay at a nearby park to wait for me while I went to the office. I arrived a few minutes before 9:00 a.m. The secretary brought me to a room with a desk and a chair, and said, "This is your office. Please go ahead and sit behind your desk. I want to be the first to see you behind this desk. This seat is for the people you will help complete their documents for the United Nations Refugee Program."

The husband and wife from the day before came to my room with a bouquet of flowers in a vase and welcomed me. The wife put the flower vase on top of the desk, and said, "In Istanbul, you can find the most beautiful flowers. They come from farms from all around the city. You should see the flower girls that sell them. They are as pretty and beautiful as the flowers themselves."

I looked at the flowers and said, "Thank you very much. They are very beautiful, and you are right, the flower girls are very beautiful in their dresses, which show that they are from the different villages. In fact, yesterday after the concert, I bought a bouquet of various colorful flowers for my wife who was very happy to receive them."

As I sat behind the desk, I suddenly remembered my office in Iran. For a moment, I lost track of time and location, buried deep in my thoughts, until the secretary walked in with a fresh hot cup of Turkish coffee and a small plate of cookies. She placed both on my desk for me. For the first time, I really missed my country and my friends.

However, my thoughts were quickly interrupted by a young man who called out my name in Farsi. He extended his hand to shake.

I shook hands with him and before I had realized it, I had filled out a questioner with his information, which had roughly lasted a good hour. My very first file was ready for the United Nations Refugee Program. As he left, the secretary walked into my office and said, "Go ahead and take a ten-minute break, until I bring you your second case."

I looked at her and said, "Please bring him in. I am not tired."

A young man and a young girl walked into the office together. They greeted me in Farsi. I offered for them to sit down and noticed we had the only one chair for them. The door of the office opened and the secretary quickly brought in another chair. It turned out that they were really brother and sister, with real names and identification papers to prove it. They were from the same mother and father. They wanted to go to America to join their older brother, who was currently living there with his uncle. Eventually they wanted their parents to join them there as well.

I completed the third and fourth cases when the Duke and Duchess walked in. The Duchess then said, "You must be tired. Besides, we don't want to keep you away from your family for too long. We want to thank you very much for your cooperation and hope to see you again, tomorrow."

I turned to both of them and said, "I should really be thanking you, because you two have such big hearts. You left your luxury lives in Switzerland and came to Istanbul to help different people from different countries. What you are doing is very holy and admirable. I take my hat off to you two for your work."

The Duchess replied, "You know that your case is handled by the HIAS (Hebrew Immigrant Aid Society), which is a Jewish organization. We will complete your file and send it to them to arrange your trip to America. Of course, your cooperation, and how much we appreciate your help, will reflect in your file."

My wife and the kids were already in the waiting room as I came out of the office. The secretary asked, "Aren't you going to show your office to your wife and kids?"

I thanked her for her enthusiasm, and replied "Not now. Maybe some other time."

My older son asked, "Papa? Do you have an office? I thought we planned to go to America? Are we going to stay here?"

I looked at both of them and replied, "No. We are not going to stay here. But we have to be here for a few days. During that time, I will help out other people with their documents just like I did in Van. As soon as our file completes, we will go to Rome, in Italy, and then finally fly to America." I knew it was difficult for the kids to understand what I had just told them, so their mother tried to explain it in much simpler language. We got out of the office and decided to go to Aksaray, to meet with Alireza.

By now, we had learned the bus line and quickly got onto the bus. We went to the same coffee shop as before, and looked for Alireza about our passport stamps. It had been a few days, so we assumed they were ready.

"Are you looking for Alireza?" the owner of the coffee shop asked.

I replied, "Yes. Is he here?"

"No. He usually comes in at 7:00 p.m."

We had no choice but to wait, so we decided to go to the Dolmabache Sarayi (Dolmabache Palace), which is one of the most beautiful palaces in Istanbul. It's located directly on the Mediterranean Sea. The bus stopped at the end of the line and within five minutes we were right by the palace. There was a fast food restaurant directly next to the sea with colorful chairs and tables set out with large umbrellas. We decided to have lunch so the kids could taste the hamburger and French fries and soft drinks of the American-culture.

As I sat with the baskets of lunch, an old lady came by our table and looked at our food. I noticed she was hungry and seemed to be searching the other tables for leftovers. I offered her a seat next to us and gave her my basket of food. I bought another order for myself. The restaurant was filled with tourists and young people, and they all appeared to be surprised by my action.

When she finished her lunch, she looked at us and said something in Turkish. I couldn't understand her, but I knew she was grateful for the food. A young Turkish man who was there with his girlfriend and understood what she said noticed I was puzzled by the old lady's comments, He told me, "She thanks you for the lunch and wishes you and your family good luck. She especially prays for your kids."

I thanked him and said, "Please thank her on our behalf and tell her that it was our pleasure that she had lunch with us." I think having lunch with that old lady was one of the sweetest memories for all of us while in Istanbul.

We walked around the area until we finally headed back to Aksaray, to meet Alireza in the Happy Coffee Shop. We arrived at the coffee shop and met the owner. He approached us, and said, "I know you're here to meet Alireza, but unfortunately, he hasn't come in yet. He is late. Actually, he didn't come in last night either. All I can say is to just please sit down and have a cup of coffee and some soft drinks for the kids until he gets in."

We waited for three hours but there was no sign of Alireza. Finally, we left the coffee shop and headed to our hotel. On the way to the hotel my wife and I were very quiet. I turned around to my wife and said, "Honey. I don't know what's going on. We are here legally and the government of Turkey knows that we are escapee refugees. We actually don't need any passports. Let's not go crazy about it and lose sleep over it. I heard any passport from any country in Aksaray is very valuable. Some of the young tourists were murdered for their passports by thieves and smugglers. But don't you worry. At least we are here and our case is with ICMC. The worst scenario that can happen is that we have already lost our passports, but we are alive and well."

Although I was trying to cheer up my wife, in my head I was going crazy about having been so naive and stupid that without any research of whether we truly needed our passports to be stamped or not, I had handed them over. We arrived at the hotel and were very tired and exhausted from the day's activities. The kids wanted to watch television so we went into the lobby and sat down. My wife brought fresh clothing for all of us and said, "Now that nobody is here, I can take a bath and then you can give a bath to the kids and then watch television." We waited until she finished her bath and then I bathed the kids. We were very relaxed. After we had our dinner we watched television.

The following day, we had breakfast and I returned to the ICMC office. I met different refugees from Iran and completed their files so they were ready to be submitted to the United Nations for approval. It became routine that I completed at least five or six files to be sent to The United Nations each day. As usual, my wife and the kids spent time in the park where the kids enjoyed themselves and then came to the office to join me for the rest of the day. We had lunch in Taksim Square and then enjoyed a young English group's band until we finally headed back to Aksaray.

We entered the same coffee shop and the owner hurriedly rushed towards us, and said, "I have a message from Alireza for you. He told me your case is going to be ready tomorrow. Try to be here at 7:00 p.m., and have the money on you."

We left the coffee shop and headed to our hotel. As we arrived at our hotel, the manager called my name, and then added, "You have a message." He handed it to me on a piece of paper. There was a phone number and a name written on the paper. The manager dialed the phone number for me, and I ended up being connected to a young man. He was very excited that I had returned his call. "I went to Ankara, to the United Nations Refugee Program, and wanted to talk to someone regarding my escape from Iran. The head of the department is a man named Mr. Paterson. I can't speak English, so he gave me your name and the telephone number of your hotel, and told me to come to you and that you would write my biography and complete my file. He also told me to remember to not speak to you about money because you help out all the refugees who can't speak English as a humanitarian gesture. He told me to then bring him the file when it was ready."

"Where do you live, now?" I asked.

"In one of the hotels very close by within walking distance from you."

I walked to his hotel and wrote down his biography and completed his forms he had received from Mr. Paterson. I then returned to my hotel and noticed my wife and the kids were watching television in the lobby. We headed back to our room, which was on the second floor with a view of the street. It had a small sink and faucet, which was very helpful for us to wash our hands. This room was one of the best rooms the hotel could offer.

The next day as soon as we woke up, the kids got ready. My older son turned to my younger son, and said, "Hurry up. We have to go to breakfast and then Papa has to go to his office to work." The kids took my helping out at ICMC very seriously.

The day started and I completed another five to six files for different Iranian escapee refugees who all had different destinations. Some wanted to go to Canada, while others needed to get to England or different states in the United States. The majority of the refugees had relatives in either California or New York. Many of them asked me about America as soon as they heard that I had lived in America. Helping ICMC had become a joyful task for me.

I also was very anxious, however, to hear about the progress of the case for my family and myself with HIAS. At the end of the workday, which for me usually ended at 1:00 p.m., the Duke and Duchess thanked me for helping them, and the Duchess added, "We have already sent your documents to HIAS in Rome. We are waiting for their response. I have to let you know that HIAS usually takes three to four weeks to send back any news regarding any file. As I understand it, they have a lot of cases for Jewish refugees from different countries, but as soon as we get an answer from them we will let you know promptly."

Then the Duke turned to me and with a large smile said, "It's not that we want to keep you here to help us. We appreciate all the help and cooperation you have given us so far."

My family and I headed to Taksim Square, which had become the center of our attention. As we walked into the area, I saw the friend who had introduced Alireza to us. He walked up to us and asked, "Did you get your passports stamped by Alireza?"

I replied, "Unfortunately, not yet. We went to the coffee shop a few times, but there was no sign of him. In fact, we are worried about our passports. The last time we went to see him, the owner of the coffee shop had a massage from him for us that today at 7:00 p.m. we should be there with the money.

My friend said, "I'm sure he will be there with the stamped passports. I'm going to give him a call, too." That was very good news for us.

There were always different activities going on in Taksim Square. It had very good restaurants, and musicians who played on the sidewalk. There were all sorts of people walking up and down the streets, which made the atmosphere pretty cheery. When we entered a restaurant for lunch, our waitress told us about a park on a hill with a view of the sea which, wasn't very far from where we were. She said "When you are at the park, the waiter will bring you a samovar and a pot of tea atop it from the coffee shop and will set it on your table. You serve your own tea and if you have sweets or cookies you can enjoy the good weather and the view while the children play." She then offered, "In fact, why don't you buy some cookies from here and take them with you? You can have a very relaxing afternoon."

We decided to go to the park to kill some time until 7:00 p.m. when we were to go get our passports from Alireza at the Happy Coffee Shop. We stayed until it was about time to go meet Alireza, and then we left.

We arrived at the coffee shop and entered ten minutes earlier than our appointment. The shop owner approached us and said, "Alireza is on his way, and will be here in about thirty minutes." We had no choice but to sit and wait for him.

Alireza finally walked into the coffee shop from the back door at about 7:30 p.m. He came directly to our table and greeted us. Then he reached into his pocket and brought our passports out. "Here you are. Sorry it took longer than I expected, but sometimes my connection guy goes out of town for a day or two and unfortunately it happened right when your passports were with me." He handed me the passports and pointed at the stamps.

I paid him $75.00 cash for the passport stamps and we left the coffee shop. We got on the bus and headed to our hotel. It was dark.

But the beauty of Istanbul at night with its sparkling lights both on the streets and across its homes, along with the reflections of the ferry boats upon the sea, appeared more and more stunning. We purchased some food-to-go from a nearby restaurant and returned to our hotel. Sitting in the lobby, we had our dinner while we watched Turkish singers on television. Although we didn't understand the words, the melody of the song and the dancers in the band made it really very interesting and enjoyable.

It had become a routine schedule for us to go to ICMC every morning after breakfast. In fact, helping the refugees not only kept me busy for a few hours, but it also made me feel like I wasn't wasting my time. Every afternoon, after my work at the ICMC was done, my *family and I discovered a new and interesting place to visit. We decided to go to the Kapali Carsi* (Turkish, *Grand Bazaar)*, of Istanbul. It reminded us of the bazaar in Tehran, Iran. One could spend hours and hours at the Grand Bazaar and not feel tired. The glow of the jewelry shops' gold and diamonds on one street, or the numerous leather shops on another, along with the hustle and bustle of visitors from everywhere, made it a very interesting visit on any day. The bargaining of customers with merchants at the bazaar was also another reminder of those in Iran. Although we had become accustomed to bargaining with merchants, it was still interesting to see the European or American tourists try to bargain for something they wanted to purchase.

I have to mention the amazing coffee shops and restaurants with their different menus and dishes along with their appetizing smells, which seemed to pull everyone in to enjoy their meals. The kids noticed a restaurant with rotisserie chicken in the window, which rolled in front of a fire pit cooking, so we decided to have chicken for lunch. A meal of chicken, French fries, bread and soft drinks was so favored by the kids that we had to go every other day for them to have some.

Days and weeks passed and almost every other day we went to the telephone station to make phone calls to our relatives in Iran, the United States, and Israel. The telephone station had many telephone booths. As I entered the station, someone directed me to a booth. After I picked up the receiver, the operator would then ask, "Where do you want to call? And what is the number?" I would tell her and then she would connect me. At least I didn't have to have a lot of change and someone next to me to drop coins into the phone for me to speak. Calling and being able to speak to our relatives was a way of releasing the pressures from our situation.

But after a while, I noticed my wife, the kids, and myself included, all getting tired of the same schedule every day. I talked to the Duke and Duchess about our case and if they had heard anything at all from HIAS. "It's been almost more than two months. I have tried to complete many files for the refugees who come into your office. Many of them went to Ankara themselves and met with Mr. Peterson. They called me and asked me to complete their files for them. Mr. Peterson also recognizes my handwriting whenever a refugee calls me over to complete their file for them. From the refugees Mr. Peterson always asks, 'Did Mr. Hakimi complete it for you, and did he write your biography for you?' I should add that helping the ICMC and others who came by after hearing about me from their friends was also a blessing for me too. I want to ask you to, please, call HIAS and make sure that we are still on their list and let them know that we are waiting anxiously for their response."

Both Duke and Duchess were very much moved with my request. "Believe us, Mr. Hakimi, we understand very well what you are talking about. You have been a great help to us and we appreciate it. We are going to call them and put pressure on them."

Being in a strange land, especially with kids, for almost four months moving from one village to another, taking refuge in different homes and traveling from one city to the next, and then finally end up here in Istanbul with all its charms and beauties, was all becoming tiresome. We tried to keep the kids as happy and cheerful as we could. My wife and I could understand the bureaucratic system and red tape, but how could one expect small kids ages five and six to understand it? We knew that we should've been very happy that our kids were cooperative and understanding. We tried to remember that, but on some days, unfortunately, the beauty of the city of Istanbul would become dull. When the weather was cloudy and cold, one could feel the smell of the burning coal smog in the air. It was very strong and made everybody cough. Nobody liked the cloudy weather and looked forward to seeing a sunny and breezy day to take the smog away. On sunny days, people went to the coast and had picnics.

One morning, after I had already completed my second case at the ICMC, the Duchess walked into my office with a note and said, "I have good news for you from HIAS. I know that you and your family have been waiting for this. I just received a message that your file has been approved and within two to three weeks you will be flying to Italy." She then added, "You are welcome to go to the park and join your wife and kids for the rest of the day."

I noticed that there were three other Iranian refugees waiting for me to complete their files. "No. Thank you. By the time I finish these three files, my wife and the kids will arrive and then you can tell them the good news." I was very happy and was able to complete the remaining files very quickly. The secretary walked into the office with a cup of coffee and cookies. She put them on my desk and said, "We just got used to having you in the office and to seeing your family every day, but pretty soon you will be leaving us. I never thought that time would fly by so fast. I can't believe it's already been two and a half months since the first day you and your family came to ICMC."

A few minutes later, my wife and kids walked into the waiting room and the secretary brought them to my office. Then the secretary called in the Duke and Duchess so they could give my wife the good news. I could see relief and happiness in my wife's face.

The kids looked at us with curious faces, wondering why the Duchess hugged them and said, "You two were very good children for your parents. Also, your parents tried to make the best for you. We are glad to tell you that very soon you will be going to Italy and from there to America."

Again, the Duchess turned to me and said, "In the morning, I am going to send your file to the Chief of Police in Istanbul. He will arrange a police escort in a civilian suit for you. That is going to take about a week. While we wait for a final travel schedule from HIAS, the police documents will become ready, too."

As we left the office, I said, "Tomorrow I will be here 9:00 a.m. sharp. I know there are other files to be completed. I will try to help you as much as I can before my family and I leave Turkey." We thanked them for the good news and left.

Under our circumstances, every bit of good news made us very happy. We decided to enjoy another concert in the park and danced with the kids amongst the other attendees. We celebrated the good news in a luxurious and fancy restaurant on the second floor of Taksim Square. I will never forget that night. A complete dinner starting with an appetizer, soup, salad, and fresh fish served with chilled white wine complimented the night in a very relaxing environment, which also included live Turkish musicians who came to our table and sang Turkish songs for us. I handed each of the kids some paper money to tip the musicians.

After the dinner, we walked into the Taksim area. Even the kids were so happy and excited about the good news that they wanted to continue the celebrations and not go back to the hotel at our usual time. But it was late. I called a taxi and we headed back to our hotel. As we walked into the lobby, the manager approached me and handed me a message on a small piece of paper. As I read the message, he dialed the telephone number on the paper. A family of four refugees wanted me to complete their files. I spoke to the man of the refugee household and asked him to come by ICMC with all their documents the next day at 9:00 a.m. sharp.

Another day started. Everybody was very happy and energetic. Although we still had to wait for at least another two to three weeks to leave, we knew we were already on our way. We were now one more step closer to our main goal. I went to the office and the family of four walked in on time as I had requested. I started their files and finished all of them as quickly as I could. Three more applicants were already waiting in the waiting room and I completed their documents and files as well. I wanted to help as many as I could while I was still there in Istanbul.

It was Thursday and we had to go to the police station. The Duchess had already notified me to be there by 1:00 p.m. When I finished my work at ICMC, I called a taxi and within fifteen minutes arrived in front of the police station. We walked into the station and asked for the police chief. The officer at the reception desk asked for my name and the reason why we were there. When I explained it to him he said, "Sit down until we call you."

We waited about an hour before they finally called us in. The police chief looked at our passports and with a smile on his face said something in Turkish and the other officers in the room laughed. I ignored them and stayed quiet. The officer then spoke to me in Turkish.

I looked at him, and said, "I'm sorry. I don't speak Turkish. I speak English." Although he knew our file was already there through ICMC, it seemed he was trying to give us a hard time. He looked at me, and sarcastically said, "No English. No English. Turkish. German." As soon as I heard German, I spoke in German to him, and said, "I speak German." Then I asked, "What seems to be the problem? We are here from ICMC, and the Duke and Duchess are very good friends of ours."

With an angry voice and speaking in German he shouted, "Go and sit down! I will let you know about your papers!"

We sat and waited for another hour until he finally asked me to approach his desk. He then said, "You have to pay $100.00 for the airport tax."

I stared at him and said, "No way. The airport tax is in the airport, and it's not $100.00. It's around $10.00. When I get to the airport to depart, I will pay the taxes then."

He noticed that I was getting upset and that I was familiar with the procedure. One of the other officers said something to him in Turkish. He then looked at me and then suddenly handed me all our documents with all their required stamps. We hurriedly left the police station and I could feel my body shaking from the anger caused by that officer. I was really upset. We quickly headed to Taksim Square, as though if we had missed being there one day our day would not have been complete.

Another task was quickly added to my list of activities in Istanbul. A young man came by the hotel and asked me to help him with the American Consulate for his visa. I eventually made a few trips to the American consulate for him and other refugees during the last two weeks of our stay in Istanbul. The first time I was at the American Consulate, I introduced myself and told them that they could call the ICMC and ask about me. I just wanted to help the refugees. They must have already spoken with ICMC because as soon as I walked into the consulate one of the employees called me over. I must have made ten trips total to the consulate. The following day at the ICMC, the Duchess became very upset when I told her about the behavior of the police officer at the police station.

I said, "It's okay. The officer tried to cheat us out of $100.00, but he couldn't. We don't care. We just want to get on with our journey."

We knew that the following Friday, in seven days, we were going to fly to Rome. When I was about to leave the office, the Duchess came to me and said, "Come with your family to the office Monday morning at 9:00 a.m. because Mr. Peterson is going to drop by. He wants to thank you in person for your assistance, on behalf of the United Nations Refugee Program. He is very happy with you. He will see you Monday morning. Have a good weekend."

We left the office and headed back to the hotel to have dinner and relax.

Monday morning came. We all dressed nice, had breakfast, and then headed to the ICMC office. On the way there, I bought a bouquet of flowers. Mr. Peterson, the Duke, and the Duchess were all waiting in the lobby to greet us. The Duchess approached, turned to Mr. Peterson and said, "I present to you Mr. Hakimi and his beautiful family." She then turned to me, and added, "This is Mr. Peterson who flew in from Ankara just to meet you and your family."

I shook hands with Mr. Peterson and said, "I am very honored and happy to meet you, Mr. Peterson." He then shook hands with my wife and said "We are very proud for what you and your husband did for the Iranian refugees during your stay in Istanbul. I understand he was given the same assignment in Van. Many Iranian refugees have come by my office and told me about him."

My wife waited a few seconds and said, "I really didn't do much. That was my husband who helped in Van and here."

"You get the same credit as your husband," said Mr. Peterson, "because you took care of the kids so he would be able to help us."

The secretary invited all of us into the conference room. There were both American and Turkish coffees, tea, and different kinds of baklava, as well as other sweets and cookies. Mr. Peterson turned to me again. "You are a very kindhearted person. I'm sure you will be successful in your life. But if you ever need any help, remember that we are all here for you and your family."

I was genuinely moved by all the appreciation and gratitude. Mr. Peterson excused himself and left to the airport to get back to his office in Ankara. My wife and the kids spent some time with the Duke and Duchess while I completed four more files for the waiting families at the office.

Afterward, we shopped for souvenirs from Istanbul and when we got back to our hotel we were in the mood for traveling again. Six of the young men who lived nearby came to our hotel and offered their help with our suitcases for when the taxi came to take us to the airport. I turned to them and said, "We are not leaving until Friday. We still have time."

Wednesday was my last day of work at the ICMC. When I finished and my wife and kids arrived, we all said our final goodbyes to the Duke and the Duchess, as well as to the secretary. Before we were out of the ICMC building, the Duchess turned to me and said, "You have to be ready with all your suitcases and outside of your hotel at exactly 7:30 a.m., Friday morning."

"I know," I replied, "and believe me, we will be ready when the police come by with a taxi to take us to the airport."

My wife turned to the Duchess and said, "Mr. Hakimi will be ready outside of the hotel at 7:00 a.m. I know him. He always wants to be early, rather than being late."

It had been almost three months since the first day we had walked into the ICMC building and I still couldn't believe that time had flown by so fast.

It was Friday morning and we were ready and waiting outside of our hotel with all our suitcases at 7:00 a.m. Our young friends had brought our suitcases down for us and stayed with us as we waited. It was 7:30 a.m. but still no sign from the taxi. 8:00 a.m. came and still nothing. We started to worry about our scheduled 10:00 a.m. flight. I called the ICMC several times, but it wasn't until 8:45 a.m. when the secretary finally picked up the phone. As soon as I said "Hello" she answered, "Good morning, Mr. Hakimi. I hope that you are calling from the airport."

"Unfortunately, not yet. We have been waiting for the police to arrive with our taxi since exactly 7:00 a.m. sharp, but there hasn't been a sign of them." I then added, "What are we going to do now?"

"The Duke and the Duchess just walked in. Please talk to The Duchess."

The Duchess took the phone. "Hello, Mr. Hakimi. What's going on?"

I told her we were still waiting for the taxi.

"You just stay put and give the telephone receiver to the manager of the hotel. I promise you that your plane is not going to take off without you and your family."

I gave the receiver to the hotel manager. After he talked and hung up the manger told me the instructions he had received from the Duchess. The Duchess told the manager to keep his telephone line open just for me and my family, because she was going to call back in a few minutes. The Duchess called back about thirty minutes later and said, "I spoke to the top police chief of Istanbul and he has promised to send another policeman along with a taxi right away. I also talked to the airport about you and your family and they are going to delay the flight until you get on board. Meanwhile, I made arrangements with the customs officials at the airport so that they take care of you as soon as you arrive so you can leave quickly and don't have to wait. I also would like to let you know that the police officer who caused the delay by not showing up will be punished for it."

The Taxi arrived at our hotel and as soon as the trunk of the taxi opened, my young Iranian friends transferred everything we had into it and we quickly left. It took us a good thirty minutes to get to the airport. The officer that was in a civilian suit had all our documents and our tickets. He started to go from one window to another calling my name. The checking in didn't take more than ten minutes. It was the law that the passengers had to pay for taxi fare both ways if they were refugees. I had more than the needed Turkish lira to pay for the fare. I gave my extra Turkish lira to the officer. He escorted us right up to the plane. All of the other passengers had already been on board for more than an hour and a half. The official of the airport announced that the reason for the delay was mechanical and as soon as we boarded the plane, the mechanical difficulty was fixed and we readied for takeoff.

CHAPTER 11

The Trip to Italy

As our plane took off from the Ata Turk Airport to our last stop before our final destination of Rome, my family and I felt pretty exhausted. Maybe it was the aggravations caused by the delay with the police that made us feel this way. We thought for sure we were going to miss our flight. When I called the Duchess and spoke to her, I didn't realize how important and influential a person she was in Istanbul. She had many different authority contacts to call the airport and have them delay the flight. When we arrived at the airport, the officer moved from one window to another mentioning my last name so that the officials were aware and ready with our family's necessary papers. In ten minutes, we were ready to board the plane. Within fifteen minutes, the hostess came to our seats with refreshments and different cookies for the four of us and welcomed us on board. She then said, "We were worried about you. We had your names and your family name on our list of passengers. You were the only passengers absent and the head of operations at the airport called us and ordered us to delay the flight until he called again and gave us permission to fly. We know you had a bad start today and waited so long without having breakfast so please relax and enjoy your flight."

Another hostess approached us soon with hot breakfast for me and my family. I turned to my wife, and said, "Honey, the Duke and Duchess are very, very, influential people in this country. What we expedited this morning is incredible. I am so happy that I helped them with their holy mission during our stay in Istanbul."

As soon as we finished our breakfast the plane started its final approached into the Athens Airport, in Greece. We had a layover which gave us a chance to walk into the passenger transit area and buy several souvenirs. We got back on board and I was happy to see that most of the passengers were new, because some of them had been somewhat upset about the delay of the plane's takeoff, and I could see they blamed us for it.

We finally arrived in Rome. As we finished up with the formalities of going through customs, we grabbed our suitcases and walked out. There we saw an Italian man who had a sign in his hand with my name on it, waiting for us.

I approached him and introduced myself and he introduced himself as Mario. "I work for HIAS. I am here to take you to your *pensione* (Italian for *boarding room*), in Rome. Your place is ready and it's located very close to all the tourist sites and attractions." While he drove us out of the airport towards the city, he turned to me, and asked, "Have you ever been to Rome before?"

"Yes. My wife and I were in Rome when we were on our honeymoon and we loved it. We also spent some good times in Venice and Milan, along with other nearby European countries. It's another chance for us to see Rome again."

Mario drove while he listened to the car radio. There was extraordinary excitement in the city of Rome. I noticed that people were jumping up and down and congratulating each other. I had a feeling there had been some type of good news on the radio that caused celebration. I asked Mario, "What is going on that the people are so happy about?"

He replied, "Don't you know that the Italian football team has won one of their games? That's why everybody is happy."

On the way to our new temporary home, Mario tried to show

us the city as much as he could, but it was obvious he wanted to listen to the radio and enjoy the accomplishments of the Italian team as well, which was okay with us.

We finally arrived at our Italian boarding room, a five-story building with luxurious rooms and a lobby that had a television on which to watch the 1984 Olympics in Los Angeles, California. It was then I realized that the Italian team had won a game in the Olympics and that was why the people were so overjoyed.

Mario helped us with our suitcases to our room, and before leaving said, "Monday morning I will pick you up at 9:00 a.m. to go to HIAS."

We freshened up and at 7:00 p.m. had dinner at the dining room of the *pensione*. We then left to go sightseeing. Being in Rome at that time was like a dream come true after what we had gone through with the revolution in Iran. My wife and I looked at each other and then to our kids. I turned to her, and said, "Honey, let's go to Fontana. The last time we were here was on our honeymoon and now being with our kids is going to have a special merit for them. I am sure the kids would like the statues and the fountains. It's fun to watch the tourists throw coins into the fountain. Maybe someday our kids will get the chance to come back and see this place again as adults. We did it a few years ago and now thank God we are here again with the fruits of our lives, our kids. Above all, we are all healthy and well."

We walked to Fontana and strolled around it until we sat on the edge of the main Fontana statue and enjoyed ice cream. Before we left, we explained the story behind the Fontana to our kids. We told them that when someone throws coins into the Fontana, they wish that someday in the future they will get the chance to return and see it again. I turned to my wife, and asked, "Remember when we were here for our honeymoon, and we threw coins into the Fontana? Our prayers have been answered. We are both here again, but now with our kids."

On the way home, we enjoyed walking amongst the many people of Rome. Once back, we headed to our room, but the manager called me over to the reception desk. "I know that this is your first day here," he said. "Breakfast is served from 7:00 a.m. until 9:30 a.m. Try to make it, otherwise we won't be able to serve anything until 12:30 p.m."

I thanked him and on the way into the elevator, I turned to my wife and said, "This guy is worried about breakfast and us being on time. He doesn't know what we had to go through to get here. It was like a fictional story, but he has to do his job."

Saturday and Sunday were the weekends and we enjoyed the parks, shops, and restaurants. Finally, Monday morning arrived. We had our breakfast and waited for Mario to come back and take us to HIAS. He arrived at 9:00 a.m. sharp and we headed to HIAS.

Once there, we entered the building and went into a waiting room. A few minutes later we met Mrs. Toneh, who was the person in charge of our case. My family and I looked very sharp and well-dressed. Mrs. Toneh greeted us and said, "Finally, you are here and on your way to America.'"

"I hope very soon," I replied, "because it has been a very difficult escape for all of us, especially for the kids. Thank God we are one step closer to our destination."

She turned to my wife. "It must have been a difficult situation for you and your kids. It might have been much easier for all of you if you had left by plane legally, and your husband, who had problems with the Iranian regime, would have escaped by himself."

My wife didn't like Mrs. Toneh's comments. She turned to her and replied, "First of all, my husband wasn't in trouble with the regime. Secondly, he had a very responsible and important job position. In fact, he was given a promotion after the so-called 'revolution' had been going on for a while. He is Jewish and his boss appreciated his work, but there were some low-class, uneducated *pasdars* who created problems for him at work. Unfortunately, the bosses couldn't stop them, because they would cause problems for everyone. My husband wanted me to leave the country with our kids, but I didn't want to leave him behind. Besides, our passport was confiscated on account that we were Jewish. I'm not sorry about my decision. I'm glad that we are all here together."

Mrs. Toneh shrugged and said, "I'm sorry. I didn't want to criticize you. Of course, every family has their own alternatives. We are very happy that you are out of that revolution-stricken country. We have heard similar stories from different people who have escaped or somehow were able to leave the country legally by plane or by bus many times over again."

It took us about three hours to go through the formalities of completing the necessary documents at HIAS. Finally, Mrs. Toneh said, "You will stay in the same *pensione* for one week and next Friday you will have to go to Ladispoli, a resort city by the beach, which is about one hour from here. Of course, we will see you before Friday anyway. Now that you have put your hard times behind you, enjoy yourselves and share good times with your kids until you go to Ladispoli."

In the late 1970's and until the 1990's, Ladispoli served as a refugee transit point for Soviet emigrants, most of whom were seeking better economic opportunities as well as political or religious freedom in western countries, mostly The United States, Canada, and Australia. Among them were refugees from Iran who had to wait for their documents to be completed by the HIAS. There was actually a good program that allowed refugees to stay in a *pensione* for a week, and enjoy the luxury of being in Rome, but not have to worry about room and board. This allowed refugees to sightsee in Rome at the same time. During the week of our stay at the *pensione*, we had to go see Mrs. Toneh two more times until it was finally time to go to Ladispoli. To get to Ladispoli, it was procedure that from the time one leaves the *pensione* the refugees are on their own until the HIAS sends word through a messenger to finally meet up.

It was Friday and we packed our suitcases and took the bus to Ladispoli. The sky was cloudy and it felt like it was going to rain. The HIAS had previously given us an address of a building in Ladispoli where mostly Iranian Jews stayed. A Rabbi from Chabad was there, who had made a small synagogue in the building. Most of the Iranian Jews were observing the Shabbat and had good knowledge of Judaism. We were halfway to Ladispoli when it started to rain. We arrived at the last bus stop in Ladispoli and waited for a while in the station, hoping the rain would stop soon. There was a small break in the weather and we were able to head to the address we were going. There were no taxis or any other forms of transportation therefore we walked. By the time we had finally arrived at the address, all of us were soaking wet from the rain. We head into the building, which was located right next to the beach.

The Rabbi approached us and said, "You must be tired, and as I can see you're wet." He then asked, "Who sent you here?"

I replied, "Your address was given to me by the HIAS."

The rabbi asked a couple of young men to help us carry our suitcases to the second floor to a large room set up for all four of us. It had a view of the beach as well as its own bathroom and shower. It was really like a blessing to be there. We took the kids out of their wet clothing and gave each of them a shower. We then freshened up ourselves and readied for a good Shabbat night.

We walked down to the large room and started helping with the setup for Shabbat. The rabbi along with the congregation performed the Shabbat reading and everyone sat at the long tables that had been prepared, to start the Shabbat dinner. The ceremony of the wine blessing and the challah bread ritual were carried out and dinner was served for all of the participants. The rabbi welcomed my family and me, and introduced us to the others. We knew some of the people who were there and, in fact, some of them happened to be my wife's relatives.

The rabbi started his speech about the morning's Torah reading and then the joyfulness of Shabbat was completed with the singing of different religious songs. I looked at my wife and said, "Quite different from the first Shabbat night we had in Istanbul."

She said, "Forget about it. We are here and hopefully in the near future, we will be in America to start a new, free, happy life."

Everybody helped clean up and then set the room up for the upcoming Shabbat Morning Prayer. The sounds of *Shabbat Shalom*

(Hebrew for *Peace on Shabbat)* could be heard everywhere as people greeted each other. We arrived into our room and within a few minutes we all fell asleep with the sounds of the waves crashing on the shore in the background. It was a beautiful and holy Shabbat night. It was made even more so because we had the opportunity to be amongst our fellow Jews, especially after the difficult escape that we had endured.

I woke up in the morning to the sounds of the ocean breeze and the waves crashing on the shore. It was a beautiful Shabbat morning with fresh air and the sky was sunny. I put on casual clothing and went to walk on the beach. I walked a good half hour by the ocean and enjoyed the cool relaxing weather.

Afterward, I came back to our room. We all got dressed and went down for breakfast and the Saturday morning Shabbat services. After breakfast the room in which we ate was cleaned (with the help of the congregation) and converted into a synagogue for the Shabbat services.

Shabbat services started and the rabbi asked me to carry the holy Torah through the congregation so that everyone could get a chance to touch it. When it was time for the third *Alliah* (blessing), the rabbi asked me to approach the Torah and read it out loud. That moment while reading the blessing made me find and make peace with myself and forget about the last five years of hardship and misery that my family and I had been through. It was one of the best days of my life that I will never forget. At the end of the services, everybody celebrated the resting day with songs and dancing.

The rabbi asked me to help him with the work of the synagogue and the Iranian Jews. Every day, and especially on Shabbat services, he made speeches in English. I translated these speeches for the others in attendance. The congregation, which was mostly made up of Iranians and included Russians and Romanian refugees, as well, ended its services with happy songs sang both in Hebrew and Farsi.

One day the rabbi said, "You have to be in the HIAS tomorrow, at 9:00 a.m. Mrs. Toneh wants to speak to you. She has some questions regarding your file."

That was a good excuse for my family and I to go back to Rome. The next morning, we arrived at the HIAS on time and met with Mrs. Toneh. She turned to me and said, "You know that we have many Iranian families that come to us because they want to go to America. Most of them need someone to translate for them. If you agree, I want you to be here when they arrive. I will send a message to you through the rabbi. Of course, we know you have to pay for your own transportation, therefore you will be compensated. If you agree to help us, we will be very grateful."

I said, "I have been helping everybody on our escape route and I worked for the ICMC everyday four to five hours, just to help them as a humanitarian act. Of course, I will help you."

Mrs. Toneh said, "There is actually an Iranian family here and we can start right away."

My wife and the kids waited in the waiting room and I met with the Iranian family. I completed their files for them and gave them instructions about the *pensione* that they had to stay in and told them not to worry about anything while their preliminary processing is carried out. I told them they would eventually head to Ladispoli after a week.

My family and I left and spent the day sightseeing in Rome. We called our relatives in different countries and hearing their voices was a real boost of morale for us. Although we were at the last stop of our trip before leaving for America, I felt that each one of us wanted to get to our destination as soon as possible.

I had to go to Rome and complete the files of the newcomers roughly four times a week. One day, I met a new family who had arrived in Rome by plane with a fixed passport and they had no idea how difficult it had been for the many others who had escaped from the borders through the mountains to gain their freedoms. As I completed their files and told them about the *pensione* they would be staying at, the husband turned to me and asked, "Where do you live?"

"In a city within an hour from here, called Ladispoli," I replied.

He then turned to Mrs. Toneh, and in Farsi said, "We will not go to a *pensione*. I want to go to Ladispoli." While pointing at me, he then added, "Where he lives." It seemed we had a dilemma right away. I tried explaining to him, but he didn't want to listen at all.

Finally, Mrs. Toneh said, "Okay. It actually saves some expenses for a family of four living seven days in a *pensione*. But he has to pay for everything in Ladispoli, just like everybody else." Mario, the driver for the HIAS, came to take their suitcases into his van. Before we knew it, all of us were on our way to Ladispoli. It was about 1:00 p.m., on Friday.

As soon as we got to the synagogue, I asked the lady and her kids to stay in our apartment with my own wife and kids. I went with her husband to look for an apartment to rent for them. The husband and I transferred the suitcases with a four-wheeled bicycle into the apartment we had found and rented for this man and his family, and then returned to my apartment.

My wife had previously purchased chicken from the store of the synagogue and had already made the Shabbat meal. It was a good thing she made more than enough for ourselves so that we could feed our unexpected guests. Soon afterward, we were in the synagogue and the Shabbat night services had started.

I later heard that the seven-day *pensione* service in Rome was cancelled for Iranian refugees after the experience of the family who didn't want to go to it. Anytime I got a call from the HIAS, I had an apartment readied for a newcomer family because after the completion of their files, Mario would bring us all back to Ladispoli.

We had a visiting rabbi from Milan in Italy who had heard about the Iranian refugees. The visiting rabbi's name was Namezar, He was born in Iran, moved to Italy and was very active in helping the young Jewish boys and girls before and during the revolution. He was very happy to see a large Jewish Iranian group of men, women and children gathered in Ladispoli and helped the rabbi there with the synagogue.

Rabbi Namezar stayed in Ladispoli for a few weeks and enjoyed his visit with the congregation. He shared his thoughts with us on Shabbat services, but spoke in Farsi, so I had to translate for the English-speaking Russians. We really had very good memories with him during his stay in Ladispoli.

Every once in a while the synagogue had a rabbi visit from Rome. The main rabbi in Rome came to our synagogue and was impressed by its setup. Men sat in front of the congregation and women were separated by a small distance behind them. The rabbi from Rome took the holy Torah to the women so they could touch and kiss it. He then placed the Torah on the podium and read from it for the congregation.

Time passed, and The Month of Av of the Hebrew calendar arrived. The Ninth of Av is the fasting day of the Jewish people to observe the unfortunate destruction of the holy Jewish temple called the Beit Ha Mighdash, which was destroyed twice within four-hundred years. The First Temple was totally destroyed by the Babylonians when they sacked the city. The construction of the Second Temple was authorized by Cyrus the Great after the fall of the Babylonian Empire the year before. The Second Temple was destroyed by Antiochus who wanted to Hellenize the Jews. The Jews rebelled and Antiochus, in a rage, retaliated in force. The Jews became incensed when the religious observances of Shabbat and circumcision were officially outlawed. When Antiochus erected a statue of Zeus in their temple and Hellenic priests began sacrificing pigs (the usual sacrifice offered to the Greek gods in the Hellenic religion), their anger began to spiral. Greek officials ordered a Jewish rabbi to perform a Hellenic sacrifice. The Jewish rabbi refused to perform one, so then he was killed at once. Many of the rabbis were killed within days for refusing to bow to the statue of Zeus and not performing the Hellenic sacrifice.

The entire congregation gathered in the sanctuary of the synagogue. All the chairs were folded and put away. Everyone had to sit on the ground as a symbol of mourning for the loss of our Holy Temple. Then the rabbi had a pile of hard-boiled eggs, which we had to dig in the ashes representing the ashes of our Holy Temple and eat them. All the reading of that night and the next day was done while the congregation sat on the ground.

Unfortunately, I noticed that a lot of our Russian Jews did not know the ceremony, due to the fact they were under strict regulation of practicing Judaism, but they were eager to hear about it. The rabbi explained to them in Russian, and when he explained the Ninth of Av in English, I translated for the Iranian Jews. I turned to my wife and said, "It really breaks my heart to see how these Jewish Russian brothers and sisters were denied their religion, and yet are so eager to find their roots and their history. Thank God at least under the religious suppression, they stayed Jewish and know that they are Jewish and that they didn't dissolve among the other religions in Russia."

"You are right," replied my wife, "and they really should be very grateful for The United Stated, and through political negotiation with the Russians, securing their freedom and permission to go to America."

During our stay, the congregation of the synagogue always stayed almost the same. There were newcomers and at the same time some were en route to their destinations in different states of the U.S. There were days that we walked to the beach and enjoyed a relaxed day, having a picnic by the beach with sandwiches and soft drinks. That gave me a good chance to teach my sons to swim. There were other times that my wife stayed at the apartment and I went with my sons alone to the beach. When we came back to the apartment, my wife had a beautiful table set with her delicious lunch ready for us. I could see that she missed her own house and tried to make us feel good. Every time I thanked her for the delicious lunch, and to complement her cooking brought her a bottle of red or white wine. "Honey, I promise you very soon, we will have our own house in America and you can cook your delicious lunches and dinners just as before."

The following Monday morning I went to Rome to take care of the newcomers, but this time a bunch of young boys and girls (more than usual) arrived at the HIAS. Some of them spoke a little English, but Mrs. Toneh wanted me to handle their files anyway, and bring them to Ladispoli. The young bunch brought a new spirit to our congregation. Previously, there were only two young men who had been in Ladispoli about five or six months and both of them had knowledge of Hebrew laws. In fact, one of them was a Cohen who completed our congregation. The rabbi was very excited with the arrival of the young people. We were getting more and more newcomers, but at the same time some of the people whose visas had come through were leaving for America.

Soon Rosh Hashanah (the Hebrew New Year) was around the corner. Rosh Hashanah was a day of joy and happiness and the young crowed made it more fun for everybody. The rabbi had two young rabbis from one of the yeshiva Jewish schools as a guest for a week.

On Friday afternoon we noticed that the two young rabbis brought some fabrics and covered the separation between men and women and said we had to have a *mekhisa* for the Friday night and Shabbat services. The congregation, which mostly consisted of Iranian Jews, didn't like the idea because we always sat separate in the synagogue. All the Iranians were looking at the work of the two young rabbis with surprise. I walked into the synagogue and everybody rushed to me. One of them said, "Look! Look at what they are doing. They are separating the women completely from the men and even the Russians are surprised by the young rabbis."

I tried to calm them down. "We are not going to be here forever or these two are not going to be here more than a week. They are young and very orthodox. Please wait until the rabbi comes. I'll talk to him about it." I tried to reassure them, but really I didn't like the idea myself.

The rabbi came in and he looked around and started to talk to them in Russian. All I could understand from the expression on their faces was that the rabbi didn't like the idea. One of the Russians who spoke some Farsi came to me and said, "I was surprised by the rabbi, because he said that if I wanted to make any changes in his synagogue, that I should talk to you first. This congregation is mostly Iranian and they are very knowledgeable people about Jewish tradition. I don't want them to be upset, they observe all the Kashrud, the Jewish Law, and amongst them there are Hazanim Jewish leaders in this synagogue."

I wasn't sure what to say, so I didn't comment.

Instead, when the afternoon prayer started and I waited outside. The rest of the Iranians stayed outside with me. The two young rabbis kept inviting everybody inside, but nobody entered the synagogue. The rabbi came to start the prayer noticed that everyone was outside. He came out and asked me, "What is going on here?"

I replied we decided to do our prayer outside in fresh air, inside is a little hot and the air is heavy."

One of the Hazanim started to read and we followed until it was over. Next we saw the two young rabbis walk out of the synagogue and at a corner of the front yard started their ritual. Our rabbi came to me and said, "Please talk to your people and asked them to come in for the continuation of our service."

I didn't have to say anything to the Iranian congregation. All I had to do was go inside and the men and women all followed me, including our Russian congregation. The Shabbat night services concluded with singing and drinking until midnight. When everybody left, the sound of *"Shabbat Shalom"* could be heard the whole time.

Next morning when we gathered in the synagogue the same scenario occurred. Unfortunately, the two young rabbis pulled the drapes and separated the men from the women. One of the Russian ladies walked up to them and spoke very angrily with them. Once again, we stood outside until the rabbi arrived. He walked in the synagogue and brought down the curtains and talked to the two young rabbis very angrily. However, they stayed in Ladispoli until the Shabbat was over, continuing their rituals, and finally then left for Rome. This was such an experience that I will never forget, especially the behavior and understanding of our rabbi.

Yom Kippur or the fast day (the day of atonement) was approaching. The rabbi had asked the men to go to his house in the afternoon for the ritual of asking forgiveness from God. I shaved, took a shower, and put on good clothing. Along with the other men of the congregation, we walked to the rabbi's house. Unfortunately, as we neared the rabbi's house, it started to rain. We got soaked. But once inside the house, the rabbi invited us into the room with a blanket spread on the floor and explained to us the ritual of receiving the lashes for our sins during the past year. I knew about this ritual, but actually had never experienced it. I looked at the congregation and said, "This is only a ritual and symbolic. What is important is that we say the words and then the rabbi will hit us with the rope he is holding. I will go first so you can see it's just a symbolic act."

The rabbi asked me to take my shirt off. I did and then knelt on my knees and hands. He said, "Repeat after me. Anything I say you repeat."

Although I had a good idea that the rabbi was not going to hit me hard, I seriously had my doubts.

The rabbi said the words and I repeated them. With every word he lightly hit me once with the rope. It took about five minutes and finally everybody went through the same ritual. When the last person finished with the lashing ceremony, the rabbi turned to me and said, "Now it's my turn. I kneel and you hit me with the rope, but first I say the words and you repeat them and I say it again, then you hit me." Jokingly he added, "This is the time to take your revenge."

Somehow we were happy about this experience of rituals we never had done before. We wanted to leave his house, but he turned to us and said, "Now we go for washing ourselves in the beach." He had one towel for each one of us and we walked in the rainy and windy weather to the beach.

I said to the rabbi, we all had showered, put on clean and fresh clothing ready for Yom Kippur."

He turned to me and said, "That is not the Jewish way. Come

on everybody I will show you."

Everybody nagged me about this and I said to them, "Just come to the beach, and if you want, don't do anything, but please respect the rabbi's kindness toward all of us. If there is anything we have to do that you don't want to do, I will do it on everyone's behalf."

When we got to the beach, the rabbi had setup a special place for us to take cover and change and get naked. The rabbi said, "I bet none of you ever had such an experience?"

We all turned to him and said, "No."

I turned to him and jokingly said, "I have been to beach many times, but not in rainy and cold weather like this. I swam in the beaches in sunny Los Angeles. But not naked."

The rabbi took all his clothes off and started to walk in the water. He looked at us and said, "Come in, everybody. Come in."

I took my clothes off and had nothing on except my underwear, which was brand new. I said to the others, "You all stay here and I will go in the water just for the rabbi's sake." I ran and dove in. It was very cold and full of leaves, debris, and other stuff because of the blustery weather. I called to the rabbi, "Are you happy now? What else do I have to do?"

The rabbi answered, "You have to submerge all your body under the water three times, including your head."

I did that and asked, "Can I go back now?"

"Did you take off your underwear?"

"No. Don't tell me that I have to do that too?" Apparently I had to take my underwear off in the water and submerge three times. I didn't ask the rabbi anything anymore. Instead, I put on my underwear on with all the debris, which was very uncomfortable. I then walked out of the water, dried myself, and put on my clothing. We all walked to our apartments wet and cold for another shower and new clothing. I couldn't wait to get into the shower. As I walked to my apartment, my wife was surprised when she noticed my wet clothes and hair, which had some debris on it. She looked at me and said, "What happened to you? Were you hit by a train that you are covered with debris and wet?"

I turned to her and answered, "I'll tell you later. All I need is a hot bath and fresh clothing. You won't believe what I had to go through when all the men got to the rabbi's house.

The next morning, we all gathered in the synagogue and the rabbi, with his Iranian helpers, started the Yum Kippur ceremony. It was one of my most memorable Yum Kippur ceremonies, which up to this day, I remember on every fasting day. The reading of the holy Torah and *Dvar* Torah or elaboration of the Torah and translation of the speeches by me, made the time pass so fast. I also talked about the situation of the Jewish people in my homeland, which many of the congregation could empathize with in the last four or five years, especially on Yum Kippur. I had to translate from Farsi to English for those who didn't speak Farsi. We had Russians in the congregation. They spoke in Russian about their hardship in Russia and the rabbi translated their comments into English and I had to translate it into Farsi. We all lived as one, big Jewish family. We all had one thing in common that brought us together and that was our Judaism.

Yum Kippur was over and the sound of blowing of the Shofar as always gave the message that atonement of everyone was hopefully accepted by the Almighty God. Hoping that our names are sealed in the book of life for another healthy and happy year. Everyone congratulated each other and headed to their homes and apartments to break their more than twenty-six hour fast.

When we arrived at my apartment, we said the blessings and enjoyed our leftovers from the night before, because no one is allowed to cook on Yum Kippur. My wife, the kids, and I talked about how the next Yum Kippur will be in our new home in America. The kids loved to hear motivational talks. My older son asked, "Papa. When are we going to America? Haven't we been here a long time?"

I reached at both of my kids and while I looked at my wife with a concerned expression answered, "You are right, my dear one. Anytime I go to the HIAS, I talk to Mrs. Toneh regarding our visa. But unfortunately, we have to wait, because it's not our turn yet. I promise you the next time I have to go, I will ask her again and will tell her that you questioned me." According to my calculation, our visa should've have arrived more than a week or two ago. We decided to go in the morning to the HIAS and then spend the rest of the day in Rome.

Recently, I noticed that many of the people whose files I'd completed, and who had arrived after my family and I got here, had received their instructions to go to the American Consulate for their visas. And very soon they would be on their way to America. But strangely, there was a young man who had been here more than seven months. During his stay he helped the rabbi a lot. But he wanted to be on his way, and any time I had to go to Rome he asked me to question Mrs. Toneh about his visa. On his behalf, I had repeatedly asked Mrs. Toneh about his visa and about mine and my family's.

"They haven't arrived," was all Mrs. Toneh had said.

I had seen this young man stand in front of her, almost crying and pleading for his visa to go to America. That's when he rushed to me once again for help. By now I knew there was something fishy and I didn't appreciate it.

The next morning, I walked to Mrs. Toneh's office, knocked on the door and went in. Mrs. Toneh was surprised at my presence. She rushed to me and said, "I didn't send word for you to come today. What are you doing here?"

The people whom I had helped process their files were all sitting in the room, getting instructions for their exit. I looked at them and then at Mrs. Toneh and said, "These people came two or three months after I had arrived, but their appointment for visa is here? Yet this young man who has been here for more than seven months, and has helped the synagogue and the rabbi all the time, his appointment hasn't arrived? I have helped everyone as a translator since I got here, for you and for them. I've helped the rabbi in the synagogue, and still my family and I have to wait for our visa appointment? Something is not right. Is this the way you show gratitude when someone helps you out of the goodness of their heart? You take advantage of them? Either that young man and me and my family go for the visa appointment to the American Counsel as soon as possible or I will make appointment through my American friend myself."

Mrs. Toneh was caught off-guard. "Please calm down," she said, "your appointment for visa, along with the appointment visa for the young man, just arrived this morning. I was going to call you and let you know. In fact, the young man will leave in a week and you and your family will leave in two weeks. I looked at the others and asked, "When did you hear about coming to this office? One of them answered, "A week ago. We were surprised that you were not among us."

I was furious. "This is what I get for helping you people out of the goodness of my heart? None of you remembered to mention anything about it to me since a week ago? Thank you. You are really very appreciative people."

Mrs. Toneh turned to me and said, "Actually we want to ask you to take everybody to the American Consulate the day after tomorrow. All their files are here and you are going to be the leader of a group of thirty-six people."

My wife looked at me with eyes that said, "Okay. You made your point and she is ashamed of her actions."

Mrs. Toneh addressed my family and kissed the kids and said, "Did your dad tell you that very soon you are going to America?" Then she kissed my wife and very quietly said to her, "Thank you," and stretched her hand to me to shake. Then she handed me a pile of files and said all of you have to be in American Consulate at 9:30 a.m. sharp, the day after tomorrow." Mrs. Toneh turned to me and said, "Tomorrow night I will send you the files by a messenger and you can take everyone to the American Consulate the next morning."

We walked out of the building and headed to Fontana because my kids liked the area and loved to have ice cream there. I was very upset with the situation that Mrs. Toneh created for me. She took advantage of me and didn't care about the fact that my kids had to go to school at the earliest time possible. I didn't want to spoil the happy moment of the good news about the visa appointment for my family. I can't stand it when someone tries to help others, but then people take advantage of that act of kindness. But what bothered me most was the young man who wholeheartedly helped the rabbi, and yet they kept him from leaving for more than seven months.

However, my wife wanted me to move on. "I know you very well and I know you get disappointed when you come across injustice. Please forget it and let's enjoy ourselves until the time we leave all these charades behind and go to our destination."

I looked at her and said, "I should be thankful to our son who reminded me about the delay of our departure. That was the only reason I decided that all of us should come to Rome, otherwise we never would've found out about what was happening behind our backs. Such is the luck of the young man. But now I am very happy for him."

We enjoyed the day in Rome and came back to Ladispoli very late on the last bus. In the morning, the rabbi came to me and inquired about our absence for the night prayer. I explained everything to him and told him how much I was disappointed with what had happened. The rabbi also was sorry about what he heard. He turned to me and said, "I told you many times, if you stay here with me, you will be the leader of the refugee program and a member of our Chabad, but you said that you escaped because of the future of your kids. I understood that and appreciate your concern as a father. Therefore, I wish you and your family all the best in America and I appreciate all the help you have given me with all the Iranian refugees during your stay in Ladispoli."

CHAPTER 12

The Trip to America

Visa appointment day arrived and all of the refugees whose names were on the list headed to the bus station, along with their files. The bus driver already knew almost all of us. The driver turned to me and asked, "Are you going to Rome for a sightseeing tour and picnic?"

"First to the American Consulate and then a picnic," I answered. Amongst many trips we had done to Rome, this trip had its own merit and happiness. Somehow deep in our hearts my wife and I thought about the goal we had planned for since the time the uprising and devastation started in our country. I had the feeling that Iran would never be the same country that I came back to fifteen years ago when I finished my studies and returned home to do my duty as an Iranian.

We arrived at the American consulate. I walked to the guard, presented my paperwork and said, "We all are here for our visa appointment with the console."

He looked at all of us and asked, "You are all here together?" I replied, "Every family has their own appointment made through the HIAS. The HIAS asked me to bring them along because most of them don't speak English."

The guard checked all the papers and the names then asked us to go into the building. We were asked to sit in the hallway on the benches and wait to be called. One of the ladies who worked in the consulate called my name. As I stood up, she asked me, "Is your family here with you?"

"Yes. My family is my wife and my two sons."

She then opened the door of the console's office and asked us to go into the room. As we walked into the office, the console stood up and asked us to sit down on the chairs across his desk. There were four chairs in two rows and a chair on the side where a lady sat. My wife and I sat in front row and the kids in the back row. The console opened my file and looked through it. I noticed he was shaking his head. He looked at me and said, "I see you were in The United States and you acquired your university education in California. Do you mind if we have the interview without the translator?"

"Of course not. Actually, I think it's a good idea because I can answer your questions myself." There was a lady from Afghanistan as a translator who helped the Farsi-speaking people who didn't speak English. Afghan people speak Farsi, but not the exact Farsi that Iranian people speak.

The console asked about the time I was in America as a foreign student,. He wanted to know why I decided to go clear across the world to school, especially in Los Angeles. "What made you decide to go to California?" he asked.

"English is one of our subjects that we have to take during high school and when I was in my last year of high school, we had a teacher who studied in America. He was very familiar with the educational system in America, especially California, because it was very affordable for students. One day he came to English class and drew a map of America and then pointed at California. I think all of the students in class made a trip to California right there in their thoughts. The teacher elaborated about the weather, beaches, freeways, and different cities in the state. That class changed into a presentation of California and Los Angeles. Time passed and then I decided to travel to the United States, of course to California and Los Angeles. My I-20 student visa acceptance was from Los Angeles and I ended up in Los Angeles for years."

The console then asked, "Tell me about your fourteen years of experience at the Oil Company in different positions."

I explained the times I was in the refinery and different offices, the scope of my jobs, the responsibilities and the performance of my duties by referring to commendations, which were in my file from the oil company at which I worked."

Finally, the console asked, "Tell me a little about the revolution, because I was looking forward to meeting someone from Iran to ask him firsthand about the revolution of 1979 in Iran."

I looked at the console with a smile and said, "You don't know the real reason behind the so-called revolution?" I took a deep breath and our conversation lasted almost two hours. My wife was nervous that disclosing so much might make a bad impression on the console and he wouldn't grant us the visa to enter America. Twice the secretary knocked on the office door and came in reminding him about other people who were waiting eagerly for their visa appointments. I tried to make my explanation so vivid that the counsel could picture everything in his head.

At the end of our talk, I asked the counselor, "Are we getting our visa? The schools in America started a few days ago, and we don't want our kids to fall behind. They've already lost one year by escaping. Are we going to America?"

The counselor looked at both of us and said, "It would be my pleasure to take you to the airport tomorrow with my own limousine and put you and your family on a plane to America. But you have to wait until the HIAS arranges your schedule. Of course, you will be granted your visa and you all will travel to America together." Then he looked at the pile of the files on his desk and said, "I see every one of these requests is written in your handwriting. You must be familiar with all their cases?"

I nodded. "Yes. That's right. I know every file by heart, because I interviewed them and they showed me all the necessary papers and documents in the HIAS. They all have relatives; sons, daughters, brothers, sisters, uncles, aunts, in different states and they will join them."

The counselor called for the secretary and said, "Please issue visas for all of these files and hand them to my good friend so all of them can go to America as soon as possible."

The counselor stood up and shook hands with my wife, me, and the kids. He walked with us to the door and when we got in the hallway, everyone rushed to me and very anxiously asked, "What happened? You were in the office of counselor more than two and half hours. Are you going to translate for us when we go in for our interviews?"

I turned to all of them and said, "Unfortunately, the console denied visa to all of us. We have to go to another country or go back to Iran." I noticed some of them took my joke very seriously and right away I said, "I'm joking. You don't have to go for an interview at all. We all got our visas. The counselor asked about your files and I answered all the questions and he ordered all our visas."

Everyone in the group jumped up and down and hugged and kissed my wife and me. We all left the American consulate and headed for a group picnic in Rome.

Our group arrived at Ladispoli late that night. The news of our meeting with the counselor had reached the rabbi and the rest of the people who had come for evening prayer. Next morning when everyone gathered in the synagogue, the rabbi approached me with a smile and said, "I heard about your two and half hour meeting with the counselor. Do you want to tell me how it started?"

I looked at the rabbi and said, "The counselor was very friendly and had an Afghan woman translator for us. The counselor looked at my file and noticed my university studies in America, he requested to conduct the interview directly with me, and asked questions about Iran's revolution. I told him what happened and we continued to discuss it until my kids fell asleep in their chairs. The lady translator almost fell asleep, too. The only people participating in the conversation were the counselor, me, and sometimes my wife. That's it."

The rabbi had a bag in his hands. He took out two navy blue bags. The larger one had a *tallit* (Hebrew for *prayer robe*) and in the small bag there was a set of *tefillin,* which consists of the arm-*tefillin* and the head-*tefillin.* He handed both bags to me and said, "I know you had to leave your *tallit* and set of *tefillin* back in your country. Since you used the ones in the synagogue while you were here, I am giving you these as a small token for all the help and hard work you have done for this synagogue and everybody. I hope always you use them in health with all good wishes for you and your family."

I was very moved by his action and the way he hugged me and kissed my face. I noticed that the face of the rabbi was wet with his tears rolling down on his thick and long beard. Right away he said, "Don't forget, the day you and the rest of the people get on that plane to America, promise me that you will put on the *tefillin* for them at the airport before you board."

I said to the rabbi with a smile, "You just gave me a very precious present and right away want me to work for it? Put on *tefillin* for all the men in the airport?"

He then said, "I know when the bus comes to take you all, and by the time you get to the airport and go through the formalities, you will have more than enough time to perform the *tefillin* for them."

I promised the rabbi that I would do it for his sake and the sake of the other passengers who were on the same plane with us.

Finally, the ten days of waiting was over and in the morning all of us waited anxiously for the bus to take us to the airport. It was about 8:00 a.m. when the bus stopped in front of the synagogue. I had all the documents for the group with me, which was delivered to me the night before. I made sure everybody had all their belongings and I checked their names on my list. I asked everyone to get on the bus in a very orderly manner. When everybody was on the bus, my wife, my kids, and at last I said goodbye to everybody. Plus, I said a final farewell to the rabbi whom I haven't seen since then. I saw the rabbi laughing, but at the same time tears were rolling down on his beard.

We got to the airport and very soon, with the help of the HIAS representative, all of us checked in and waited to board the plane. I remembered the promise I made to the rabbi and asked the men to put on the *tefillin*. It was time to board the plane to our destination of America. I presented the tickets for everyone and we all got on. As we sat in our assigned seats very close together, I looked at the group. I can't forget the look on their faces. One by one, they all said, "This is the moment we had dreamed of for years. Heaven knows what we went through to get to this last lap of our trip."

I looked at all of them and said, "I have the same feeling, just like a little boy who has been waiting for new year to come and get that new bicycle as a present. We all went through a lot of hardship, agony, some disappointing moments, and even sometimes when we thought everything was finished, and we were going to be arrested and executed without reason. But let's forget the past and look forward to a very bright and healthy future. Let's enjoy the flight and good Kosher food!"

As soon as the plane took off and the passengers could walk around, our kids came to us and sat in our laps, even though we were all in the same row. Our flight was very smooth and we were well-cared for by the hostesses.

About 6:00 p.m. New York time we landed at JKF International Airport. I had to get all of our group together and enter the airport immigration office. The time had come for some of the member of our group to separate from us. Some of them went to New York, some had to go to Miami, others to Texas, but most of the group was in the same connecting flight to Los Angeles. As I brought an elderly couple to their connecting flight to Texas, the immigration officer said, "I notice you spoke English with the immigration officer and at the same time Farsi with a group of people. Can you help me with this gentleman who has a letter in Farsi?"

"I am at your service," I replied. "What can I do for you?"

He then said, "I want you to raise your right hand and promise that you read this letter and translate it word by word for me."

I raised my hand and said, "I promise to translate it as it is written."

He then asked me "Do you know this man?"

I said, "I don't know him at all and this is the first time I met him."

The officer handed the letter to me and I translated it for him. It took about twenty minutes and when it was finished, the officer said, "I thank you and welcome to America. Then he asked, "I see the university ring on your finger. Where and when?"

In two minutes, I told him. After he realized that I came back to America after fourteen years he said, "Let me shake hands with you and welcome you again."

I got back to the group and our final boarding the flight to Los Angeles started. The airport was very busy and it took our plane half an hour to take off. While the plane taxied down the runway, I was very tired and fell asleep. I woke up and noticed my wife was with the kids. She turned around and said, "You were tired and you slept about two hours. The kids and I decided to let you rest. The last two days you had many different tasks and responsibilities."

I hugged the three of them and said, "In three hours we will be in Los Angeles and start a new life in the land of free and the home of the brave, the city that I know and lived in for almost seven years. I am sure a very good and successful life is ahead of us."

We arrived at the Los Angeles International Airport and were welcomed by our family. I was excited and relieved that our situation turned out the way it did. I turned to my wife and said, "Honey, you and I have made one of the most difficult decisions of our lives by taking such a big risk, escaping through dangerous and enduring times. If there is a will, there is a way to success, and we have made it."

We were finally home.

EPILOGUE

Our lives in the United States of America had begun. During the course of our escape, I met many people, starting from the first day of our dangerous escape in Iran to meeting with the young man with the fancy sunglasses and Levi's, Pahlavan, who had initially evoked fear into us at the Khoy post office at our rendezvous point with the human smugglers. He has since become a very good friend of the family. My family and I had the opportunity to get to know his mother and his younger brother very well in Istanbul and we became good friends. We all live in Los Angeles now and have kept in touch either by telephone or meeting each other occasionally.

Nader and Sarah, who had fictitious names and were Armenian, whom I had tried to help cover for in Turkey during our group's arrest in Van by the Turkish police, and for whom I had explained the history of Passover in case the undercover police had any suspicions of their faith, eventually were able to escape to Germany. The last time we saw them was the day they wanted to arrange to help my family's group of four with our entry stamps through a connection they had in Istanbul, which would've ended up with a very high cost for us and some eventual commission for them. The last I heard of them, they wound up with acquaintances that made arrangements for them to go by train to the border of Germany. They had been given instructions to get off at a specific station and meet through a connection to enter East Germany. I haven't heard about them or seen them since.

Ghasem joined us from the first day of our journey inside the border of Turkey. He became a great help to our group, especially with his command in the Turkish and Kurdish languages. At the times when I had exhausted my English or German, Ghasem was my help and translated my request or comments for the authorities or common people. Our last goodbye was in Istanbul at the hotel. No one saw him after our first arrival at the hotel in Istanbul. His last comments before we said goodbye were, "I will remember you and your family forever and ever. I am looking forward to the day that we all gather in our country of Iran someday with freedom. I never will forget your kindness and hard work for all the escapees." Ghasem was a big man both in size and in character, and a humble man, as well.

The young pregnant couple, the one in which the husband had been arrested by the police for carrying a gun to protect his pregnant wife when they had entered Turkey illegally, and who had eventually been released, had their baby in Van. The last I heard of them was from the colonel before I left Van. They had been scheduled to leave Van soon to join the husband's brother in Germany.

After a few days of our arrival in Istanbul, I did not see or hear from any of the other escapees who had made it with us to the hotel.

In the city of Ladispoli, Italy, the only person I saw or heard from again was the young man who had been kept in Ladispoli for seven months waiting for his visa. On my last visit to the HIAS I noticed he was upset and was crying, so I talked to Mrs. Toneh about him. She decided to release his visa and send him to New York, where he eventually continued his studies and became a dentist. But unfortunately, I haven't seen or spoken with him since. Although I have been in New York and have tried to find him. Unfortunately, I wasn't successful.

The couple with the son and daughter who were on the same

plane with us and then went directly to Ladispoli, flew to the United States from Italy, and then continued on our flight with us to Los Angeles. Since then, we occasionally meet in different family and community gatherings. Their son is now a chiropractor and their daughter is married with two children.

My mother and grandmother remained in Israel until July 4th of 1984. Through a hired lawyer, they entered the United States legally, where they lived in a rented apartment. My mother very happily always said, "My arrival in America was on the Independence Day of this great country." And the day my mother, my wife, and I became naturalized, she was very excited to answer the immigration officer's question, "Do you know the date of America's independence?" She excitedly answered, "The fourth of July', 1776." She then added, "My arrival to America was also on the fourth of July, but in 1984." The immigration officer was happily impressed by her comment.

Unfortunately, my grandmother died six months after her arrival to the United States. Before her passing, she was very happy to see that my wife, my kids, and I had made it to America.

My brother-in-law, the one who had given me the red *tasbih* on our last night in Tehran, and told me, "Take this with you and wear it around your fingers. It goes with your look, your beard, and your Islamic revolutionary persona. It might help you," eventually immigrated to the United States with his wife and two kids. They live in California. Every time we get together we share memories of our last meeting in Iran.

As I had promised my mother-in-law in Iran, I made arrangements for her to come to America as soon as we settled into our new home in Los Angeles. I began working fervently in that endeavor and she was able to join us in 1987.

My family is and always has been very excited about living in America, the land of democracy and freedom. It is a privilege to be free and to be involved in the future of one's country. As a free man I enjoy the right to vote without any pressure from authorities, unlike in some modern-day, dictator-like countries.

My wife and I have lived in the same house since 1987 and our kids are university graduates; my older son is in the field of computers and my younger son is an attorney. My wife and I are semi-retired and try to help our community as much as possible.

Istanbul. Year 2015 as a tourist. 31 years after my first visit to Turkey as a refugee.

ABOUT THE AUTHOR

Parviz Hakimi was born in Sanandaj, a province of Kordestan of Iran. He acquired his early education in Iran. He traveled to the United States of America as a foreign exchange student. He finished his university work at the California State Polytechnic University. He went back to his homeland of Iran to help his country which was progressing toward the twentieth century under the Shah's rule. He had to finish his compulsory army duty as an officer and returned to his old job at the Abadan Refinery.

After four years of service in Abadan, he was transferred to Tehran. By the time of Islamic Revolution, he had 10 years of experience at the Iranian oil Company. After the revolution, he was interviewed and transferred to a new position in the company where he worked for four years. Finally, due to the situation in the country and the treatment of the Islamic revolutionary people he decided to escape from his homeland "Iran", and return to the U.S.A.